The AKC Classifications

The American Kennel Club (AKC) currently recognizes 150 separate breeds of dogs. The AKC has categorized the breeds into seven groups, based primarily upon original purpose: Sporting, Hound, Working, Terrier, Toy, Non-Sporting, and Herding. In addition, the AKC has a separate interim classification of Miscellaneous.

Sporting group

- American Water Spaniel
- Brittany
- Chesapeake Bay Retriever
- Clumber Spaniel
- Cocker Spaniel
- Curly-Coated Retriever
- English Cocker Spaniel
- English Setter
- English Springer Spaniel
- Field Spaniel
- Flat-Coated Retriever
- German Shorthaired Pointer
- German Wirehaired Pointer
- Golden Retriever
- Gordon Setter
- Irish Setter
- Irish Water Spaniel
- Labrador Retriever
- Pointer
- Spinone Italiano
- Sussex Spaniel
- Vizsla
- Weimaraner
- Welsh Springer Spaniel
- Wirehaired Pointing Griffon

Hound group

- Afghan Hound
- American Foxhound
- Basenji
- Basset Hound
- Beagle
- Black and Tan Coonhound
- Bloodhound
- Borzoi
- Dachshund
- English Foxhound
- Greyhound
- Harrier
- Ibizan Hound
- Irish Wolfhound
- Norwegian Elkhound
- Otterhound
- Petit Basset Griffon Vendeen
- Pharoh Hound
- Rhodesian Ridgeback
- Saluki
- Scottish Deerhound
- Whippet

Working group

- Akita
- Alaskan Malamute
- Anatolian Shepherd Dog
- Bernese Mountain Dog
- Boxer
- Bullmastiff
- Doberman Pinscher
- Giant Schnauzer
- Great Dane
- Great Pyrenees
- Greater Swiss Mountain Dog
- Komondor
- Kuvaz
- Mastiff
- Newfoundland
- Portuguese Water Dog
- Rottweiler
- Saint Bernard
- Samoyed
- Siberian Husky
- Standard Schnauzer

Herding group

- Australian Cattle Dog
- Australian Shepherd
- Bearded Collie
- Belgian Malinois
- Belgian Sheepdog
- Belgian Tervuren
- Border Collie
- Bouviers des Flandres
- Briard
- Canaan Dog
- Cardigan Welsh Corgi
- Collie
- German Shepherd Dog
- Old English Sheepdog
- Pembroke Welsh Corgi
- Puli
- Shetland Sheepdog

Breeding Dogs For Dummies®

Cheat Sheet

The AKC Classifications (continued)

Terrier group

- Airedale Terrier
- American Staffordshire Terrier
- Australian Terrier
- Bedlington Terrier
- Border Terrier
- Bull Terrier
- Cairn Terrier
- Dandie Dinmont Terrier

- Irish Terrier
- Jack Russell Terrier
- Kerry Blue Terrier
- Lakeland Terrier
- Manchester Terrier
- Miniature Bull Terrier
- Miniature Schnauzer
- Norfolk Terrier
- Norwich Terrier

- Scottish Terrier
- Sealyham Terrier
- Skye Terrier
- Smooth Fox Terrier
- Soft-Coated Wheaten Terrier
- Staffordshire Bull Terrier
- Welsh Terrier
- West Highland White Terrier
- Wire Fox Terrier

Toy group

- Affenpinscher
- Brussels Griffon
- Cavalier King Charles Spaniel
- Chihuahua
- Chinese Crested
- English Toy Spaniel

- Havanese
- Italian Greyhound
- Japanese Chin
- Maltese
- Miniature Pinscher
- Papillon
- Pekingese

- Pomeranian
- Toy Poodle
- Pug
- Shih Tzu
- Silky Terrier
- Toy Manchester Terrier
- Yorkshire Terrier

Non-Sporting group

- American Eskimo Dog
- Bichon Frise
- Boston Terrier
- Bulldog
- Chinese Shar-Pei
- Chow Chow

- Dalmatian
- Finnish Spitz
- French Bulldog
- Keeshond
- Lhasa Apso
- Lowchen

- Poodle
- Schipperke
- Shiba Inu
- Tibetan Spaniel
- Tibetan Terrier
- Bouviers des Flandres

Miscellaneous

- Beauceron
- Black Russian Terrier
- German Pinscher
- Glen of Imal Terrier

- Neopolitan Mastiff
- Nova Scotia Duck Tolling Retriever
- Plotthound

- Redbone Coonhound
- Toy Fox Terrier

Copyright © 2002 Wiley Publishing, Inc. All rights reserved.

Item 0872-5.

For more information about Wiley call 1-800-762-2974.

For Dummies: Bestselling Book Series for Beginners

ces for the

BESTSELLING BOOK SERIES

Do you find that traditional reference books are overloaded with technical details and advice you'll never use? Do you postpone important life decisions because you just don't want to deal with them? Then our *For Dummies*® business and general reference book series is for you.

For Dummies business and general reference books are written for those frustrated and hard-working souls who know they aren't dumb, but find that the myriad of personal and business issues and the accompanying horror stories make them feel helpless. *For Dummies* books use a lighthearted approach, a down-to-earth style, and even cartoons and humorous icons to dispel fears and build confidence. Lighthearted but not lightweight, these books are perfect survival guides to solve your everyday personal and business problems.

> *"More than a publishing phenomenon, 'Dummies' is a sign of the times."*
>
> — *The New York Times*

> *"A world of detailed and authoritative information is packed into them..."*
>
> — *U.S. News and World Report*

> *"...you won't go wrong buying them."*
>
> — *Walter Mossberg, Wall Street Journal, on For Dummies books*

Already, millions of satisfied readers agree. They have made For Dummies the #1 introductory level computer book series and a best-selling business book series. They have written asking for more. So, if you're looking for the best and easiest way to learn about business and other general reference topics, look to For Dummies to give you a helping hand.

Wiley Publishing, Inc.

Breeding Dogs FOR DUMMIES®

by Richard Beauchamp

Wiley Publishing, Inc.

Breeding Dogs For Dummies®

Published by
Wiley Publishing, Inc.
909 Third Avenue
New York, NY 10022
www.wiley.com

Copyright © 2002 by Wiley Publishing, Inc., Indianapolis, Indiana
Published by Wiley Publishing, Inc., Indianapolis, Indiana
Published simultaneously in Canada

For general information on our other products and services or to obtain technical support, please contact our Customer Care Department within the U.S. at 800-762-2974, outside the U.S. at 317-572-3993, or fax 317-572-4002.

Wiley also publishes its books in a variety of electronic formats. Some content that appears in print may not be available in electronic books.

Library of Congress Cataloging-in-Publication Data:

Library of Congress Control Number: 2001093698

ISBN: 0-7645-0872-5

Printed in the United States of America

10 9

1O/RV/QT/QT/IN

About the Author

Richard G. ("Rick") Beauchamp has been successfully involved in practically every facet of purebred dogs. He has bred them as well as trained and handled them professionally in the show ring. For many years, he owned and managed a publishing house devoted almost entirely to books and periodicals about purebred dogs. He is a published author of numerous breed and all-breed dog books and has lectured extensively on purebred dogs throughout the world.

As a breeder-exhibitor, he has been actively involved in breeds of nearly all the variety Groups, including top quality Chow Chows, Dachshunds, Salukis, and Irish Setters. His Beau Monde Kennel has produced champion Boxers, American Cocker Spaniels, Poodles, Wire Fox Terriers, Bull Terriers, Pembroke Welsh Corgis, Cavalier King Charles Spaniels, and Chinese Shar-Pei. Rick is particularly associated with the Bichon Frise, a breed he has specialized in since its earliest days in America.

As a judge of all breeds with the Federacion Cynologique Internationale, Rick has had the distinct pleasure of judging championship events in Mexico, throughout the United Kingdom, Scandinavia, Europe, Australia, New Zealand, South Africa, the Orient, Central America, and South America. Rick now judges throughout North America for the American Kennel Club, the Canadian Kennel Club, and the United Kennel Club.

In his other life, Rick has had a lifelong interest in film and theater and spent several years as a copy editor and reporter for the television and film industry bible, *Daily Variety*. He lives in Cambria, California, a coastal village situated midway between Los Angeles and San Francisco.

About Howell Book House

Committed to the Human/Companion Animal Bond

Thank you for choosing a book brought to you by the pet experts at Howell Book House, a division of Wiley Publishing, Inc. And welcome to the family of pet owners who've put their trust in Howell books for nearly 40 years!

Pet ownership is about relationships — the bonds people form with their dogs, cats, horses, birds, fish, small mammals, reptiles, and other animals. Howell Book House/Wiley understands that these are some of the most important relationships in life, and that it's vital to nurture them through enjoyment and education. The happiest pet owners are those who know they're taking the best care of their pets — and with Howell books owners have this satisfaction. They're happy, educated owners, and as a result, they have happy pets, and that enriches the bond they share.

Howell Book House was established in 1961 by Mr. Elsworth S. Howell, an active and proactive dog fancier who showed English Setters and judged at the prestigious Westminster Kennel Club show in New York. Mr. Howell based his publishing program on strength of content, and his passion for books written by experienced and knowledgeable owners defined Howell Book House and has remained true over the years. Howell's reputation as the premier pet book publisher is supported by the distinction of having won more awards from the Dog Writers Association of America than any other publisher. Howell Book House/Wiley has over 400 titles in publication, including such classics as The American Kennel Club's *Complete Dog Book,* the *Dog Owner's Home Veterinary Handbook, Blessed Are the Brood Mares,* and *Mother Knows Best: The Natural Way to Train Your Dog.*

When you need answers to questions you have about any aspect of raising or training your companion animals, trust that Howell Book House/Wiley has the answers. We welcome your comments and suggestions, and we look forward to helping you maximize your relationships with your pets throughout the years.

The Howell Book House Staff

Dedication

This book is dedicated to the many breeders I have known and learned from over nearly a half century's involvement in purebred dogs. Their triumphs and bitter disappointments have enabled me to preserve, to accomplish, and to contribute to this wonderful world of dogs.

Author's Acknowledgments

No words will ever be able to express my appreciation for those wonderful books with dog heroes in them written by the late Albert Payson Terhune. His books not only inspired a love of all nature but a fascination with the magic of the written word.

The enthusiastic and supportive people at Wiley and Howell Book House have helped tremendously in translating my fascination with purebred dogs and the words we use to describe them into what I sincerely hope is a real guide to breeding quality purebred dogs and understanding the huge responsibility involved in doing so.

I particularly wish to thank my editor, Tim Gallan, who assisted me so well in consolidating all the bits and pieces of my experience in dogs, in general, and dog breeding, in particular, into this book.

Publisher's Acknowledgments

We're proud of this book; please send us your comments through our online registration form located at www.dummies.com/register.

Some of the people who helped bring this book to market include the following:

Acquisitions, Editorial, and Media Development

Senior Project Editor: Tim Gallan

Acquisitions Editors: Mike Singer, Kira Sexton, Tracy Boggier

Copy Editors: Ben Nussbaum, Patricia Yuu Pan

Technical Editor: Marcia Halliday

Editorial Managers: Pam Mourouzis, Christine Meloy Beck

Editorial Assistants: Nívea C. Strickland, Melissa Bennett

Illustrator: Marcia R. Schlehr

Cover Photos: Image Bank/g.k./Vikki Hart

Production

Project Coordinator: Erin Smith

Layout and Graphics: Brian Drumm, Stephanie Jumper, Mary J. Virgin

Proofreaders: Andy Hollandbeck, Linda Quigley

Indexer: TECHBOOKS Production Services

Publishing and Editorial for Consumer Dummies

Diane Graves Steele, Vice President and Publisher, Consumer Dummies
Joyce Pepple, Acquisitions Director, Consumer Dummies
Kristin A. Cocks, Product Development Director, Consumer Dummies
Michael Spring, Vice President and Publisher, Travel
Brice Gosnell, Publishing Director, Travel
Suzanne Jannetta, Editorial Director, Travel

Publishing for Technology Dummies

Richard Swadley, Vice President and Executive Group Publisher
Andy Cummings, Vice President and Publisher

Composition Services

Gerry Fahey, Vice President of Production Services
Debbie Stailey, Director of Composition Services

Contents at a Glance

Cartoons at a Glance

By Rich Tennant

The 5th Wave — By Rich Tennant

"She's a model dog, alright. When she's not on a catwalk, she demands a lot of attention, requires constant grooming, and is a picky eater."

page 209

The 5th Wave — By Rich Tennant

COMMON DOG BREEDS

FAIRWAY RETRIEVER

BACKSEAT TERRIER

POMERANIAN CONDODOG

BEDROOM MASTIFF

page 87

The 5th Wave — By Rich Tennant

PAVLOV'S DOG

"Watch—I can make him ring that bell just by drooling a little bit."

page 253

The 5th Wave — By Rich Tennant

"Can I look at this dog's pedigree papers again?"

SAL'S KENNEL

Quack...

page 55

The 5th Wave — By Rich Tennant

"I got him a bowl, a collar, and since he's a dalmatian puppy, a small fire extinguisher to make him feel right at home."

page 119

The 5th Wave — By Rich Tennant

He's a mix.

page 279

The 5th Wave — By Rich Tennant

"She's not a registered breed; however, she has been booked by several animal control agencies."

page 7

Cartoon Information:
Fax: 978-546-7747
E-Mail: richtennant@the5thwave.com
World Wide Web: www.the5thwave.com

Table of Contents

Part VI: Business or Pleasure? *253*

Introduction

*1*f, after reading this book, you decide *not* to breed dogs, part of my mission will have been accomplished. Throughout these pages, I hope to introduce you to the information that will help you decide whether or not you have the stuff that it takes to be a dog breeder. Speaking from experience, I can assure you, it's no bed of roses.

But understand, I have a great deal of respect for the person who takes the time to understand what dog breeding is all about and decides that it's just not their "thing." So much better than the person who plunges ahead and does a haphazard job of it, letting the pieces fall where they may. In dog breeding, those "pieces" are living, breathing, and very dependent beings.

I also want you to know that, regardless of how little or how much you may know about dog breeding, I do not consider you a dummy. The reason I think this book is appropriately titled is that when I compare what I thought I knew in the beginning to the knowledge I've accumulated over the years, well, I haven't found a better word to describe my naiveté back then!

The complex breeding programs responsible for consistently producing the kind of dog that you and I can rely on to behave and perform in a certain way takes intelligence and careful planning. Dog breeding sense is at once an art and a science, and it's one that takes a whole lot of study and many years of experience to master. Common sense alone indicates it's not something that should be jumped into on a whim.

Breeding Dogs For Dummies was written for everyone who has an interest in dogs. If you are simply curious about what dog breeding entails, I hope that what I've included will show you what a huge responsibility it is. If you've already decided that you are going to breed purebred dogs, I hope what you read here will send you out to find an experienced mentor to guide you. And perhaps the experienced breeders will find some valuable bit of information here and there to assist a small step forward on that illusive journey to breed that perfect dog

What I Assume about You

I'm assuming you love dogs and think you might like to have more than one scampering around the house. Or you may have been "bitten by the dog bug" as those of us in the biz are inclined to say. Your mind is already made up as to which of the many is your breed of breeds, and you're thinking about making more — exactly like yours. Other than that, you don't know exactly where or how to start.

That might well be a foolish assumption on my part, and you may already have done some research, such as visited kennels or homes of people who live with that breed you admire, and you would like to try your hand at this breeding thing. Like myself, you might see dog breeding as an art or a science or perhaps even both.

Regardless of what I've assumed, I do believe there is something that tells you dog breeding is worth considering, and if it is worth doing, it is worth doing well — or even better. If so, there's something here for you.

How to Use This Book

You can read this book straight through from front to back if you want, but you don't have to read it that way. Feel free to use this book as a reference. Just look in the table of contents or the index for the topic you're interested in. Then jump right to that specific section in the book. You'll see cross-references to other sections or chapters for more or related information about the topic.

It's probably very unlikely that many of you will be able to arrange the time to sit down and read this book from cover to cover at one sitting. So for that reason, there are a few things that may appear somewhat repetitive. After all, the chapters are modular and are meant to stand on their own. Also, there are a few things that I fully intended to repeat, both because of their importance and because I want to make sure you don't forget!

How the Book Is Organized

Breeding Dogs For Dummies is divided into seven parts. You can read the parts consecutively or in the order that appeals to where you feel you are with all this breeding stuff. Here's how they go:

Part 1: Should You Be a Dog Breeder?

In other words, do you have what it takes? There's a lot to consider before you start — financially, environmentally, and even emotionally. This is where you'll have an opportunity to look before you leap.

Part 11: Understanding Purebred Dogs

Time, effort, and a lot of thought, to say nothing of thousands of years, have gone into the development of our modern dog breeds. All of them come down from the same basic ancestor, and how they got here is a fascinating story that will help you determine how they'll fit into your lifestyle.

Part 111: Breeding Stock

This part gets down to the nitty gritty. I provide advice and instructions to help you find quality foundation stock so that you can produce dogs worthy of their breed name.

Part 1V: Getting Your Breeding Program Started

In this part, I present methods that will enable your breeding program to produce top specimens. I show how breeders' experiences and scientific discoveries can help pave the way to your success, and I help you determine the ways to increase your chances of producing dogs that live up to the standard of their breed. Along the way, I show you how to avoid the pitfalls that nearly every breed is susceptible to.

Part V: Prenatal Care, Whelping, and Raising Puppies

There's a great deal more involved than passing out cigars before, during, and after the pups arrive. This part deals with care of the mom-to-be before she gives birth and what to do from the big day on.

Part VI: Business or Pleasure?

Raising good stock costs money — a lot of money. It makes sense to organize your expenditures and income in a businesslike manner. This part may help you do so. Even if you don't consider your breeding efforts a business, I explain the kinds of records you are required to keep.

Part VII: The Part of Tens

I've assigned the magic number ten to things like characteristics that can make you a good breeder, tips to help you breed better dogs, and much, much more.

After the Part of Tens, I include a couple of helpful appendixes: a list of additional resources and a glossary.

Icons Used in This Book

As you read along, you'll come across little signs not unlike you see along the highway when you're driving. Some are important, some not so important, and others are just interesting or fun things to know. Here's what they'll mean:

Useful bits of information that could make your life a bit easier.

These important blocks of text are strings for your memory fingers, like remembering to record the dates on which your female came into heat, when she was bred, and how many days from that date she whelped.

Danger lies ahead, and I'm telling you to proceed with caution!

Geeky facts that may not have life-and-death implications but are just interesting to know.

Auntie Mame told us that "life's a banquet," so why not enjoy a few hors d'oeuvres? This icon flags fun facts and anecdotes that I've thrown in.

Where to Go from Here

You may be the Capricorn type who isn't about to let go of A until you have a firm grip on B. If so, start at the beginning of this book and proceed on through step by step. Or you may like "new news" to come in small doses on an as-needed basis. If so, just check out the index to ferret out what you want to know when you want to know it.

Then too, some of the information I've included may appear a bit too elementary for the level of knowledge you've already attained. Could well be, but a lot of it is the basic stuff — information that a breeder or potential breeder should have firmly in place. And as lo these many (many!) years of involvement with purebred dogs have taught me, *no one knows what they don't know!* So even though I'm encouraging you to skip around, you may want to skim over the stuff you think you know, just in case I may have a few extra pearls of wisdom for you.

Part I
Should You Be a Dog Breeder?

The 5th Wave   By Rich Tennant

"She's not a registered breed; however, she has been booked by several animal control agencies."

In this part . . .

Mother Nature has supervised the procreation of her animal kingdom, dogs included, for eons, so why do we have to step in at this late date and interfere? What makes dog breeding so different now than it was when good old Nell whelped out in the shed? Why all this preparation? Why whole books on the subject?

Well, fellow dog lovers, this part of *Dog Breeding For Dummies* answers all those questions and more. Time, space, zoning laws, and cost are just a few of the external factors that can hinder you from just jumping into dog breeding. You'll also need to think about all the personal issues like your temperament, work habits, and family needs. Nowadays, Nell and her brood are pretty much members of the household, so compatibility has become an important part of both dog owning and dog breeding.

This part helps you take a good look at all the issues that today's dog lover has to carefully consider before becoming today's dog breeder.

Chapter 1

Passing the Responsible Dog Breeder Test

So what's the big deal with breeding dogs? Old Nell did just fine by herself whelping and raising her litter of tail waggers. The pups grew like weeds and once they started eating on their own, off they went to their new homes. That was that!

That, however, was then, and this is now. Cities or counties that let you keep any number of horses, cows, and goats place strict limits on the number of canines that you can house on your property.

Attempts are being made everywhere to control the number of dogs that are born. If you think that there's no reason for these controls, all you need do is pay a visit to your local humane society or animal shelter.

We certainly don't need anyone else adding to the country's ever-increasing canine population unless they're breeding a certain kind of dog for specific reasons and under sensible guidelines. The American Humane Society reports that well over 15 million healthy and friendly dogs and cats were euthanized in the year 2000. Most of the dogs were mixed breeds, but many of them were purebreds that were born into caring homes but who fell into the hands of irresponsible disappointed owners.

I say "disappointed" because a good many of the purebred dogs in the shelters are there because they failed to live up to the romantic expectations their owners had. Even a pricey dog won't be Lassie or Rin Tin Tin. Purebreds in shelters are there because they didn't arrive pretrained or pan out quite as heroically as the owners expected.

This chapter is intended to make you think long and hard about taking on all the responsibilities connected with dog breeding. If, after careful consideration, you do decide to breed dogs, this chapter contains valuable tips and advice on who you can contact to help you with your goals.

Why Purebreds Make Sense

All puppies are cute. Just about anything naughty they do is forgivable, because they do it in such an innocent and beguiling way. Who wouldn't melt at the sight of puppy? Unfortunately, all this puppy cuteness lies at the bottom of many problems.

Puppies like the ones shown in Figure 1-1 grow up, and not all of them grow up to be cute or have the temperament that you may want them to have. (Although what's attractive and compatible to one person is not necessarily seen in that light by another.)

Figure 1-1: These Cavalier King Charles Spaniels puppies, like most purebreds, offer a strong degree of predictability in how they'll act and look as adults.

Bred by Carol Williams; photo courtesy of Jerry Vavra.

Size and temperament can vary a bit within any of the purebred breeds. However, the results of hundreds of generations of selective breeding pretty well insures the buyer of what the puppy he purchases will look and act like as an adult. Therefore, the surprises and disappointments that you have with the surprise package of a mixed breed just aren't as prevalent.

Just as important as the predictability of size and personality, and even more important to some people, is the fact that you can purchase a purebred dog for a specific purpose and feel reasonably certain that the pup will grow up with the ability to fulfill that role. There are hunting dogs and guard dogs, dogs inclined to bark at most any unusual sound, and dogs that live to do nothing more than bring a ray of sunshine into your life. You can get a better sense of this in Chapter 3.

In fact, many breeds are amazingly specialized. There are field dogs that freeze at the first scent of hidden game and point it out to the hunter. Other breeds will swim through icy water to retrieve winged fowl that the hunter has brought down. Some breeds of dogs protect by attacking on command, while other breeds knock intruders to the ground and stand guard and call for assistance by barking.

There are companion dogs so small and light in weight that even the most elderly person can manage them easily. There are breeds with such an inborn need to please and assist that they are easily trained to become guide dogs for the blind.

No doubt exists in my mind that practically any dog, purebred or not, is capable of becoming a great companion. However, common sense would indicate that if we are going to perpetuate any kind of dog it should be one that has a high potential of finding exactly the right kind of home and owners who will be satisfied that they got what they really wanted

Who Should Breed Dogs

Many people believe that the only real requirement for breeding dogs is just being a dog lover. I wish I could say that's true. Unfortunately, it's not. Granted, being a dog lover is an essential component of a good dog breeder's makeup. Who else would be willing to put up with the all the disappointments, setbacks, and sheer drudgery that is often involved?

Much more is involved in becoming an accomplished breeder of dogs than loving them. In fact, a mighty long list of characteristics mirrors the one that I give to people who ask me where they should go to buy a well-bred dog.

If I were forced to select just one word to describe the characteristic that overrides all the other important characteristics of a good dog breeder, that word would have to be *responsibility.* So much that's involved in breeding dogs can be done haphazardly or not at all. Practically no laws or licenses exist that *force* anyone to be a good breeder. Other than those that are self-imposed, there aren't many sanctions for a lack of ethics in dog breeding.

The Responsible Breeder Checklist

- ✔ The Responsible Breeder is a member of the national breed club and participates in activities that support the breed: Conformation Shows, Obedience Trials, Agility Competitions, Breed-specific events.

- ✔ The Responsible Breeder follows all breed-club recommendations for hereditary defect testing of all breeding stock.

- ✔ The Responsible Breeder does not release any dog, puppy or adult, to a new home before it is sexually altered, unless the dog is specifically designated as show or breeding stock.

- ✔ The Responsible Breeder does not release any dog, puppy or adult, who has not had an identifying microchip implanted.

- ✔ The Responsible Breeder takes all necessary steps to insure that each and every dog bred is given all the socialization that's appropriate for the dog's age.

- ✔ The Responsible Breeder maintains proper housing for the breed with adequate room for exercise.

- ✔ The Responsible Breeder is vigilant in maintaining clean and sanitary conditions at all times.

- ✔ The Responsible Breeder is always prepared to make appointments for prospective buyers or those interested in breeding to view the dogs.

- ✔ The Responsible Breeder guarantees in writing the health of all stock sold.

- ✔ The Responsible Breeder is available for the lifetime of the dog to answer questions related to dogs sold.

- ✔ The Responsible Breeder will take back any dog sold if the buyer is unable to keep the dog.

- ✔ The Responsible Breeder uses a sales contract in all instances that clearly defines the rights and expectations of both buyer and seller.

- ✔ The Responsible Breeder has all registration and veterinary documents relating to the dog available for inspection at the time of the sale.

- ✔ The Responsible Breeder does not permit any dog to go to a home or environment that is not entirely suitable for the breed of dog.

- ✔ The Responsible Breeder has completed all inoculations appropriate for the age of the dog being sold.

Why Responsible Breeding Is an Issue

The responsible breeder gives each and every dog bred or owned all the care and attention it needs. That care even precedes the birth of the dog. Many hidden hereditary factors must be considered when mating two animals. I find it hard to believe that an irresponsible person would take all the time and endure the high costs involved in determining if the breeding stock about to be used is clear of some of these debilitating physical problems or temperament flaws.

You must understand that no breed, no dog, no animal (human or otherwise) is entirely free of hereditary defects of some degree or another. Chapter 9 takes a closer look at what can be inherited, both positive and negative.

Contributions you can make

Breeders who consistently produce mentally and physically sound dogs and who adhere to guidelines similar to those listed in the accompanying Responsible Breeders' Checklist can derive great satisfaction from the dogs they breed. Breeding and owning that dog of your dreams is a point of great pride, but the satisfaction can and does extend far beyond those few dogs who you're able to keep.

You can't help but take pride in knowing that you have established a line of dogs that's positively altered the course of the breed. That contribution lives on long after you have bred your last litter — even beyond having said a final goodbye to the last dog of your line.

Everyone who breeds championship-caliber dogs takes pride in the accomplishments of their dogs, but an even greater thrill can be derived from seeing what those outstanding dogs are capable of doing for the breed.

Stories of encouragement

Some years back I was invited to judge in Sydney, Australia. My first breed of the day was Bichon Frises, a breed that I had some measure of success with back at home in the United States. Among the entries was a dog of such outstanding quality that he stood heads above anything else that was competing.

I placed the dog Best of Breed and at the conclusion of the judging told the exhibitor that she should be extremely proud of having bred the dog. In my opinion, I told her, the dog was undoubtedly the best specimen of the breed I had ever seen.

She thanked me profusely and told me the dog had done a great deal of winning in Australia. She then said, "You have reason to be proud as well. Everything in this dog's pedigree goes back to your stock!"

I learned that dogs I had exported to England had produced well for their new owners there, and they had exported offspring to Australia who produced the dog that I had just awarded a top prize to.

Or consider the letter a friend of mine who raises Pugs received from the mother of a young man who was a paraplegic. The young man's injuries were the result of an automobile accident he was in while still a teenager.

The mother wrote, "Pugsley (the name of the dog) is absolutely devoted to my son and never leaves his side. When my son is due back from school, Pugsley sits at the window watching and waiting until he sees the van drive up. I think the greeting between the two is a high point in both their days. I can't thank you enough for sending this wonderful, wonderful dog into our lives. He has been a godsend!"

Other friends and breeders have told me wonderful stories about how their dogs have protected children or sounded the alarm when fire threatened. Bee Godsol, a dear friend of mine and a famous breeder, had her life spared because of the devotion and intelligence of two Newfoundlands who she had raised since the day they were born.

If you're not familiar with the breed, a Newfoundland is a very large (120 to 150 pounds), heavy-coated dog with a very calm and gentle nature. You'd never think it to look at the big old fellow but, when the need arises, the "Newfie" is a devoted and protective companion to those whom the dog loves and a heroic rescue dog for even an absolute stranger in need.

Bee was driving home from a friend's with just the two dogs in her car. It was late at night and snowing heavily. Her car hit a patch of ice and skidded off the road and down a steep embankment. Part of the way down, the car hit a tree and the impact threw Bee out of the car. Bee couldn't move her arms or legs. She was paralyzed and helpless in the blinding storm.

Between long periods of unconsciousness, she realized that her two Newfoundlands were lying close on each side of her. Occasionally, they would go off and she would hear barking in the distance.

When she woke up in the hospital, she was told that someone driving along the lonely stretch of road had stopped to investigate why a huge black dog was alone and frantically barking at the side of the road — obviously in a frenzy about something. The passerby soon realized that something was amiss at the bottom of the ravine and called for help.

When Bee awoke in the hospital, the ambulance driver told her that if it hadn't been for the dogs, she couldn't possibly have survived. The only problem he encountered, the driver said, "Was those two black beauties who couldn't decide whether we were there to help you or do you harm. It took a whole lot of coaxing and petting to get them to let us put you on the stretcher!"

To be responsible for bringing dogs into existence who have as great beauty, persistent devotion, and intelligent bravery as the dogs in these stories is something that most breeders aspire to. Naturally, every dog who you breed isn't going to be responsible for stories like these. Having that type of impact really isn't the point of breeding dogs. But the stories do illustrate that remaining loyal to what the creators of our breeds intended the breeds to be and do is a sign of great respect and, in a way, preserving the breed shows a love of mankind as well.

Working with a Mentor

Breeding dogs with the beauty, the brains, or the abilities that the breed is intended to have isn't something that you can do easily. In fact, just breeding one dog that combines *most* of what the breed standard requires is a genuine accomplishment. It doesn't just happen by accident.

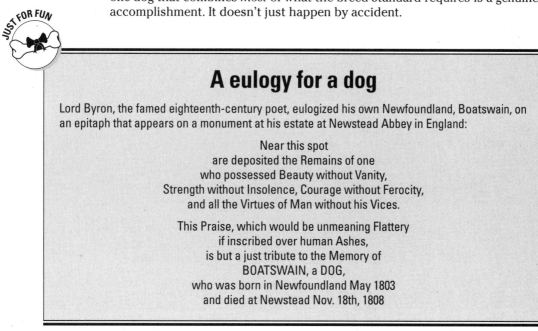

A eulogy for a dog

Lord Byron, the famed eighteenth-century poet, eulogized his own Newfoundland, Boatswain, on an epitaph that appears on a monument at his estate at Newstead Abbey in England:

Near this spot
are deposited the Remains of one
who possessed Beauty without Vanity,
Strength without Insolence, Courage without Ferocity,
and all the Virtues of Man without his Vices.

This Praise, which would be unmeaning Flattery
if inscribed over human Ashes,
is but a just tribute to the Memory of
BOATSWAIN, a DOG,
who was born in Newfoundland May 1803
and died at Newstead Nov. 18th, 1808

In a perfect world, the beginning dog breeder would spend at least a few years reading, studying, and observing the rights and wrongs of a breed. A newcomer would fully acquire the knowledge that old-timers in that breed have to pass along. The study time would also help the beginner learn some of the lingo that goes along with all the different breeds. ***Note:*** If I start to use some of that lingo, there's a glossary in the back of the book.

Where to start

Most of us have not yet achieved nirvana, entered paradise, or otherwise become perfect. We're inclined to get started where most dog fanciers get underway — somewhere near the middle.

Most of the people I know who are now established breeders have told me that they were well under way and already owned a number of dogs before they came to the realization, "Uh oh, what I *should have done* was. . . ." Fortunately, all of us learn (or should learn!) from our mistakes. The time and courage it takes to retrace your steps and go back to where you may have veered off course can put you on the short route to success.

Once you've decided on the breed that you want to raise, get your hands on everything that you possibly can that has been written on the breed. But here's a strong word of caution: DO NOT BUY, and I repeat, *DO NOT BUY,* ANY DOGS! Don't even take any freebies!

You don't even know enough at this point to know whether you're buying that pig in a poke you always hear about. In fact, at this early stage of the game, you may be better off if you do wind up with a pig, because the animal that could be foisted off on you may not even meet the standards of our porcine friends.

Where to go

After the dog bug starts nipping away at you, you'll undoubtedly want to start seeing some dogs. The most logical place to go always seems to be a dog show. Do go, but leave your wallet at home!

Why do I say that? Invariably, the first person a novice gets hooked up with at a dog show is exactly the last person they should get hooked up with. Accomplished breeders and exhibitors are successful because they've kept their noses to the grindstone and worked hard at what they do. If they take time off from their busy schedule at home or at the kennel to go to a dog show, it's because they have something important to do at the show — like show a dog, judge, or watch someone they admire judge.

The best breeders don't have time to lurk around corners and pounce on unsuspecting beginners to try and sell them a dog. There's a reason these people don't have anything better to do at shows and I don't think it would take a whole lot of explaining to have you figure out what that reason is. You wouldn't think of handing over your hard-earned cash to that guy who approaches you on a street corner and says, "Wanna buy a watch? Solid gold and cheap!" would you? Probably not. You won't find any solid gold dogs waiting for you *anywhere,* and even if there were some out there for sale, you can take my word that they're never available at bargain prices.

Who to meet

Respectable and successful breeders always have time for novices, but invariably they arrange that time by appointment. They have you come to their home or kennel to view their dogs and discuss the breed.

This arrangement gives them an opportunity to size you up and determine just how serious you are about becoming involved in their breed. Most major breeders are delighted to find someone genuinely interested in joining their ranks, someone who will breed conscientiously and well. They want to see their good dogs go to such a person. You can rest assured that they're not going to take a chance on placing a dog or puppy of the quality that's taken them half a lifetime to breed with someone they suspect jumps into every new hare-brained notion.

A successful breeder who determines that you're sincere about becoming involved in their breed — in possibly becoming a breeder or an exhibitor — will bend over backwards to help you. If you can locate someone like this to act as your mentor, it's worth every minute of the time you invest in doing so!

You can't imagine how much time and money I've watched people spend on dog after mediocre dog, breeding one unsuccessful litter after the next. They do so because they've had no one to guide them in the right direction or upon whom they could rely for sound advice on how to go about planning a breeding program.

The most successful young breeders I know are those who in their early years of breeding simply followed the directions of their mentors. Only after they learned how it had all been done successfully in the past did they feel equipped to try some well-thought-out experimenting. And they are still willing to have their mentors evaluate their efforts.

Solo Flights

I can only imagine that along about now you're wondering if I'm not making a bigger deal out of all this than I need to. You just want to breed one good litter of puppies to have something to show or to hunt with or to do whatever your breed is supposed to do with.

You're probably also feeling that I've not only sent you back to prep school, but that I want you to remain there under the headmaster's thumb *forever.* Will you never be able to do this on your own?

All this information and the recommendations to seek guidance are here to encourage you to do *whatever* you plan on doing in dogs at your best possible level. This includes those who plan on breeding one litter or many.

So, when I'm talking solo flights, I'm talking to both those who plan to breed just one time and to those who look at all this as something they will be doing for the foreseeable future. I'm sure there are some of you among the latter who hope to eventually succeed to the point where your success warrants you becoming a mentor to someone else.

I feel equally certain that some of you reading this wonder just how important one litter of puppies can actually be. How can one litter of three or four puppies have any impact on the future of dogdom?

Even a single litter from a breeder who didn't have sufficient knowledge of the breed or disregarded hereditary problems can have disastrous effects. Offspring of such a litter — or even of one dog in that litter — can contribute untold problems to a gene pool and cause a great deal of heartbreak and financial burden as well. I'd like to give you an unfortunate example.

A newly married couple I know called me for recommendations on where to buy a Rottweiler puppy. I told them that I would be happy to get them some names of responsible breeders because there are a good many problems in the breed that they should be aware of before buying. I wanted to be sure that they got a dog that was as trainable and intelligent as the best Rotties are.

Before I had had any time to locate someone I felt confident in recommending, the husband called back to let me know that they had found "just what we were looking for!" A friend of a friend had mated their female to someone's male who had advertised the services of a "huge registered male" in the local paper. A litter of ten resulted. (Why are there always more puppies in the litters that shouldn't be than in the litters that should be?) The young couple chose Bruno, who was, according to the husband, "The biggest, bossiest male of the bunch."

Fortunately for the buyers, Bruno didn't grow up to be the biggest, bossiest adult! In Rottweilers, this can prove to be more of a handful than most people are prepared to cope with. Actually, the dog grew up to be very sweet tempered. However, that's the only thing about the dog that one could list on the positive side of the ledger.

By the time I was able to see Bruno, he was two years old and his owners had spent well over $6,000 on veterinary bills. He proved to be extremely dysplastic (*dysplasia* is a crippling hip disorder) and he needed complicated surgery. (I go into the details about some of these hereditary problems in Chapter 10.)

To complicate matters, Bruno was unable to keep food down after eating. Prolonged and expensive testing by several different veterinarians revealed he had a malfunctioning digestive system that required regular medical supervision and an expensive specially formulated diet. They were given no hope for improvement.

Just before my arrival, their vet had advised the couple that Bruno was now developing severe problems in his stifles (knee joints) and the problem required more surgery. Although I certainly don't claim any medical background, I could easily see from Bruno's very awkward movement that something was radically wrong.

The young couple was devastated. They were just getting established financially and they were expecting their first baby in only a few months. Now they faced the possibility of more huge veterinary expenses.

They were at a loss and asked me what they should do. I knew what the truth of the matter was: that the dog should be put down. I also knew that doing so was absolutely out of the question in their minds. Instead of telling the truth myself, I suggested they see a veterinarian friend of mine, knowing full well what his honest advice would be.

Fortunately, my friends had made no attempt to breed Bruno. However, I don't even want to think about the breeding plans the owners of Bruno's nine brothers and sisters have for their dogs.

Going back to my question of how much difference just a single litter of puppies can have — I'll let you think about the answer.

Chapter 2

Important Stuff You Need to Know

*C*all me impulsive if you will, but once I've made the decision to begin a project, I want to start now, not later. Forget about reading carefully before I begin.

If I buy one of those "some assembly required" gadgets, I'm more interested in using it than I am in assembling it. That, I can assure you, has led me to doing the "some assembly" twice, if not three or four times.

Dog breeding is like a "some assembly required" gadget. You have to know certain things before you leave the starting line. Even though some of the things you need to know take time and may put a bit of a damper on your plans, trust me when I say that investing time upfront is worthwhile. Get the basics out of the way first so that you aren't totally submerged in your project before you realize that you're drowning in mistakes and rescue is impossible.

This chapter is about those pesky rules and regulations that you have to be familiar with. They apply to any breed of dog. Some of the rules are imposed by the community you live in; others by the canine registering organization — probably the American Kennel Club — governing the breed you choose; and last but far from least, there are those self-imposed rules that separate the respected breeder from the backyard breeder.

What separates the respected breeder from the backyard breeder? Can't a good breeder keep his dogs in the backyard? The term *backyard breeder* actually has little to do with where the dogs are kept, but rather with how and why they're kept. Backyard breeders are those people who breed dogs for no other reason than to make money. They are not involved in any activities to promote or improve the breed and make no effort to test their breeding stock for genetic health problems. They couldn't care less what kind of homes the dogs they breed go to, just so long as they go. See Chapter 1 to read more about the traits that separate responsible breeders from irresponsible ones.

All too often, well-intentioned parents will decide little "Ruffles" should have a litter — "Just to introduce the kids to the miracle of birth." There are now books and videos available that will make the same introduction without all the work and responsibility involved in raising a litter and finding proper homes. No matter how you cut it, bringing puppies into the world just for the fun involved or even for educational purposes does not relieve you of having to find the right home for each and every puppy in the litter.

Bottom-Line Breeding Goals

If you're going to breed dogs, you need to have at least two broad goals in mind.

Mental and physical health

The absolute bottom, bottom line of breeding is a clear understanding that at least 95 percent of the dogs you breed will go into homes where they will become *companions*. The dogs you keep may become breeding stock or show dogs and, in some cases, the dogs that leave your home or kennel may have duties beyond companionship. In the end, however, the vast majority of the dogs you breed will wind up in homes as somebody's pal.

That fact tells you something very important: The dogs you breed have to be physically and mentally sound. I don't care what kind of home the dog is in or what the designated role of the breed is, no one — and make that NO ONE — needs an uncontrollable or ill-tempered dog running around the house or being near children. A dog who will take the owner's life savings to pay never-ending vet bills also isn't what people need.

In addition to what the originators of a breed had in mind regarding looks and performance, there were specific ideas of how the breed should behave. No matter how tough, how aggressive, how whatever-the-creators-thought-the-dog-should-be, they also knew that the dog had to be controllable and healthy.

Respect for the origin and purpose of the breed

Written records called *breed standards* make it clear that the people who first fashioned our breeds expected that those who followed them would maintain the breeds' characteristics. Living up to those expectations has a high and mighty title called *respecting the integrity of the breed.* In less lofty terms, this means a current breeder respects what the founders had in mind for the breed physically and mentally and strives to maintain these characteristics.

I find what the creators of some of our breeds accomplished absolutely amazing. I often stop to wonder what genius inspired these people to put this and that together in order to get what they were after. If you were to research the origins of many of our breeds, I think you would be astounded at what lies behind them.

I see the breeders who were instrumental in the formation of our breeds as artists — artists who, in my mind, stand right alongside Gauguin and Picasso. The only difference is that the artists of the dog world subtly blended colors and shapes on a living canvas that produced a unique and distinctive new breed. Their brushes produced dogs that looked like what they wanted, behaved in the manner they felt was appropriate, and were able to perform in the way intended. Tampering with what they created in order to suit our whims is as disrespectful as chiseling away at Michelangelo's *David* to modernize its look or painting over a Monet to have its colors suit a room's decor.

Changing a breed means eliminating or adding physical or temperamental characteristics. The standard of perfection is altered to suit the whims of the breeder. There is no way to view this other than complete disrespect for the genius that was obviously involved in the breed's creation.

The need to respect origin and purpose is usually clear enough to those people who have breeds that were originally intended to work for a living — the hunting, hauling, protecting, and herding dogs. But all too often breeders who have the purely decorative breeds feel they are exempt from these rules. They assume that since their breed has no working purpose, they can redesign it to please themselves.

This thinking could not possibly be more off track. The way our companion breeds work for their owners is by providing a very specific picture and presence. I don't know of any breed that man has designed for which there was nothing specific in mind — that is, that had no purpose. It is that purpose that a breeder must be dedicated to protecting.

Getting to Know Breed Standards

The presiding kennel club of each country of the world has a registering system for the purebred dogs that are born and bred in the country. The AKC is the recognized authority in the United States. England has the forerunner of all dog clubs in The Kennel Club and Canada's dogs are registered with the Canadian Kennel Club. Each major country in the world has its own registry. These registering systems issue certificates of registration that are probably best described as canine birth certificates. Dogs' birth certificates are just as important as ours are. The only way a dog can be considered a purebred and be registered is if the dog's father and mother (*sire* and *dam* in dog parlance) are registered. The only way the sire and dam could have been registered is if their parents were registered, and so on.

In order for a breed to have been accepted by one of the registering organizations in the first place, the supporters of the breed had to provide credentials certifying their dogs had been bred true to form and free of *outcrosses* (introductions of other breeds) for at least five generations.

Before the breed is given official recognition, the sponsoring club is also required to submit a written description of the breed that gives a word picture of both what the breed should look like and how it should interact with humans. This written description is the breed standard.

The disqualifications that appear in many of the official breed standards are there for two primary reasons:

- ✔ To breed out the undesirable characteristics obtained from early crosses to other breeds
- ✔ Probably even more significantly, to eliminate any dogs from the breeding pool who display physical or mental characteristics that prevent them from performing the task or maintaining the form that is the breed's essence

Because the standard describes the ideal specimen, it isn't based on any particular dog. It's a concept against which a dog is compared. Breeders use it as a goal. Judges compare the dogs in the ring to this standard of perfection and award those who come closest. In most cases, the people responsible for creating the breed wrote the original standards. Necessary revisions that take place through time are usually made by members of the national breed organizations formed to oversee the well-being of the breed.

Time, Space, and Financial Considerations

I read somewhere that two dogs are just as easy to keep as one. Hmm, interesting. I don't know where that idea came from, unless it was from someone trying to sell two dogs!

The initial purchase price of two dogs is double the cost of one unless someone is selling you two for the price of one, and if that's the case, scoot. No good breeder will do that. Two dogs eat twice as much, have two times as many vet bills, and cost you twice as much to "vacation" at the Doggie Dude Ranch while you're away. Now multiply that by three or four or a dozen and I think you'll get the idea that raising and breeding dogs is not inexpensive by any stretch of the pocket book.

Time

Before we get to all the financial considerations, let's take a look at some of your other major considerations: accommodations for your dogs and the time it takes to care for them. The latter becomes really important when puppies are involved. You think having that first baby was a time consuming job? Just wait until you're responsible for three or four, or even *sixteen* canine babies — as my good friend in Australia was presented with all at one time!

Someone has to take care of the dogs you'll be using in your breeding program. They need food and someone to prepare it. They need grooming and someone to do it. They most definitely require individual attention that goes beyond just being brushed or prepared to go to a dog show or out hunting.

Dogs who are involved in activities with their owners are the best off of all. Dogs that go to dog shows or participate in activities like Agility, Obedience Trials, or Herding and Hunting events get to spend all kinds of time with their owners. Owners who are involved in these events are the best "parents" a dog can have. They share their lives with their dogs and it is exactly that kind of treatment that brings out the very best in any breed of dog.

Dogs who have the benefit of regular close association with humans develop a personality that's very different than that of dogs who are solely kennel raised with minimal human interaction. There's a certain responsiveness, a willingness to please, and greater tractability with dogs whose socialization process began early in life and continued on a regular basis.

I've been involved in a breed or two that I felt wasn't the most brilliant in the world. I based this opinion on my kennel bred and raised foundation stock. My opinion definitely changed as time went on and I saw how home-raised dogs of that breed blossomed and achieved a level of awareness and compatibility that had been untapped in the kennel dogs.

When puppies from my first litters went to their new homes as companions, testimonial letters soon came back praising how quickly they learned and how responsive the puppies were. What these glowing testimonials told me was that rather than lacking brainpower, these were breeds that needed a great deal of individual human attention in order to fully develop their personalities.

This was a great lesson for me and one that made me reevaluate how the breeds should be raised. As early as was practical, I separated the puppies in a litter from each other and gave each as many human experiences as I could possibly manage. A ride in the car, a trip to the post office, a night of watching television with me — all part of the socialization process.

Did it take time? Lots of it. Socialization, combined with trips to the vet and the regular feeding and never-ending cleanup chores took up the part-time effort of two adults. Was the time invested worth it? You bet.

Because I was so involved, I was able to catch health problems and those minor skin flare-ups before they became situations requiring veterinary care. The dogs themselves were just more fun to be around. But above all, the happiness they brought into the lives of their new owners made every minute of the time that I invested worthwhile.

Space

Will you be raising St. Bernards or Chihuahuas? It makes a difference in how your dogs will be housed and how much space will be required to house them. You also have to consider the matter of adequate and escape-proof areas for the dogs to exercise.

What part of the country you live in and what the average temperatures are in winter and summer make a difference. Bulldogs would have great difficulty surviving the heat of some southern climates without the aid of air conditioning. Although St. Bernards are in seventh heaven outdoors on an average northern winter day, a Chihuahua could easily become a pupsickle in less than an hour under the same conditions.

"Family" considerations

Females in heat must be kept in safe, separate quarters from your males to avoid mismatings or unwitnessed matings. In order to insure identification of parentage, the AKC requires that all females in heat be segregated from males. Accidental breedings are bound to happen otherwise, and you don't want to put up with the lovesick moaning and groaning (if not outright howling) of the male who knows his ladylove is around somewhere but he can't get at her.

Some males, denied access to females, go on a complete hunger strike and can become a bag of bones in nothing flat. Once your boy gets even the faintest whiff (and the signal is airborne!) of a potential liaison, you'll be hard pressed to divert his attention. Also, females in heat excrete a highly traceable odor through the pads of their feet. This means that unless the visiting female comes and goes on the same day, she will not only have to be admitted to your property through a separate entrance, she'll also have to be quartered in an area your male will not use.

If you keep stud dogs whose services are offered to outside females, you have to provide safe and separate quarters for the females who spend the night or nights. You are entirely responsible for visiting females while they are in your care, unless you have a signed contract that states otherwise.

Newborn puppies should be kept in an area that is away from your own adult dogs. They should definitely be kept separate from outside dogs and people who have been around outside dogs to prevent their becoming infected with communicable diseases. My advice is keep puppies away from outside dogs until breed- specific permanent inoculations have been completed. Until your puppies are adequately immunized, quarantine conditions should exist.

Housing issues

Housing your dogs in secure facilities with adequate space for exercise may require having separate kennel buildings and runs, depending on the breed. In northern and southern locations, this may entail a major financial investment if you stop to consider the added expenditure of thermostatically controlled heat or air conditioning.

In the right climate, some of the larger and heavier-coated breeds are able to survive quite nicely with individual doghouses surrounded by secure fencing. These private "bungalows" can be purchased from any number of companies. Many of the modular houses that are offered are made of materials that are able to modify extremes in temperature to some extent.

Security

Security is also an important consideration. Your dogs must be kept safe from would-be thieves and out of the reach of children. Very young children may not know whether it's safe to be around your dogs. This isn't to say that you would keep dogs of a dangerous disposition, but there are many very playful breeds that don't know their strength. Then too, older children who love dogs may not think that there's any harm in letting one of your dogs out of its enclosure for some playtime.

Toy breeds need space too

Breeding the Toy breeds doesn't eliminate the space problem, even if you plan on conducting the entire operation within your own home. Even the tiniest dogs need a place to call their own. Also, you probably don't want dogs underfoot 24 hours a day.

Most Toy dog breeders have allocated a separate room or rooms within the home for their dogs and have collapsible enclosures called *exercise pens* in which their dogs can exercise.

Adequate fencing of your property and the individual runs keep unwelcome visitors out and your dogs in. Some breeds of dogs are notorious climbers or diggers. These escape artists could put Houdini to shame with their talent for getting out of just about any enclosure you can get them into. These breeds require special covered runs for the climbers and jumpers and fencing that extends below ground level for the diggers.

Most major fencing companies can supply exactly what you need, but rest assured that good standard fencing is expensive and specialized equipment costs even more. Still, there's really no choice in the matter when you weigh the expense of a good fence against the theft or disappearance of one of your valuable dogs.

The breeder from whom you purchase your foundation stock is the best source for sound advice on what kind of security measures you will have to take to insure the safety of your breed. The experienced breeder will also be able to counsel you on what kind of housing, inside of your house or in a separate doghouse, that your breed requires.

Financial considerations

The unfortunate mistake that far too many potential breeders make is assuming that the dogs that they do not want to keep can be sold to finance the overhead of the operation. Please think again if this assumption is part of your plan.

The first mistake people make is to multiply the selling price of a hypothetical number of puppies by what they paid for their first foundation female. Say the figure you paid for a top quality foundation bitch was somewhere in the area of $800 to $1,000. You may have thought, "Wow! What a great source of income!"

Think again! First off, it will take you a long time to establish yourself well enough so that your stock is in demand. You won't be able to charge a top price until you've produced many champions and your trophy room is brimming with blue ribbons and trophies.

You put yourself into the hands of the most experienced and most successful breeder you could find when it came to purchasing your foundation stock. You were willing to pay that extra dollar to ensure you got the best possible dog. You can expect the next beginner to do likewise.

Occasionally, the breeder from whom you purchased your original stock may not have the right puppy for a buyer and may refer the buyer to you. The breeder making the referral may even tell you what to charge for the puppy you sell. But even when this is the case, the higher price, even though entirely justified, is apt to be due to the reputation of the person making the recommendation.

Another thing to consider is that there are many times when you'll have to keep a puppy or puppies for many months before the right buyer comes along. Food costs and veterinary expenses continue right on while the puppies live with you. Large litters that are quickly placed somehow seem balanced by the next litter that is plagued with unexpected costs and great delays before the right homes are found.

Breeding dogs ain't cheap

For your consideration, here's a breakdown of the average costs involved in raising a litter of five Pembroke Welsh Corgi puppies to eight to ten weeks of age:

Cost of show quality female	$1,000
Cost to acquire championship title for female ($3,000 divided by 3 litters)	$1,000
Prebreeding vet examination (of the mother), including brucellosis test	$75
Shipping to/from stud dog	$300
Stud fee	$600
Prenatal costs, whelping box, gauze pads, heating pad, emergency supplemental feeder, mother's-milk replacement, rectal thermometer, sterilized scissors, cotton thread, baby scale, infrared lamp	$200
Post-whelping vet examination (dam & puppies)	$75
Tail/dewclaw docking/removal	$125
Inoculations (3 shot series for each puppy)	$350
Advertising	$150
Food costs (mother and puppies)	$200
	$4,075.00
Possible caesarean delivery	$ 650
	$4,725.00

Note: Most potential buyers of puppies are inclined to go to an established breeder if they are looking for a female to breed or show. First-time breeders are most likely to attract customers who are interested in obtaining a pet-quality puppy at a cost of about $500.

Unless all the costs involved in producing the puppy you sell are totally ignored, most breeders will tell you that breeding dogs is undoubtedly the greatest nonprofit venture you can embark upon. Almost invariably, that rare year your breeding operation shows more income than expenditure is balanced by several years in which expenditures far outweigh what few dollars do come in.

Stop to consider the cost of a stud fee and prenatal veterinary expenses, and then add the cost of possible whelping problems, health checks, and the necessary inoculation series for the puppies. These are all significant cost factors that must be taken into consideration and they are the same factors that will put a very large dent in any anticipated profits. This is to say nothing of everything you've spent getting up to the point when your dam produces that first blessed event.

City, County, and State Animal Regulations

Before you start tracking down your town's leading architect to design the kennel building of your dreams, there are a few things that you have to look into.

One of the first telephone calls you must make before you initiate any kind of a breeding program is to the Animal Control Service that has jurisdiction over the city in which you live. If you do not live in a city proper, you'll have to speak to the County Animal Control Department.

There are city zoning laws that may limit you to keeping no more than two or three dogs at any one time. There are licensing fees that vary according to the number of dogs you keep and whether or not you are going to breed. If you are going to breed dogs, the number of litters you produce in a given period may up your status from that of a "hobby" to a "commercial" breeder. Permits and regulations differ for hobby and commercial breeders. The dollar amount you charge for the dogs may also constitute a deciding factor determining which category of breeder you fall into.

In most states, it is the County that imposes regulations that will govern the kind of breeding you will be permitted to do where you live. If there are any regulations other than those imposed by the County, the County office will normally be aware of what they are and who you should contact if you require more information.

Regulations affecting dog owners and dog breeders who live within a city's boundaries can be considerably different than regulations applying to someone who may live just a few blocks away but outside of the city's limits.

Governing Kennel Clubs

Big Brother is watching you! You can boast about the royal blue bloodlines of the dogs you breed until it's you that's blue (at least in the face!), but unless you can produce a certified registration certificate and have a means of proving that the registration certificate you hold belongs to the dog in question, you may as well forgeddaboudit! Without the right paperwork, the blood of your dogs is no more royal than that of the Heinz 57 mutt down the street.

If you live in the United States and you're planning to breed dogs, one thing you have to understand right from the get-go is that the New York City and Raleigh, North Carolina–based AKC not only makes all the rules governing purebred dogs, but it keeps a close eye on you to make sure that you follow those rules! The AKC is in charge of registering the dogs you breed and it has some very well- thought-out rules to keep what you do as a breeder on the up and up.

Other domestic registries exist in the United States, but none of them has the international affiliations and acceptance that the AKC does. Heading the list of alternative domestic registries is the United Kennel Club (UKC), headquartered in Kalamazoo, Michigan. The UKC is the second oldest and second largest purebred dog registry in the United States. The organization registers all breeds, but has historically focused on the many Coonhound breeds developed in North America. As a result, the UKC legitimately claims the largest Coonhound registry in the world.

The records the AKC wants you to keep on each dog you own and breed and the way it wants you to keep these records is fully described in a pamphlet titled *Regulations for Record Keeping and Identification of Dogs.* The pamphlet can be obtained free of charge directly from the North Carolina offices of the AKC and is on the Web at www.akc.org. You can call the AKC at 919-233-9767 to order a copy of the pamphlet.

This pamphlet is an extremely important publication for every dog breeder. It lists everything you must do to stay in compliance with AKC rules so that your dogs can be eligible for registration. Noncompliance can result in a wide range of penalties — often very costly and never very pleasant.

Domestic dog registries

There are a number of domestic dog registries in the United States other than the AKC — each with its own system of registration and area of specialization. Their addresses and contact information can be found in the Appendix at the back of the book.

- United Kennel Club (UKC). The second oldest and second largest all-breed dog registration. The organization strongly supports the *total dog* concept, meaning that the ideal dog is one who looks and performs equally well. Single breed and multibreed shows are sponsored by the UKC throughout the United States.

- American Rare Breed Association (ARBA). As its name implies, ARBA specializes in the less-common breeds. Breeds developed in foreign countries are judged by the standard used in their country of origin. ARBA itself decides which standard should be used for breeds developed in the United States. The organization holds all-breed dog shows throughout the country.

- States Kennel Club (States KC). The youngest U.S. kennel club, founded in the mid-1980s and organized to give exhibitors one more choice in respect to registries and shows in which to exhibit. The organization recognizes all other registries.

You have to provide all the information required for the registration certificate, such as breed, registration name and number, sex, color, markings, and so forth as well as a the name and address of the person from whom you directly acquired each dog. The AKC reserves the right to visit your home or kennel for the purpose of inspecting the records it requires and it expects you to have those records up to date and available at all times.

Above all, you have to be able to accurately associate all the information they require with the dog the information describes. That is, there must be some method of marking, tattooing, tagging, or microchipping the dog so that identification is possible.

The consequences of failing to comply with these requirements are rough. They range from fines on through to the AKC refusing to register a dog who you bred. It's even possible that the AKC will completely suspend all your privileges to breed or show dogs. As you can see from the following list, the AKC isn't kidding around when it comes to proper records and identification of your dogs:

- In the United States, an American-born puppy must come from a registered litter in order to be registered by the AKC. Figure 2-1 shows a registration certificate, which lists all pertinent information concerning the dog's vital statistics: name, breed, color, sex, date of birth, sire, dam, breeder, current owner, registration number. The reverse side of the Certificate includes all information required for transfer of ownership.
- The AKC provides official registration application forms to breeders for all litters, as shown in Figure 2-2.
- After the application to have a litter registered is approved, individual registrations (see Figure 2-3) for each puppy in the litter are sent back to the breeder.
- The AKC also provides Litter Record forms (see Figure 2-4), which must be carefully maintained for every breeding an individual makes. These records must be produced should the AKC have need to inspect them.
- It is important to keep individual records of every dog a breeder owns. The form supplied by the AKC (see Figure 2-5) provides space for all the information the breeder must maintain.
- A properly completed registration form and three-generation pedigree (shown in Figure 2-6) must accompany each puppy a breeder sells. Although breeders normally supply a typed or written pedigree with each puppy or adult dog they sell, a pedigree Certified by the AKC insures the buyer that there are no spelling errors or incorrect information on the form.

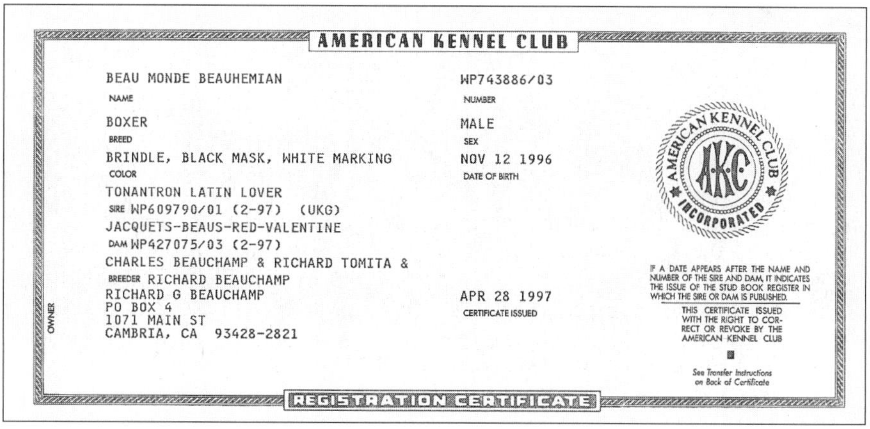

AMERICAN KENNEL CLUB

BEAU MONDE BEAUHEMIAN
NAME

WP743886/03
NUMBER

BOXER
BREED

MALE
SEX

BRINDLE, BLACK MASK, WHITE MARKING
COLOR

NOV 12 1996
DATE OF BIRTH

TONANTRON LATIN LOVER
SIRE WP609790/01 (2-97) (UKG)

JACQUETS-BEAUS-RED-VALENTINE
DAM WP427075/03 (2-97)

CHARLES BEAUCHAMP & RICHARD TOMITA &
BREEDER RICHARD BEAUCHAMP

OWNER RICHARD G BEAUCHAMP
PO BOX 4
1071 MAIN ST
CAMBRIA, CA 93428-2821

APR 28 1997
CERTIFICATE ISSUED

AMERICAN KENNEL CLUB AKC INCORPORATED

IF A DATE APPEARS AFTER THE NAME AND NUMBER OF THE SIRE AND DAM, IT INDICATES THE ISSUE OF THE STUD BOOK REGISTER IN WHICH THE SIRE OR DAM IS PUBLISHED.

THIS CERTIFICATE ISSUED WITH THE RIGHT TO CORRECT OR REVOKE BY THE AMERICAN KENNEL CLUB

See Transfer Instructions on Back of Certificate

REGISTRATION CERTIFICATE

Figure 2-1: Every dog properly registered with the AKC is issued a Registration Certificate.

LITTER REGISTRATION APPLICATION

To register a litter born in the U.S.A. out of an AKC registered female and sired by an AKC registered male of the same breed.

PLEASE READ REVERSE SIDE BEFORE COMPLETING APPLICATION

PRINT IN CAPITAL LETTERS ONLY - USE INK

Mail with fee to: **THE AMERICAN KENNEL CLUB, P.O. BOX 37901, RALEIGH, NC 27627-7901**

OR FAX TO: THE AMERICAN KENNEL CLUB (919) 233-3627

FEE: $20.00 Litter registration applications must be received within six (6) months of the date of birth or an additional $60 penalty fee with explanation and records will be required. Fee subject to change without notice. Do not send cash.

Charge my ☐ AmEx ☐ Master Card ☐ VISA

Account number   Expiration   Signature

BREED _____ PLACE OF BIRTH ☐ U.S.A. ☐ FOREIGN (print country) _____

THIS LITTER IS A RESULT OF:
☐ a natural breeding
☐ artificial insemination
SEE REVERSE SIDE FOR INSTRUCTIONS

Number of living dogs

MALES   FEMALES

Date of Birth

MONTH   DAY   YEAR

REGISTERED NAME OF SIRE   NUMBER OF SIRE

REGISTERED NAME OF DAM   NUMBER OF DAM

SEC. A. OWNER OF SIRE ON DATE OF MATING COMPLETES THIS SECTION.

PLACE OF MATING ☐ U.S.A. ☐ FOREIGN (print country) _____

Date of Mating

MONTH   DAY   YEAR

I CERTIFY that the above named Dam was mated to the above named Sire and that the Sire was owned/co-owned by me on the date of mating, and further understand that if the above Sire has sired 6 or more litters in a lifetime or 3 or more in a calendar year, a DNA profile will be required to register this litter.

FIRST NAME   LAST NAME

STREET ADDRESS

CITY   STATE   ZIP   EMAIL _____

TELEPHONE NUMBER   FAX NUMBER   Owner/Co-Owner Signature

SEC. B. OWNERS OR LESSEES OF DAM ON DATE OF BIRTH COMPLETE THIS SECTION.

FIRST NAME   LAST NAME

STREET ADDRESS

CITY   STATE   ZIP   EMAIL _____

TELEPHONE NUMBER   FAX NUMBER

Please print the name and address of the owner to whom the registration applications will be mailed.

I(we) apply to register this litter and CERTIFY that I(we) was(were) the owner(s) or lessee(s) of the above named Dam on the date of birth of the litter and that this Dam was not mated to any other dog during her season. I(we) further CERTIFY that all of the representations on this application are true. I(we) agree to comply with AKC rules and regulations. I(we) have read the "Notice" and instructions on the reverse side of the application.

FIRST NAME   OWNER   LAST NAME   Owner Signature

FIRST NAME   2nd OWNER   LAST NAME   2nd Owner Signature

FIRST NAME   3rd OWNER   LAST NAME   3rd Owner Signature

FIRST NAME   4th OWNER   LAST NAME   4th Owner Signature

☞ * IF OWNERSHIP OF DAM CHANGED OR LEASE TERMINATED WHILE DAM WAS IN WHELP, YOU MUST COMPLETE SECTION C ON THE REVERSE SIDE OF THIS APPLICATION.

The American Kennel Club reserves the right to correct or cancel for cause the registration of this litter.
Any misrepresentation on this application is a cause for cancellation and may result in loss of all AKC privileges.

Figure 2-2:
After a litter is born, a Litter Registration Application must be correctly filled out and submitted with the necessary fees.

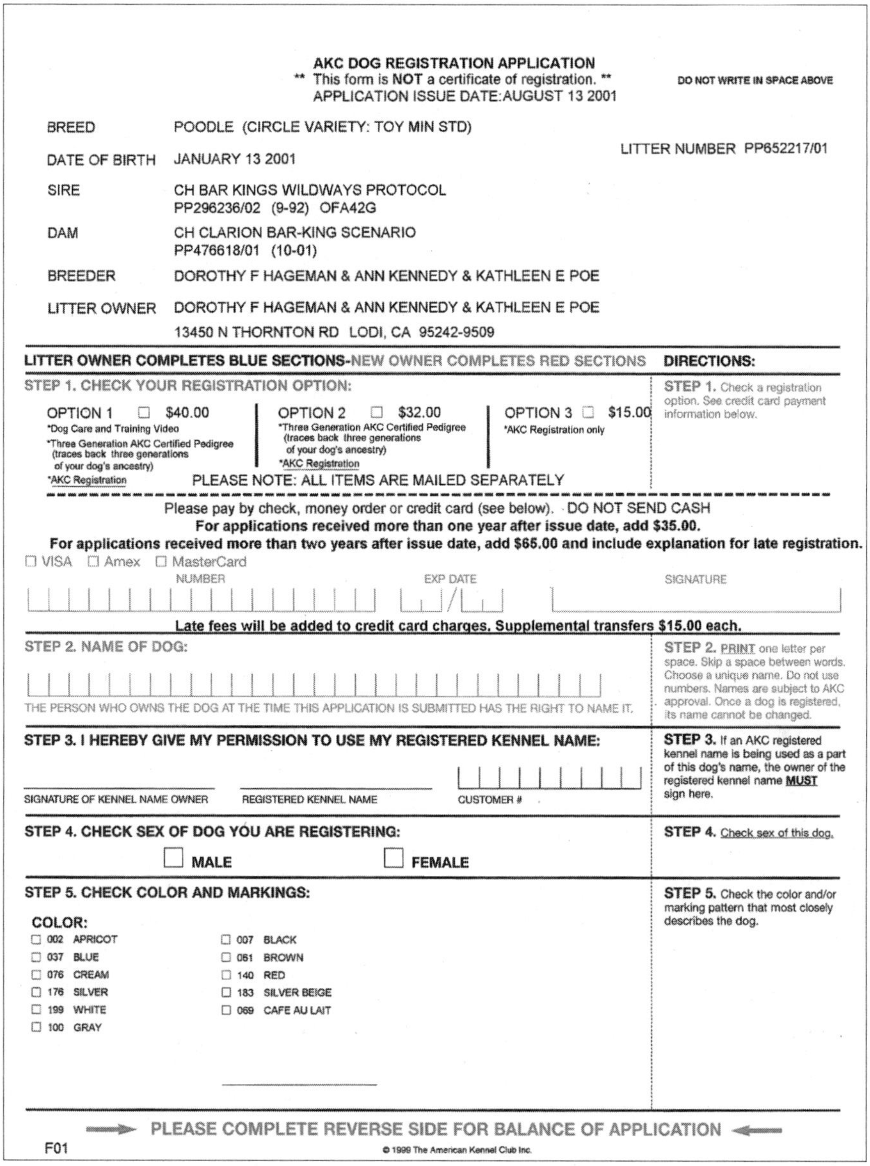

AKC DOG REGISTRATION APPLICATION
** This form is **NOT** a certificate of registration. **
APPLICATION ISSUE DATE:AUGUST 13 2001

DO NOT WRITE IN SPACE ABOVE

BREED   POODLE (CIRCLE VARIETY: TOY MIN STD)

DATE OF BIRTH   JANUARY 13 2001

LITTER NUMBER PP652217/01

SIRE   CH BAR KINGS WILDWAYS PROTOCOL
       PP296236/02 (9-92) OFA42G

DAM   CH CLARION BAR-KING SCENARIO
       PP476618/01 (10-01)

BREEDER   DOROTHY F HAGEMAN & ANN KENNEDY & KATHLEEN E POE

LITTER OWNER   DOROTHY F HAGEMAN & ANN KENNEDY & KATHLEEN E POE

       13450 N THORNTON RD LODI, CA 95242-9509

LITTER OWNER COMPLETES BLUE SECTIONS-NEW OWNER COMPLETES RED SECTIONS

DIRECTIONS:

STEP 1. CHECK YOUR REGISTRATION OPTION:

STEP 1. Check a registration option. See credit card payment information below.

OPTION 1 ☐ $40.00
*Dog Care and Training Video
*Three Generation AKC Certified Pedigree
 (traces back three generations
 of your dog's ancestry)
*AKC Registration

OPTION 2 ☐ $32.00
*Three Generation AKC Certified Pedigree
 (traces back three generations
 of your dog's ancestry)
*AKC Registration

OPTION 3 ☐ $15.00
*AKC Registration only

PLEASE NOTE: ALL ITEMS ARE MAILED SEPARATELY

Please pay by check, money order or credit card (see below). · DO NOT SEND CASH
For applications received more than one year after issue date, add $35.00.
For applications received more than two years after issue date, add $65.00 and include explanation for late registration.

☐ VISA ☐ Amex ☐ MasterCard

NUMBER   EXP DATE   SIGNATURE

/

Late fees will be added to credit card charges. Supplemental transfers $15.00 each.

STEP 2. NAME OF DOG:

STEP 2. PRINT one letter per space. Skip a space between words. Choose a unique name. Do not use numbers. Names are subject to AKC approval. Once a dog is registered, its name cannot be changed.

THE PERSON WHO OWNS THE DOG AT THE TIME THIS APPLICATION IS SUBMITTED HAS THE RIGHT TO NAME IT.

STEP 3. I HEREBY GIVE MY PERMISSION TO USE MY REGISTERED KENNEL NAME:

STEP 3. If an AKC registered kennel name is being used as a part of this dog's name, the owner of the registered kennel name **MUST** sign here.

SIGNATURE OF KENNEL NAME OWNER   REGISTERED KENNEL NAME   CUSTOMER #

STEP 4. CHECK SEX OF DOG YOU ARE REGISTERING:

☐ MALE   ☐ FEMALE

STEP 4. Check sex of this dog.

STEP 5. CHECK COLOR AND MARKINGS:

STEP 5. Check the color and/or marking pattern that most closely describes the dog.

COLOR:

☐ 002 APRICOT   ☐ 007 BLACK
☐ 037 BLUE   ☐ 051 BROWN
☐ 076 CREAM   ☐ 140 RED
☐ 176 SILVER   ☐ 183 SILVER BEIGE
☐ 199 WHITE   ☐ 069 CAFE AU LAIT
☐ 100 GRAY

→ PLEASE COMPLETE REVERSE SIDE FOR BALANCE OF APPLICATION ←

F01   © 1998 The American Kennel Club Inc.

Figure 2-3:
Using this form, the breeder of record may individually register each puppy in the litter or transfer this form on to buyers who may register the puppy themselves.

Figure 2-4:
This important form helps you to record vital information about the puppies in your litter.

Litter Record

Breed		Date of Whelp
Dam's AKC Number	Dam's Name	Male Puppies
Sire's AKC Number	Sire's Name	Female Puppies
AKC Litter Number	Date of Mating	Owner of Sire	Total Puppies

AKC Puppy or Litter ID Number	Sex	Microchip ID Type & Number Or Tattoo Number	Colors & Markings	Date Puppy Died	Appl	Cert	Bill of Sale	Ltd? Yes or No	New Owner Name, Address & Telephone	Name of Puppy if Registered by Breeder
1										
2										
3										
4										
5										
6										
7										
8										
9										
10										

OWNERSHIP RECORD OF INDIVIDUAL DOG (MALE OR FEMALE)

BREED	REGISTERED NAME (LITTER NUMBER IF NOT REGISTERED)		REGISTRATION NUMBER

NAME AND NUMBER OF SIRE		NAME AND NUMBER OF DAM	

DATE OF BIRTH	SEX	COLOR AND MARKINGS	

NAME OF PERSON FROM WHOM DOG WAS OBTAINED	DATE OBTAINED

ADDRESS OF PERSON FROM WHOM DOG WAS OBTAINED	BREEDER

FINAL DISPOSITION OF DOG- Check (✓) APPROPRIATE BOX AND GIVE DATE IN SPACE PROVIDED	DIED	SOLD	GIVEN AWAY	DATE	NAME OF PERSON TO WHOM SOLD OR GIVEN

ADDRESS OF PERSON TO WHOM SOLD OR GIVEN

GAVE BUYER FOLLOWING PAPERS ON DATES SHOWN IN APPROPRIATE BOXES	REGISTRATION CERTIFICATE	REGISTRATION APPLICATION	BILL OF SALE	DOG IDENTIFICATION-MARK, TAG OR TATTOO NUMBER

BREEDING RECORD OF ABOVE DOG

DATE OF MATING	NAME AND REGISTERED NUMBER OF DOG MATED WITH ABOVE DOG	NAMES OF PERSONS HANDLING MATING
NAME AND ADDRESS OF OWNER OF DOG MATED		
DATE OF MATING	NAME AND REGISTERED NUMBER OF DOG MATED WITH ABOVE DOG	NAMES OF PERSONS HANDLING MATING
NAME AND ADDRESS OF OWNER OF DOG MATED		
DATE OF MATING	NAME AND REGISTERED NUMBER OF DOG MATED WITH ABOVE DOG	NAMES OF PERSONS HANDLING MATING
NAME AND ADDRESS OF OWNER OF DOG MATED		
DATE OF MATING	NAME AND REGISTERED NUMBER OF DOG MATED WITH ABOVE DOG	NAMES OF PERSONS HANDLING MATING
NAME AND ADDRESS OF OWNER OF DOG MATED		
DATE OF MATING	NAME AND REGISTERED NUMBER OF DOG MATED WITH ABOVE DOG	NAMES OF PERSONS HANDLING MATING
NAME AND ADDRESS OF OWNER OF DOG MATED		
DATE OF MATING	NAME AND REGISTERED NUMBER OF DOG MATED WITH ABOVE DOG	NAMES OF PERSONS HANDLING MATING
NAME AND ADDRESS OF OWNER OF DOG MATED		

Figure 2-5:
You need to keep an Ownership Record for each of your dogs.

Figure 2-6:
Certified
Pedigrees
can be
obtained
directly from
the AKC for
a nominal
fee.

Registration rules and procedures vary from country to country. Very often a breeder will become interested in a breed or in a particular bloodline that's not easily obtained in the breeder's country and will choose to import a dog from another country. The registration systems used by the United States, Britain, Australia, and Canada are compatible. Normally, a dog properly registered in any one of those countries can be registered in any of the others.

However, there is no actual guarantee that the registrations will cross borders, and each pedigree and registration application is carefully examined to make sure that it's in full compliance with the policies and regulations established by the Board of Directors of the AKC.

The AKC has a special division, the AKC Special Registry Services, that deals with matters of this nature and can provide you with a publication that covers most of the questions you may have in regard to other registries. The publication is titled *AKC Special Registry Services* and has a reference code of GASPEC (8/00).

The American Kennel Club

Normally just called *the AKC,* the American Kennel Club is a nonprofit organization devoted to the advancement of purebred dogs. The AKC maintains a registry of recognized breeds and adopts and enforces rules for dog events, including Shows, Obedience Trials, Field Trials, Hunting Tests, Lure Coursing, Herding, Earthdog Trials, Agility, and the Canine Good Citizen program. It is a club of clubs, established in 1884 and composed, today, of well over 500 independent dog clubs throughout the United States. Each club is represented by a delegate; the delegates make up the legislative body of the AKC, voting on rules and electing directors.

The American Kennel Club maintains the Stud Book, which is a record of every dog ever registered with the AKC, and publishes a variety of materials on purebred dogs, including a monthly magazine, books, and numerous educational pamphlets. For more information go to www.akc.org or contact the AKC at the address listed in Appendix A.

Chapter 3

Choosing the Right Breed for You

- -

- -

*T*he various canine registering organizations of the world officially recognize well over 400 distinct breeds of dogs. They run the gamut of size, color, shape, and temperament. There's a certain breed that could be just about perfect for every person wanting a dog. Unfortunately, not enough attention is paid to the breed that will prove most compatible; all the attention goes to what the dog looks like or how well it has acclimated itself to someone *else's* household.

Before you make that final decision on what is going to be your breed of choice, I want to throw up a few road signs to help guide you in the right direction.

Compatibility: The Bottom Line

You may be well ahead of this stage of the game and already be ready to search for a dog of the breed that you've fallen in love with. Or "Duke" or "Duchess" may already have taken up residence in your household. You know for certain that this is the breed for you and the one in which you are convinced that you want to specialize.

On the one hand, what's included in this chapter may at first seem redundant. However, a lot of what's included will help you immeasurably in understanding what you should and should not expect of your breed of dog. Rather than working against what generations of selective breeding have produced, this chapter may help you go with the flow.

Compatibility, quite frankly, is one of the most important considerations involved in dog breeding, or in dog ownership for that matter. If you aren't able to establish and maintain a pleasant relationship with one dog of a breed, there is absolutely no way on earth that you're going find life tolerable with two of the breed, much less with a whole house or kennel full!

Your getting along well with the dog is just as important as the dog getting on with you. Both of you have to get something out of the relationship. Actually, dogs are better at coping than their owners are. Dogs put up with all kinds of treatment and still love their masters. They'd probably be better dogs with different owners but they love and respond to their owner regardless. Owners, on the other hand, are not very good at this "coping" thing. When dogs don't adjust to their owners' life styles, the relationships seldom last. In order for dogs or their offspring to be sound, stable, and compatible representatives of their breed, an environment conducive to achieving their genetic potential is bottom line.

Dogs that go into the wrong homes do not stay there. This is something that you must know, understand, and never forget. Not every terrific dog is suitable for every terrific home. Strange? Not really. Think of the situation as if you were dealing with humans. I'm sure you've met people in business situations that you got on famously with but completely reversed your opinion of them when you were put together in a social situation.

Was your judgement off base? Not necessarily. You probably didn't know enough about the person to fully assess their character and understand just how they would react in a situation other than that in which the two of you came together. A person who does not fully understand the basic character of the dogs he breeds can hardly be expected to be capable of determining the kind of home they should go into.

A true-life example

Before dashing out to buy any breed of dog for any reason — because your good friend has one or you hear it's the smartest or cutest breed around — spend some time with adults of the breed. (All puppies are adorable, and as youngsters they haven't learned to be all that they can be!) I'll give you a little example of just why spending time with the breed is so important.

Jack Russell Terriers are little dogs who have made a huge splash lately, even though the AKC has just recently acknowledged them as a breed. So many of my "non-doggie" friends (those who don't breed and show dogs) had asked about Jack Russells that I felt learning more about them was important. All I knew was that on the TV sitcoms I've channel surfed by, JRs appear to have the intelligence level of a Ph.D. and the athletic ability of an Olympic decathlon gold medalist. No mean recommendation for any breed, I would say.

Jack and Laura, longtime friends of mine who have owned, bred, and trained dogs for years, now breed and show Jack Russells along with their first love, Golden Retrievers. So, when they asked me to spend a weekend with them when I was attending a nearby dog show, I gladly accepted. I learned a lot over those few days — about Jack Russell Terriers and about myself.

When I arrived, I was greeted at the door by my friends' three Golden Retrievers, who wagged their tails, licked my hand, and brought me offerings of tennis balls and stuffed teddy bears.

"No JRs?" I asked.

"Not at the same time the Goldens are indoors," was the response.

"Fights?"

"No — *riots!*"

I found that having three Golden Retrievers in the house at once was a snap. And *possibly* one Golden and *one* JR could work, but when the indoor dog population grew any larger than that with even one JR on site, chaos ensued.

Are JRs simply bad dogs? Not at all! They are dynamos of energy and admittedly true comedians. They want to see, smell, investigate, and do everything in sight and all at once. But in my friends' home, the JRs' energy level interrupted the Goldens' tranquil existence. When Goldens and JRs got together, the result was what Jack and Laura's five-year-old daughter called *"all over dogs!"*

One JR in the house was cute as all get out, but, quite frankly, even then there was a bit more activity than I am accustomed to. It obviously worked for my friends, but not for me. In fact, JRs work well for many people I know. They're smart little fellows, and not finding them amusing is impossible. However, their energy level on a scale of one to ten must be at least an eleven. Certainly not the "good old boy" I'm accustomed to at home who enjoys a couple of hours of totally immobile TV watching as much as I do. In fact, depending on the weather, Raif just may *prefer* a night in front of the television set.

Home considerations

If you haven't selected the breed you are thinking seriously about owning (and let's deal with owning first, before we even *think* about breeding), the first thing you want to do is sit down and think very clearly about the environment in which you live.

Do you like it the way it is or do you want it changed? Bringing a dog into your life is not unlike bringing a new baby into the home. In fact, it can be just as much work — and dogs never arrive at the age when you can send them off to school for five of the week's seven days.

If other people live with you, what do they think about owning and perhaps breeding dogs? Your significant other may not view cleaning up after a puppy as the most exciting thing in the world. If that's the case, the prospect of a litter or *litters* of puppies down the road may be "the end of a sweet love affair," as the old song goes.

You have to take so much into consideration. What if you and yours spend every weekend jogging, skiing, or mountain climbing? As unique and intriguing as the Bulldog may be, the breed is at the opposite end of the energy scale from the earlier example of the Jack Russell Terrier. A Bulldog would not only choose to snooze (and snore!) in front of the fireplace, his physical makeup does not allow for the super-jock life you lead.

Is the breed you're thinking about too big for the place in which you live? You and Sampson the Great Dane may look very smart strolling down 5th Avenue together, but what will Sampson be doing when you aren't out strolling? I once heard of a Great Dane living in a downtown Manhattan studio apartment, but I just can't picture it. I don't *want to* picture it! And if one Great Dane is really too big for a lot of residences, common sense has to tell you that a whole litter of little Sampsons could be a big problem.

If you or your mate is a fastidious housekeeper, you aren't going to be thrilled with a dog whose semiannual shedding makes like a Minnesota blizzard. A good friend once told me that she would love to patent what German Shepherd hair is made of. "It's lighter than air," she said, "can find its way over, under, around, and through the tiniest crack, and sticks permanently to everything but the place it came from — *the dog!*"

Also stop and think of how you handle, or want to handle, additional responsibility. If having a dog, and potentially *dogs,* is your idea alone, don't saddle someone else with the responsibility of care. Doing so isn't fair and could cost you your happy home. And even if the kids in the family "promise, promise, *promise!*" that not a day will go by without their giving the dog first priority — don't believe it!

Not that kids don't believe it themselves when they promise to care for a dog. They intend to. Children don't mean to mislead you (well, not always), but their first priority is one thing now and another thing in a few minutes. At eight the most important thing in little Johnny's life may well be the family dog, but at nine it's Little League. Sister Mary's thoughts turn to the better things of life — like boys — before you can imagine.

If planting the petunias or giving them an occasional drink of water after they are finally planted is drudgery to you, dog care is going to seem like indentured servitude! Petunias shrivel up and disappear after a few days of neglect. Dogs eat the new sofa cushions and dig holes in the middle of your Kentucky blue grass lawn when they're neglected. They don't do this out of spite, mind you, it's just their way out of boredom. Better think twice (or four times) about this one!

Your PST (personal suitability test)

A new dog owner must clearly understand the amount of time and work involved in the project. Again, if watering the philodendron or giving the parakeet some seed proved to be something you did grudgingly and only because you had to, a dog is going to make you feel like you're responsible for the national debt.

Can you pass the Dog Owner's Personal Suitability Test (PST)? Unless you can pass with flying colors, you may not qualify to be a dog owner at all, and certainly not a dog *breeder!* Before you leap into this, sit down with a pencil and sheet of paper. Answer these questions as honestly as you possibly can. The final results tell you a lot.

- ✔ Is the person who wants a dog the same person who will really wind up with the responsibility for providing its care?
- ✔ Is everyone you live with as anxious as you are to have a dog in the home?
- ✔ Depending on the breed, does your lifestyle allow enough time for care, training, and exercise?
- ✔ Is your living environment suitable for a dog of this kind?
- ✔ Are you physically capable of handling a fully grown dog of this breed?
- ✔ Is your own character and personality strong enough to establish the proper relationship between you and a dog of the breed you've chosen?
- ✔ Are you financially able to incur the cost of food, upkeep, and sometimes extremely expensive veterinary bills?

Don't take the questions lightly. Affirmative answers are required for every one of these questions. If any of them create doubt in your mind when answered for one dog, you have to realize that the importance of answering each question affirmatively is multiplied when it comes to dog breeding. Don't bring dogs into a situation that isn't compatible with their being there. It does not work.

What You See Is (Not Always) What You Get!

You will note that thus far I haven't dwelled on what any of the breeds look like. This is partially because beauty remains in the eye of the beholder. But more significantly, I've left aesthetics alone because more owner-dog mismatches are created because of physical appearance than by anything else. What a dog looks like usually has absolutely nothing to do with his or her temperament or personality.

If you are going to breed a particular breed, fully understanding the character of that breed is critical. The character and personality must not only be compatible with yours, but they must also be a part of your breeding goal. Those who established the breed had sound reasons for developing the character as they have, and no respected breeder would or should disregard this important breed characteristic.

There are many breed-specific books available through pet outlets, bookstores, and on the Internet. The best of these specialized books give you great detail on each breed and the specifics of their respective characters and special needs.

Beware though, not every book written about a breed may give you the information you need if you're still trying to make up your mind. Even people who are experts can be unintentionally misleading in their enthusiasm for their breed.

If Boxers or Rottweilers are breeds you're considering, you may want to pick up a book on either of the two in the *For Dummies* series. They're written by an author I can recommend without reservation. (Well, if I don't toot my own horn, who will?)

Seriously, I've done my best in both instances to detail all my experience — both negative and positive — with the two breeds. Even Boxers, my personal favorites, get the whole truth and nothing but. If you really love the breed as much as I do and they suit your lifestyle, you'll overlook the trials and tribulations of an adolescence that can very often last well into their fourth or fifth year.

Read as much as you can and spend as much time observing and interacting with as many different dogs of that breed as you can. Take all the time you can and be sure.

Do not make the fatal mistake of becoming involved with a breed whose only attraction is its looks. This can prove to be disastrous for both the owner and dog.

A perfect example of why dogs shouldn't be bought on looks came about after the release and box office success of the Disney film *101 Dalmatians.* There was an avalanche of requests for puppies. Within a year, however, an alarming number of young adult Dalmatians began to appear in city pounds and animal shelters throughout the country.

Was there something intrinsically wrong with the breed? In all fairness to the breed, it should be noted that suddenly kennels sprang up across the nation aimed at nothing less than mass producing these short-in-demand spotted puppies. Quality was not a concern! And the kennels disappeared just as quickly, when the demand died down and buyers had to deal with the results of what physically and temperamentally unsound parents had produced.

But not all the Dals in pounds were poorly bred. Many were the result of royal pedigrees, but the people who had purchased the dogs as adorable little puppies had no idea how any dog, let alone a Dalmatian, should be raised and trained. The puppy was no longer cute and cuddly and was no longer able to be contained in a little box in the corner. Next stop — the animal shelter!

Purebred Dogs and Selective Breeding

As the centuries passed on from the time man first met wolf, the more domesticated of the wolves were performing many of the tasks that humans had previously been burdened with. Certain things began to be apparent. Some of these canines were better at their job than others, and even among the best performers, enthusiasm for the tasks varied from one animal to the next.

At some point in time, man also became aware that the offspring of a sire and a dam who both excelled at a particular task were apt to be good at that task too. Intentional manipulation of the mating habits of these animals began. This was the dawning of a new type of wolf — one that history now refers to as *Canis familiaris* (the domestic dog) rather than *Canis lupus.* People took control of the mating in order to develop specific breeds of dogs that best suited their purposes.

The important thing to understand here, however, is that humans did not *invent* any characteristics that the dogs of those days displayed. Nor have we invented any since. Every characteristic our dogs have has been there since dogs were wolves and ran in the forest. Humans have simply isolated and intensified what had already been inherited. This was accomplished by adding only those animals to the gene pool who were strong in the desired traits and eliminating the animals whose characteristics opposed what was desired.

An example

Taking a brief look at the evolution of the Australian Cattle Dog shows how selective breeding has resulted in what we have today. The Aussie owes its reliability and efficiency to a unique breeding ability that British stockmen have earned a worldwide reputation for possessing.

The Brits call their breeding approach *Horses for Courses.* This simply means choosing a formula that will produce a horse best suited to the terrain of the region in which the horse will work. The formula has been successfully applied not only to horses, but also to livestock of all kinds and to the many breeds of outstanding livestock dogs that the British have developed through the years.

This breeding ability was given its greatest test in the late eighteenth century, when early settlers from the United Kingdom migrated to Australia. The emigrants took their livestock with them only to find that many of their time-proven rules governing animal husbandry had to be adjusted to this rugged, and often entirely inhospitable, land down under.

On the one hand, the vast expanses of land that were available afforded space for huge herds of not only sheep, but also more space-needy cattle. Certainly an economic boon — but the stockmen quickly realized that free-ranging cattle were not only difficult to keep track of, but also treacherous to the hands hired to work them.

Further, the highly developed stock dogs that easily controlled the laid-back sheep and small herds of cattle in Great Britain met conditions in Australia they were entirely unable to cope with. The dogs were unable to tolerate the country's scorching temperatures and rough terrain and the huge distances that needed to be covered. Nor were they ready for the fierce challenges of the hostile cattle.

The dogs somehow able to survive the adverse conditions presented yet another problem — *barking!* Their incessant barking kept the drovers' horses on edge and the near-wild cattle in such a state of nervous frenzy that it worried the marketable weight right off their bones. It was obvious a much different kind of herding dog was required for the settlers' new home — a dog more able to handle the rugged new territory.

Indigenous to the new land was a wolf-like dog that was destined to play a significant role in the development of a new breed. The aboriginal population called the dogs *Worrigals* or *Dingoes.* Anthropological evidence reveals the Dingo is a descendant of the Asian wolf rather than the northern gray wolf from which most other dogs are descended.

These wolf descendants probably reached Australian shores some 4,000 years ago, well before the white man, and easily acclimated themselves to Australia. The aboriginals never subjected the Dingo to the domestication pressure that had been put upon descendants of the northern gray wolf throughout Europe. Still, the Dingo maintained an independent, yet close, relationship with the aborigines.

The Dingo lived both in aboriginal camps and in the wild, not unlike the northern wolf descendants had in their earliest stages on the European continent. Those who lived in the camps were easily taught to track and hunt. The others in the wild existed as swift, silent, and highly successful predators who found easy meals in the white man's newly introduced sheep and cattle.

On the one hand, Australian cattlemen considered the dingo a plague that needed to be eliminated. At the same time, the more clever stockmen were not blind to the fact that many of the Dingo's survival qualities were exactly those missing in their herding dogs.

Several of the herdsmen attempted crossing their own herding breeds with the Australian native dog. The early crosses didn't work — the offspring were extremely aggressive. Left to their own devices, the offspring of these matings would attack and eat sheep and young calves, to say nothing of their unreliable attitudes toward the men themselves.

In 1840 Thomas Hall, who lived near Sydney, crossed his pair of imported blue merle smooth-coated Highland Collies with Dingoes. The Collies had proven willing and capable workers, but couldn't cope with the ill-tempered cattle or inhospitable environment.

Even the first cross revealed great promise — the offspring maintained the herding instincts of their Collie ancestry but worked silently, as the Dingo did. The one drawback was that the offspring treated the herdsmen's horses like cattle — snapping at the horses' heels while trying to get them to join the herd.

About that time, ranching brothers Jack and Harry Bagust bred the best of their Dingo and smooth Collie-cross females to a Dalmatian who had been imported from Great Britain. The cross was made in respect to the Dalmatian's long-standing rapport with horses.

The experiment was successful. The offspring did have a workmanlike relationship with both horse and horseman. In the end, through selective breeding, the Dingo's athletic conformation and constitution, along with its intelli- gence and silent way of working, were maintained while being enhanced by the Dalmatian's devotion and protectiveness.

The developing line of dogs was also heir to its sheepdog ancestors' ability to learn quickly, follow commands, and herd. Anything that contradicted that intuitive herding ability was bred out and what was brought in only assisted that instinctive ability.

The upshot

I use this example for two reasons — to illustrate the selective process responsible for the development of our modern breeds and to show how contrary to a dog's character and heritage it is to deny the dog the ability to exercise what hundreds, if not thousands, of generations of selectivity has prepared him to do.

It is important to understand that *every characteristic* a dog has been handed down for hundreds, if not thousands, of generations. Because of the hodge-podge ancestry of a mixed-breed dog, predictability is almost impossible. In the purebred dog, everything from appearance to character and temperament are as near a certainty as we can have in dealing with animals.

This predictability is extremely important in your ultimate choice of a pure-bred dog. The likelihood of having the bred-to-travel-and-travel-far Siberian Husky prefer to sit home by the hearth is remote. Asking a Rottweiler to drop his inbred protective traits is unfair. This is not to say the Rottie should be allowed to arbitrarily decide how to be protective — to the contrary. But protectiveness is an inbred part of the breed's nature.

Rather than work *against* character, choose a breed whose character you can support and maintain.

Understanding Canine Behavior

Wonder dogs — dogs who never do anything wrong — are, if anything, made, not born. Training produces these canine marvels, but their owners also carefully chose the dog to suit the owners' wants and needs. Finding a dog who suits your life is the best way to success.

The dog who lies quietly alongside my desk as I write this is about as mellow a pal as one could hope for — quiet and tractable in every way. That is, until a visitor arrives, and then Raif's response is such that you would be sure the new arrival is his long-lost love for whom he's been waiting for years. He reacts the same way whether it's a first-time visitor or someone he sees every day of the week. That is simply Raif. He's a Boxer and that's how Boxers are about life. He greets every new day like it should be celebrated as if it were New Year's Eve or the 4th of July!

Dogs with human qualities?

After adults bring a new dog into the household, they immediately seem to start endowing the dog with human qualities. They then expect the dog to start behaving like a human. Children, on the other hand, endow their dogs with human qualities but expect nothing more from their dogs than to act like dogs.

What do I believe? You can't have lived with as many dogs as I have through the years without observing what is clearly instinctual behavior at times and what is obviously rational behavior at others.

I do believe that dogs learn to obey our "laws" in a manner that is similar to, but different from, the way that humans do. They can learn that certain behavior on their part brings your approval, disapproval, and consequences; both negative and positive. However, dogs can only associate your reactions to their behavior when your response immediately follows the action.

Don't let the learning *similarities* override the fact that you are working with a dog and not a human. Keep it simple! Another thing you have to remember is that although generally speaking all dogs learn in the same way, the speed with which you get the message through to different dogs and different breeds varies.

Again we have the purebred predictability factor here. You can rest assured that probably nine out of ten Golden Retrievers will knock themselves out trying to please you by responding to your lessons. However, don't expect that same response from a Chow Chow. A Chow Chow may think your new "game" is delightful and respond with enthusiasm. On the other hand, he may not. Or he may one time and not another. And if it's *not*, you'll have to call upon every bit of patience you've got to work on getting the message across.

Of course, some dogs' attitudes toward strangers lie entirely in the opposite direction: They are extremely reticent around strangers. Although there are many explanations for both Raif's extroverted personality and another dog's wariness, selective breeding through generations could certainly be the primary factor. One breed maintains the wolf's wariness of humans, although it's now channeled into simply being reserved around people the dog doesn't know. The other breed has lost the wolf's suspiciousness completely.

Sound and stable foundation stock is far more apt to come from bloodlines that have been carefully selected for these qualities. At the same time, even the best physical and mental representative of a breed will not achieve his or her potential if the owner-dog relationship is not well structured. In this relationship, there is one leader and one follower. If the owner is not willing or able to assume the role of leader, he fails in his part of the relationship.

Yes, here we are, 12,000 or more years after domestication, and even Wang Foo the Pekingese still needs her pack leader. The leaders of the wolf packs our dogs are descended from got the job because they knew what to do to get the job and also knew what had to be done in order to keep the followers in line.

The leaders instinctively understood what the followers needed and enforced the rules. They didn't do this simply to prove who was in charge, but to contribute to the survival of the pack. Now that you're the pack leader, you must enforce the rules to insure the survival of the relationship. If you are going to breed and raise dogs, you must have a thorough understanding of how thousands of years have shaped the breed's character and, as a result, how the breed learns and how it communicates.

All dogs are born with a clean slate as far as what humans would like to have them do. Dogs aren't born knowing any of our rules so their experiences with their owners are what puts the writing on that slate. Your part of all this is to write exactly what you want on that slate!

Word association

Dogs can associate a *word* with a substance or an event. Using different words to express the same command, even if the words were to have exactly the same meaning to you, will only serve to confuse your dog — the connection cannot be made. *Car, automobile,* and *Ford Mustang* have basically the same meaning for you and me, but not for our dogs.

Rational learning

As strong a drive as instinct is, the people I know who have spent any time with dogs are fully convinced that dogs can think and come to logical conclusions. When I drive down to the end of our country road and turn right to the highway, my dog Raif sits back calmly in his seat, gazes out the window, and is ready to travel calmly to wherever I, his chauffeur, may take him. However, if I turn left from our road, this means but one thing to Raif — *beach time!* And then keeping him contained is all I can do.

What causes a dog to rush out into the street and snatch a child from the danger of an oncoming auto? Who told our dogs that bringing us their leash or a toy will inspire a walk or play time? Rationality, not instinct.

Instinct

All dogs have some instinctive behaviors because they are, in fact, dogs. This applies whether your dog is a Great Dane, Toy Poodle, or Golden Retriever. All dogs, regardless of breed, descend from the same source — *Canis lupus,* the wolf. Great-grandpappy wolf contributed certain behavior-controlling genes to his descendants that have proven so strong or so useful to dogs that the genes live on to this day. Granted, humans have manipulated some of these heredi-tary inclinations to suit themselves, but the source from which the instincts came remains the same.

For instance, just about all dogs have inherited from their lupine ancestors a desire to chase. I feel quite certain that even among the earliest wolves some had a stronger chase instinct than others. They all had a built-in ability and desire to chase, but it was undoubtedly far more prevalent in some wolves than in other wolves. So it has been with their descendants ever since.

Some dogs chase a ball or a stick, or the neighbor's cat, only if they have noth-ing else to do. Other dogs chase just about anything that moves — every time it moves! The breeds in which the chase instinct is strong can be trained not to chase, but you can never eliminate their *inborn desire* to do so. Instincts of that kind course heavily through a dog's genetic makeup.

Female dogs have read no books and have never attended a Lamaze class, yet they know everything there is to know about the birth and care of their offspring. This is instinctual knowledge. Puppies nurse by instinct. Males are compelled to breed through instinct. In nature, these are the things that animals are required to do in order to survive.

Even the most well-fed mother dog regurgitates food for her pups. This is a carry-over from the time when regurgitation was used by a mother to get the day's kill back to the den for her hungry pups. The mother of your puppies doesn't have to do this for her pups, and it may seem repugnant to you but it is a very normal instinctive behavior. Quite frankly I believe you would confuse and stress the mother were you to reprimand her for doing so.

No one teaches the modern dog any of these behaviors. The traits are within the genetic structure of each and every dog. Some traits are of little conse-quence and others conflict with how people want their dogs to appear or to behave as pets.

Why Mixed Breeds Should Not Be Bred

You won't hear long-time dog breeders say *never* very often. Most of what a breeder thinks might or should happen doesn't, and what breeders expect to happen all the time seldom happens at all. Because breeders deal with Mother Nature, they get used to the fact that *she will have her way!*

But breeders do say *never* in one situation — in the case of allowing a mixed-breed dog to produce puppies. Believe me, this isn't because breeders don't like mixed breeds. The contrary is true. In a good many cases, a mixed-breed dog was a breeder's introduction to any kind of dog at all. I've been to many homes where a treasured mixed breed holds a place of honor right alongside some of the most famous show dogs in the country.

The reason that breeders are adamantly opposed to allowing mixed-breed litters is that they have seen how tragically most mixed-breed pups end their lives. All you have to do is visit an animal shelter at pretty much any time of the year and invariably you will find a very young mixed-breed female nursing a litter of puppies — and it always seems to be a very large litter of mixed-breed puppies.

The reason posted for the mother and her puppies being in the shelter is usually "Owner moving, couldn't keep." Sure, *moving.* It's far more apt to be a case of "Owner careless and negligent. Didn't have dog spayed. Now doesn't want to cope with the consequences." If you were forced to witness the mass euthanasia of dogs that takes place across the country because there are too many puppies being born, you would *run,* not walk, to have your pet sexually altered.

Even if someone comes along who is willing to adopt a mixed-breed pup from the pound, determining what a mixed-breed puppy will look like and act like as an adult is nearly impossible. It's impossible to determine if the mixed-breed puppy's temperament is suitable for the person who will own it. Your Trixie or Spike may well be the greatest and smartest dog that has ever seen the light of day. You may feel the whole world deserves to have a dog just like her, but don't make yourself responsible for an unhappy ending for any offspring your pal produces. If the puppies grow up to be too big, too hairy, too active, or too anything for the people who take the puppies, what will their fate be?

Love your mixed-breed dog enough to make sure it will not contribute to a problem that is already out of control.

Part II
Understanding
Purebred Dogs

The 5th Wave   By Rich Tennant

In this part . . .

Whether your choice is a Pekingese or St. Bernard, a Fox Terrier or Basset Hound, all these breeds have one thing in common: their origin. All dogs trace back to that point in time when their common ancestor, the wolf, was out taking care of her daily hunting chores when, lo and behold, there stood the strangest creature she had ever seen: a human being! The rest is history, and you get a bird's-eye view of that history in this part.

Chapter 4

The Origin and Development of Dog Breeds

*Y*our mind may already be completely made up as to which breed is your breed of breeds. That one dog in a million may be sitting there at your feet as you read this. Possibly you've already done a lot of research and visited the homes of people who live with the breed you admire — and you're convinced that life would be better with one such dog in your life, and even better with many.

If so, you can feel free to skip this chapter. The information I'm presenting here, at first glance, may appear a bit too elementary for the level of knowledge you've already reached or the level of decisions that have to be made. It's the basic stuff — information that a breeder or potential breeder should have firmly in place.

Something I discovered early on in this world of dogs is that no one knows what they don't know, so you may want to keep reading just to be safe! Even though you're thinking that you've been there and done that, there may be something here that can give you a little better idea of why the various breeds of dogs are what they are or that may shed a little more light on the breed of your choice.

Knowing how dogs got here in the first place explains a great deal about why your very civilized pooch does things that seem totally out of character. It also helps you understand why some doggie behavior is very hard, if not impossible, to alter.

If you plan to live with a dog of any breed, you and the dog must find life more than just tolerable. In order for the dog and its offspring to be sound and stable representatives of the breed, they have to be raised in an environment conducive to achieving their genetic potential, so you have to know what those genetics are all about.

Breeds, Behavior, and the Human Factor

Hundreds, sometimes thousands, of years have been invested by humans in shaping how breeds look and behave. But some dog behaviors are even more firmly fixed than those imposed by humans — the things that were passed down from the very source of the world's dogs.

If you try to change the basic character of the dogs you breed, particularly in many of the instinctive behavioral areas, you only create a difficult situation and don't provide the environment that is really suitable for bringing more of the breed into existence. Even more important, if you don't fully understand the basic character of your dogs, you can hardly expect to be capable of determining the kind of homes the dogs you breed should go to. And dogs that go to the wrong homes do not remain there!

The prospective dog owner has a veritable candy store of breeds to choose from. The American Kennel Club alone recognizes over 150. And that's only a small part of what are probably over 400 breeds that are recognized worldwide. The breeds range from the tiniest of toy breeds, weighing as little as three to four pounds, on up to the giant breeds that weigh as much as most women and a lot of men.

The breeds all look different and act different — to a point. Although most potential owners and future breeders recognize the obvious differences in appearance, not many stop to consider the important differences in what I refer to as *breed character* — those things that constitute how dogs of a breed behave, how they carry themselves, and what their character demands in the way of space and activity.

Although *canine character* may sound like a Saturday morning kid's cartoon, it's something that has been refined by humans through generations of intervention — *meddling* is another word for it! The hard work that's been put into creating a breed is something that must be considered before someone brings a dog of any breed into their home. Breeders are morally responsible to respect and do their utmost to reproduce the basic stuff that makes a breed what it is intended to be.

It is highly doubtful that any breed people have had a hand in developing didn't have an original purpose. At some point in time, undoubtedly someone somewhere said, "Gol dang it — I got to have more like ole Bess!" Persistent manipulation of the gene pool (again, meddling) then took place over hundreds, if not thousands, of years to insure there were, in fact, more like ole Bess.

In order to understand what selective breeding is really all about and to see how it affects the dog who is sitting at (or on) your feet as you read this chapter, I'm going to zip back in time to the beginning of the beginning — before the man-dog relationship even started.

It's Evolution, Baby

Darwin and his bunch tell us that following all the thunder, lightening, earthquakes, and volcanic eruptions on the early days of this planet, water, water was everywhere and every once in awhile some great land mass. Living in that environment were all those squirmy things — some that swam and others that just crawled around. The next bunch to make their appearance was smarter. They waited until things had quieted down and there were some plants and things around to eat. They included large ape-like mammals.

I, for one, believe every word Darwin said. First, because I wasn't there to disprove what he said. Second, because blaming Ms. Eve for everything that's gone wrong since she offered Adam a few bites off her fruit plate is no longer politically correct.

Hot on the heels (well, hot on the heels when you're speaking in millions of years) of the apes and such came a whole series of animals who not only looked weird, their names were even weirder. Take, for instance *Cynodictis,* who most paleontologists agree is one, of if not the, oldest ancestor of the dog. Like, we're talking 40 to 60 million years ago!

Down from old *Cynodictis* came a whole line of what are known as *carnivores* (meat-eating animals). They didn't look much prettier, and their names — *Pseudocynodictis, Hesperocyon,* and *Tomarctus* — didn't do anything to help them catch on either.

But finally, finally, along came a *Cynodictis* descendant that not only looked like something you'd want to keep around, it had a name you could almost pronounce! This was the *Carnivora canidae,* which is just a fancy term for the family that includes one branch called *Canis.* This branch includes *Canis aureus,* the jackal, *Canis vulpes,* the true foxes, *Canis latrans,* the coyote, and the part of the family that we're most interested in: *Canis lupus,* the wolf.

It's a big family and, as you can see, an ancient one. Family members live on every continent of the world and under every condition imaginable — forest, desert, mountain, and steppe. They survive in almost every climate, no matter how extreme.

If you can't say anything else for this bunch, you'd have to acknowledge their adaptability. They adapted their physical structure and the way they behave to be able to survive in just about any place they wound up. Some were nomads; others stay-at-homes. Some hunted at night; others during the day. Some were loners; others hunted in packs.

Wolves Meet Humans

The jackals, coyotes, and foxes continued right on their merry ways, staying totally wild and as woolly as they'd always been, but the wolf family's path took an abrupt turn when it met humans. It was love at first sight. Well, "love" since anything less than eating each other in those days was tantamount to a love affair.

Love story or not, it's a story that began over 12,000 years ago and continues on to this day. Oddly enough, it has a lot to do with trash collection. It seems that back then, folks in the settlements had a waste removal problem. (So what's new?) A resolution to the mounting problem turned out to be none other than the wolf. It appears the big bad wolf was actually one of mankind's original trash collectors!

After dining on brontosaurus steaks or whatever cave persons dined on, the early humans threw the food discards in a big pile outside the campsite. After wolves got over the initial shock of seeing their first human, they came sniffing around the outskirts of the settlement to see what was cooking. Evidently, they found rummaging around the trash heap a heck of a lot easier and frequently more rewarding than chasing down a mastodon for lunch. So they hung out and waited for whatever came next.

As a result, the wolves helped keep the grounds free of garbage and in return for their services, humans didn't spear them on sight as they did with so many other animal visitors.

Since the wolf spent a good deal of time nearby, waiting to see what was on the dinner menu, Mesolithic men and women had some time to observe the wolf. Mesolithic man and his family recognized the fact that the wolf had some value. Instead of including wolf meat as part of the clan's diet, they offered some members of the wolf family camping privileges.

As the relationship jelled, the better-behaved members of the wolf pack moved closer and closer to the settlements, until they were almost in town. Exploring children and returning hunters perhaps would come across some roly-poly wolf cubs that were brought home and easily tamed. The clan folk undoubtedly began to realize they could select certain descendants of these increasingly friendly wolves to help around the settlement — hunting, pulling things around, sounding the alarm when animal or human midnight marauders came calling.

These were all qualities the settlement people began to prize in their wolves. By then, the folks who we might well call the original "village people" were becoming clever enough to match up he-wolves and she-wolves to create ideal offspring.

Branches of the Wolf Family

As centuries passed, wolves evolved into four separate and distinct branches or races: *Canis lupus,* the rugged northern gray wolf, *Canis lupus pallipes,* a palefooted Asian wolf; *Canis lupus chanco* or *laniger,* the woolly coated wolf of Tibet and Northern India; and *Canis lupus arabs,* a small desert wolf of Arabia.

Each of these branches had developed separate skills, slight modifications in appearance, and subtly different temperamental and behavioral traits. The great diversity of the dogs who were to follow began with these wolf groups. Humans found both desirable and undesirable characteristics existing across the groups and intentionally manipulated the gene pools to both intensify and eliminate the specific traits of the branches.

It should be understood that all wolf-domestication stuff wasn't a single isolated incident but was going on in many different parts of the world with different kinds of people and different branches of the wolf family. Further, it was occurring at different rates and times spread out over thousands of years.

The road from wolf-in-the-wild *Canis lupus* to man's best friend, *Canis familiaris* (also known as *dog*), is long and fascinating and has widely varying explanations.

There are some things that historians generally seem to agree on: Wolves were employed to assist man in acquiring food and certain descendants of these increasingly domesticated wolves could also be used by man to assist in survival pursuits other than hunting.

Canine historians Richard and Alice Feinnes' book, *The Natural History of the Dog,* is an interesting and enlightening study of the development of the dog breeds. In it they classify most dogs as having descended from one of four major groups: the Dingo group, the Greyhound group, the Arctic group, and the Mastiff group. Each of these groups traces back to separate and distinct branches of the wolf family.

The Dingo group

The Dingo Group traces its origin to the Asian wolf (*Canis lupus pallipes*). Two well-known examples of the Dingo Group are the Basenji and, through the mixture of the blood of several European breeds, the Rhodesian Ridgeback.

The Greyhound group

The Greyhound group descends from a "coursing" type relative of the Asian wolf. Coursing dogs are those who hunt by sight and are capable of great speed. The Greyhound itself, the Afghan Hound, the Borzoi, and Irish Wolfhound are all examples of this group and have become known as the *coursing* breeds. They are not true hounds in that they do not use their noses to locate or follow prey.

The Arctic group

The Arctic group of dogs is a direct descendant of the rugged northern wolf (*Canis lupus*), also known as the gray wolf. Included in the many breeds of this group are: the Alaskan Malamute, Chow Chow, German Shepherd, and the much smaller Welsh Corgi and Spitz-type dogs.

The Mastiff group

The fourth classification is the Mastiff group, which owes its primary heritage to the Tibetan wolf (*Canis lupus chanco* or *laniger*). The great diversity of the dogs included in this group indicate they are not entirely of pure blood — the specific breeds included have undoubtedly been influenced by descendants of the other three groups.

The acute scenting powers found in the retrievers, spaniels, pointers, and the true hounds (Bloodhounds, Beagles, and Dachshunds) typify this group. However, many breeds not particularly thought of as scenting or hunting breeds are also included in this group, including Bulldogs and the many mastiff breeds such as Bull Mastiffs, St. Bernards and Newfoundlands.

The Human Factor

Current archeological discoveries indicate there were at least several different types of humans that were in existence as civilization developed. However, our village people, being smarter and more experienced than their cave-dwelling ancestors and counterparts, realized that they could customize the wolves to suit more specific needs through selection. Humans were realizing what the wolf descendants looked like also had a great bearing on what they could accomplish.

Humans can't take all the credit for the changes that transpired during the wolf-to-dog transition. The unique ability of the wolf to adapt to its environment, both physically and mentally, had created the different wolf families with their own distinct characteristics and gave humans more to work with. Particular characteristics were prized and inbreeding practices were used to intensify the desired characteristics.

Long about this time in history we stopped calling the animals *wolves* and start referring to them as *Canis familiaris,* or, for the non-Latin speaking among us, *dogs.*

So much for the thousands and thousands of years of history. The important point to remember in all this is that the wolf brought a whole set of characteristics to its dog descendants that took mankind thousands upon thousands of years to modify. Succeeding generations were carefully manipulated by close breeding, weeding out undesirable characteristics, and intensifying the desirable traits. It took the best part of 13 millennia of natural transition and intentional selectivity to create dogs that have the health, intelligence, looks, and personality of some of our purebred breeds today.

Chapter 5

Categories and General Characteristics of the Breeds

. . . .

In This Chapter

▶ Early attempts to classify dogs

▶ Understanding how the list of breeds gets longer

▶ The FCI classifications

▶ The AKC classifications

. . . .

*W*hen people were in their cave-dwelling period, something was either a dog (actually a wolf, as the case was back then) or it wasn't. Life was easy — at least in respect to having no need for technicalities. Later though, as people started assigning specialized duties to their dogs, they began to realize that it was important to let someone know what kind of dog you were talking about when you were talking dogs.

After all, if you wanted someone to sell you a dog to keep on eye on the goat herd, you wouldn't want to be sold a dog that had brought down every antelope on the veldt. Things got even more complicated when the cave ladies got into the act and wanted something little and cute, something they could hold on their laps. The tiny ones had to be accepted as dogs too. Just saying *dog* was obviously not going to work anymore, so people started calling them little dogs and big dogs, mean dogs and nice dogs. No big deal really — just enough description to identify generally what was wanted.

The problem was that the minute the list was completed, somebody came along and complained that their kind of dog wasn't included. So back to the drawing papyrus. The problem and tentative solutions were passed from one generation to the next. Through the ages, all kinds of attempts have been made not only to classify dogs but to have the classifications make some kind of sense and tell a bit about what someone might expect to find within the classifications.

This chapter takes a look at the attempts to define and classify the many breeds. Some of them make sense and others are downright bizarre. I also go into detail about the American Kennel Club classifications, which are the classifications that are most often used in the United States. Having a general idea of what to expect from a breed or group of breeds can help a person considerably in deciding if a breed is the right one.

Romans Get There First

Leave it to the Romans! They not only had to be in charge of the world, they also wanted a say-so about everything in it. It should come as no surprise that they were the first to make an official list of dog breeds and made an attempt to explain what the dogs included on that list were used for.

The Romans had already begun to classify dogs by the beginning of the first century. They put the breeds into three major groups. The names sound more like what you'd read on the menu of your favorite pasta trattoria — *Venatici, Pastorales,* and *Villatici*.

The *Venatici* were what the man of the house took out on hunting expeditions. This group included three different kinds of hunters: *Celeres, Sagaces,* and *Pugnaces.* (If they don't sound like sauces for the pasta, I'll take mine plain!) Each of these had a different responsibility. The *Celeres* were dynamite at tracking, the *Sagaces* were willing to chase the prey through five counties if need be, and then the *Pugnaces* were, not surprisingly with a name like that, the tough guys — the ones who could bring down the meanest critters alive without thinking twice.

The second major group was the *Pastorales.* This group included the shepherd dogs who had two jobs. They had to protect the flocks from poachers and the marauding wolves that hadn't received the message that humans were a soft touch and would give you free room and board if you just behaved yourself. The shepherd dogs also had to run around and make sure no sheep strayed from the flock or got lost or stolen when the sheep were being moved to greener pastures

The third group, *Villatici,* included all the watchdogs. They guarded everything that didn't move. Tough customers, these dogs.

Ah, what clever things man's ingenuity had wrought. Our clever forebears had taken all those hereditary inclinations dogs had inherited from their lupine ancestors and channeled the inclinations to suit themselves.

More Dogs, Longer Lists

Just like every dog has its day, every great nation has its time to be in charge. And then it's over, and another country steps up to the plate. When you're the big cheese, you get to change everything around to suit yourself (and to prove to all the other countries just how much in charge you really are!).

When the Roman Empire faded into oblivion, England eventually had its turn to run the show. Along with everything else, the smart alecks there made up their own lists of dogs and created their own categories for all the breeds. By the time England got its turn, a whole lot more breeds had been developed, and Merrie Olde was no slouch in that department either.

In fact, the English got in so much practice at creating new breeds that they got better at it than any country before or since. If you don't believe that's true, just ask an Englishman. He'll tell you it's so in a heartbeat!

Unfortunately, these breed inventors were seldom the same people who were considered scholars and scientists capable of telling the world what these dogs were all about. So while the people with dog smarts were inventing the new breeds, scholars were writing down all they knew about the breeds. It shouldn't have taken long because, in far too many of the cases, the scholars knew nothing. At least they knew nothing about the dog breeds.

Take, for instance, John Keyes, who was an eminent physician of the sixteenth century. In fact, he was so eminent that Queen Elizabeth I hired him to make sure that she stayed patched together well enough to run the British Empire.

There were many wonderful things about Keyes, but knowledge of dogs was not one of them. Not letting this trifle stand in his way, Keyes (who wrote under the scholarly sounding name Caius) compiled *De Canibus Britannici*, an imposing but not entirely accurate tome, which stood for many years as the definitive work on all breeds of dogs.

Since Keyes's work was in Latin, it was translated and reinterpreted countless times through the centuries by men with high sounding names and *nom de plumes* like Buffon, Stonehenge, Cornevin, Dechambre, and Dalziel. Each book was an attempt to classify dogs. Although many of the works contain fascinating material for the student of dogs, the basis for some of the content raises more than just an eyebrow.

Keyes's work assigned breeds to groups based upon who owned them. His "gentle" group belonging exclusively to the nobility, and the "currs" were property of the lower classes. Buffon felt ears best categorized dogs, and Cornevin relied upon skulls to differentiate.

Wisdom from Stonehenge

John Henry Walsh, who wrote under the impressive sounding name of Stonehenge throughout the 1800s, is undoubtedly the most quoted canine historian today. Interestingly, those researchers who have not accepted his writings as gospel are apt to tell you that much of what he wrote was subsequently contradicted in what he wrote next. To Mr. Walsh's credit, however, it is his system of classification that divided the canine world into seven groups — the seven groups that are still used at dogs shows organized in England, Australia, and America.

FCI Classifications

Inaccuracies and varying degrees of literary liberty aside, the naturalists and scientific scholars of their day tried hard to create some order in classifying dogs. Their efforts were probably highly instrumental in the Federation Cynologique Internationale (FCI) finally taking the bull by the horns to classify dogs according to aptitude. The FCI is the governing body of dog activities in Continental Europe and the Latin American countries. The FCI's system prevails throughout those countries.

The FCI recognizes over 400 breeds, and those breeds are broken down into 10 variety groups. A complete list of the breeds and their descriptions can be obtained from the Federacion. You can visit the Web site at `www.fci.be/english`.

Here are the official subdivisions of dog breeds of the FCI:

Category I: Shepherd Dogs, Guard Dogs, Defense and Work Dogs

- ✔ Group 1: Shepherd Dogs
- ✔ Group 2: Guard Dogs, Defense and Work Dogs

Category II: Hunting Dogs

- ✔ Group 3: Terriers
- ✔ Group 4: Dachshunds
- ✔ Group 5: Hounds for Larger Game
- ✔ Group 6: Hounds for Smaller Game
- ✔ Group 7: Setters (excluding the British Breeds)
- ✔ Group 8: English Hunting Dogs

Category III: Pet Dogs

‖ ✔ Group 9: All inclusive

Category IV: Greyhounds

‖ ✔ Group 10: All inclusive

Home on the Range: The AKC Classifications

As of this writing, the American Kennel Club (AKC) recognizes 150 separate breeds of dogs. The AKC has categorized the breeds into seven groups, primarily based upon original purpose: sporting, hound, working, terrier, toy, non-sporting, and herding.

Miscellaneous dogs

The AKC also has a separate interim classification of Miscellaneous. This designation is for unrelated breeds being observed prior to full AKC acceptance. Since it is a stopover place, the breeds included are constantly changing. At this writing there are nine breeds included in the Miscellaneous classification:

✔ Beauceron

✔ Black Russian Terrier

✔ German Pinscher

✔ Glen of Imal Terrier

✔ Neopolitan Mastiff

✔ Nova Scotia Duck Tolling Retriever

✔ Plotthound

✔ Redbone Coonhound

✔ Toy Fox Terrier (see Figure 5-1)

Although the following comments on the characteristics of each group are generalizations, in most cases they do give a somewhat valid picture of the dogs in the group and major exceptions are noted. Countless individual breed books have been written outlining the virtues (and vices!) of most of the following breeds.

Figure 5-1:
This Toy Fox
Terrier
owned by
Olen
Nichols
looks
toward full
recognition
someday
soon.

Photo courtesy of Olen R. Nichols.

The AKC's official publication *The Complete Dog Book* (Howell Book House) is now on its 19th edition. It does a bang-up job of giving a capsule version of each breed's origin and history along with the current standard of perfection. It is a must for all dog fanciers and can be obtained directly from the AKC or through major bookstores.

Sporting group

This group (called gundogs in some countries) includes most of what you might call the jocks of the dog world: the pointers, retrievers, setters, and spaniels. Their sizes range from the smallest (Cocker Spaniel) on up to the largest (the setters and retrievers). The dogs in this group are, for the most part, sleek and good looking, like you'd expect any self-respecting athlete to be. They're attractive in an outdoorsy sort of a way and they're happy go lucky, people loving, and people pleasing. Sporting dogs are seldom aggressive, but they are athletes and do need plenty of room to stretch and flex those muscles. The breeds take training and patience in that they probably have the most extended period of adolescence of all the breeds.

Litters produced by the Sporting breeds are often large, and the resulting puppies are early bloomers. They grow like weeds. A litter of Sporting breed puppies requires plenty of time, space, and individual attention. Housing for the Sporting breeds takes some thought because they get bored easily when hunting season is not on and can find diabolical ways to amuse themselves.

AKC-recognized Sporting breeds:

- ✔ American Water Spaniel
- ✔ Brittany
- ✔ Chesapeake Bay Retriever
- ✔ Clumber Spaniel
- ✔ Cocker Spaniel
- ✔ Curly-Coated Retriever
- ✔ English Cocker Spaniel
- ✔ English Setter
- ✔ English Springer Spaniel
- ✔ Field Spaniel
- ✔ Flat-Coated Retriever
- ✔ German Shorthaired Pointer
- ✔ German Wirehaired Pointer
- ✔ Golden Retriever
- ✔ Gordon Setter
- ✔ Irish Setter
- ✔ Irish Water Spaniel
- ✔ Labrador Retriever
- ✔ Pointer
- ✔ Spinone Italiano
- ✔ Sussex Spaniel
- ✔ Vizsla
- ✔ Weimaraner
- ✔ Welsh Springer Spaniel
- ✔ Wirehaired Pointing Griffon

The Golden Retriever and Cocker Spaniel are shown in Figures 5-2 and 5-3.

Figure 5-2:
The handsome looks, amiable character, and trainability of the Golden Retriever make this Sporting Dog an outstanding all-around dog.

Mark and Tonya Struble's Ch. Rush Hills Watz Cookin' Good Lookin'; photo courtesy of Bill Meyer.

Figure 5-3:
The soulful expression of the Cocker Spaniel, smallest member of the Sporting Group, disguises the breed's merry temperament.

Photo courtesy of Wentzle Ruml.

Hound group

There are two basic subdivisions in this group: the sighthounds, which includes breeds like the Afghan Hound, Whippet, and Greyhound, and the scenthounds, which includes breeds like the Beagle, Basset Hound, and Bloodhound. Their manner of performance in the field is indicated by their names.

The glamorous and sometimes exotic looking sighthounds are relatively placid dogs who, generally speaking, could not care less about strangers. In fact, some of them act like they don't care about anything other than themselves. In reality, however, they are devoted to their owners.

The sighthounds were bred with great vision (you'd swear they see things before they even happen) and great speed (like in a speeding bullet). They have surprising strength for their long-legged, lean appearance. Sighthounds can turn on a dime, and pity the little creature that catches their eye because the sighthound will be on it in the wink of an eye. Don't expect the off-leash sighthound to stand by and watch if some fluffy little thing (the neighbor's Toy Poodle, for example) goes scurrying by!

Sighthounds are an acquired taste, both physically and temperamentally, and find loyal owners only among those who understand and appreciate their uniqueness. Finding just the right homes for the sighthound breeds' often large litters restricts most people's breeding programs to very occasional litters.

The scenthounds are almost the exact opposite of the sighthounds. They're the good ole boys of the canine world. Laid back, they get on well with the entire world. But scenthounds were bred to follow the trail to the ends of the earth if necessary and they carry this tenacity with them (some call it out-right stubbornness) to this day. Following his nose can lead a scenthound far, far from home — often so far he can't find his way back.

AKC-recognized hound breeds:

- Afghan Hound
- American Foxhound
- Basenji
- Basset Hound
- Beagle
- Black and Tan Coonhound
- Bloodhound
- Borzoi
- Dachshund

- ✔ English Foxhound
- ✔ Greyhound
- ✔ Harrier
- ✔ Ibizan Hound
- ✔ Irish Wolfhound
- ✔ Norwegian Elkhound
- ✔ Otterhound
- ✔ Petit Basset Griffon Vendeen
- ✔ Pharoh Hound
- ✔ Rhodesian Ridgeback
- ✔ Saluki
- ✔ Scottish Deerhound
- ✔ Whippet

The Dachshund and Afghan Hound are shown in Figures 5-4 and 5-5.

Figure 5-4:
Smooth Dachshund, Ch. Sheen V Westphalen, is an excellent representative of the scenthound portion of the Hound Group.

Photo courtesy of Tauskey.

Figure 5-5:
The exotic
Afghan
Hound, like
most of the
sighthounds,
has great
vision,
great speed,
and an
independent
nature.

Chris and Marguerite Terrel's Ch. Kabik's the Challenger; photo courtesy of Vicky Fox.

Working group

Most dogs in this group are what would be considered at least good sized, if not very large or giant. Dog fanciers divide the breeds into two generally inclusive groups: the protective and territorial guard dogs and the draught dogs. The guard dogs include both those whose main object of concern are their owners, like Dobermans and Rottweilers, and the flock guardians like Great Pyrenees and Anatolian Shepherds. The draught dogs include the likes of the Malamute and Siberian Husky, dogs who were employed to pull loads across the snow in northern climates.

All the dogs in this group are happiest when given a job to do. Overall, they're intelligent and easily trained to their assigned tasks and they give it their all. Most of them have good-looking muscular physiques that all too often appeal to people whose chief interest is in the macho image that some of the breeds carry. Popularity of the breeds in this group seems to shift in waves, and even though interest might run high at times, breeders often experience great difficulty in finding truly responsible buyers for each of the puppies in the frequently large litters.

Many of the large working breeds are born weighing not a whole lot more than their cousins in the other groups, but in just a few weeks have quadrupled their birth weight and size. As such, the pups demand significantly more space, more time for cleanup and maintenance, and, it goes without saying, vast quantities of food.

AKC-recognized working breeds:

- Akita
- Alaskan Malamute
- Anatolian Shepherd Dog
- Bernese Mountain Dog
- Boxer
- Bullmastiff
- Doberman Pinscher
- Giant Schnauzer
- Great Dane
- Great Pyrenees
- Greater Swiss Mountain Dog
- Komondor
- Kuvaz
- Mastiff
- Newfoundland
- Portuguese Water Dog
- Rottweiler
- Saint Bernard
- Samoyed
- Siberian Husky
- Standard Schnauzer

The Rottweiler and Boxer are shown in Figures 5-6 and 5-7.

Figure 5-6: The protective nature of the Rottweiler has earned him a strong position among the Working breeds of America.

Photo courtesy of Leslie Simis.

Figure 5-7: The Boxer's stable temperament and love for children make the breed an ideal family dog. Pictured with handler Christine Baum is Bruce and Jeannie Korson's Ch. Kiebla's Tradition of TurRo.

Photo courtesy of Ashbey Photography.

Terrier group

Terriers fall into three general classifications: short-legged (like Scottish Terriers), long-legged (as in Wire Fox Terriers or Airedale Terriers), and the bull-and-terrier breeds (the English Bull Terrier and American Staffordshire Bull Terrier). Most of the terriers have hair-trigger responses, and although they're great with people, it doesn't take much to get them to put up their dukes and challenge another dog.

AKC-recognized terrier breeds:

- Airedale Terrier
- American Staffordshire Terrier
- Australian Terrier
- Bedlington Terrier
- Border Terrier
- Bull Terrier
- Cairn Terrier
- Dandie Dinmont Terrier
- Smooth Fox Terrier
- Wire Fox Terrier
- Irish Terrier
- Jack Russell Terrier
- Kerry Blue Terrier
- Lakeland Terrier
- Manchester Terrier
- Miniature Bull Terrier
- Miniature Schnauzer
- Norfolk Terrier
- Norwich Terrier
- Scottish Terrier
- Sealyham Terrier

✔ Skye Terrier

✔ Soft Coated Wheaten Terrier

✔ Staffordshire Bull Terrier

✔ Welsh Terrier

✔ West Highland White Terrier

Airedale, Lakeland, Cairn, and Bull Terriers are shown in Figures 5-8, 5-9, and 5-10.

Breeders are aware that the boys (and on occasion the girls too) in this group are not to be trusted with each other without close supervision. Still, the people who have owned just about any of the Terrier breeds would never think of having anything else.

Figure 5-8:
These two fully mature long-legged Terriers are the Airedale (left) and Lakeland (right).

Photo courtesy of Richard Beauchamp.

Figure 5-9:
Cairn Terrier, Ch. Caithness Rufus, represents the short-legged division of the terrier group. Friends of this rugged little fellow like his always ready, easy care character.

Photo courtesy of Evelyn M. Shafer.

Figure 5-10:
Gordon and Norma Smith's Bull Terrier, Can. Am. Ch. Magor Maggie Mae, ROM, is an outstanding example of the popular "bull and terrier" cross that includes a number of different breeds.

Photo courtesy of Gordon and Norma Smith.

Toy group

These little guys love their owners with a passion and live to be with them. Toys have lots of zip and make vocal comments about most everything they see and do. They can be delicate in many cases and prone to leg injuries.

AKC-recognized toy breeds:

- Affenpinscher
- Brussels Griffon
- Cavalier King Charles Spaniel
- Chihuahua
- Chinese Crested
- English Toy Spaniel
- Havanese
- Italian Greyhound
- Japanese Chin
- Maltese
- Toy Manchester Terrier
- Miniature Pinscher
- Papillon
- Pekingese
- Pomeranian
- Toy Poodle
- Pug
- Shih Tzu
- Silky Terrier
- Yorkshire Terrier

The Shih Tzu and Pug are shown in Figures 5-11 and 5-12.

Although the tiniest members of these breeds seem to attract the most attention, they also present the greatest risks when it comes to giving birth and survival of the newborn offspring. Their fragile frames make them poor candidates for homes in which there are toddlers or children accustomed only to the bigger, rough-and-ready type dogs.

Figure 5-11:
The kewpie
doll face
and flowing
coat make
the Shih Tzu
a very
popular
member
of the
toy group.

Figure 5-12:
The Pug is
popular
among
those who
enjoy toy
breed size
but prefer
not to deal
with long
coats.

Non-Sporting group

This is the AKC's catchall group. There are so many different kinds of dogs included in this group that it's impossible to make generalizations. In it you will find a variety of attractive and exotic breeds like the Chinese Shar-Pei, Bulldogs, and Poodles. Because they originate from all different kinds of backgrounds and ancestry, there is really no way to characterize them as a group.

AKC-recognized non-sporting breeds:

- American Eskimo Dog
- Bichons Frise
- Boston Terrier
- Bulldog
- Chinese Shar-Pei
- Chow Chow
- Dalmatian
- Finnish Spitz
- French Bulldog
- Keeshond
- Lhasa Apso
- Lowchen
- Poodle
- Schipperke
- Shiba Inu
- Tibetan Spaniel
- Tibetan Terrier

The Bulldog and Bichons Frise are shown in Figures 5-13 and 5-14.

The Bulldog and his close relatives, the French Bulldog and the Boston Terrier, are a part of this group and are referred to as the *brachycephalic* breeds. That is, their skulls are very large and broad and their muzzle length extremely short. This often creates breathing problems, and the breeds have next to zero extreme heat tolerance. The unique statures of some of these breeds create a whole series of complicated breeding and whelping problems, frequently requiring artificial insemination and caesarean operations.

Figure 5-13:
Great Britain's contribution to the non-sporting group takes form in the dour-looking Bulldog.

Photo courtesy of Mij Charbonneau.

Figure 5-14:
In less than 30 years on the American dog show scene, the effervescent Bichons Frise has become one of the Non-Sporting Group's most popular companions. Pictured is Ch. Drewlaine's Eau de Love.

Photo courtesy of Missy Yuhl.

Herding group

As their name implies, these fellows were bred to work livestock. From the tall and shaggy Old English Sheepdogs to the short and perky Pembroke Welsh Corgis, the herding dogs are inclined to be very fervent in pursuing their duties and really need to be given a task to take up that intensity. In other words, they still need a job of some kind.

AKC-recognized herding breeds:

- Australian Cattle Dog
- Australian Shepherd
- Bearded Collie
- Belgian Malinois
- Belgian Sheepdog
- Belgian Tervuren
- Border Collie
- Bouviers des Flandres
- Briard
- Canaan Dog
- Cardigan Welsh Corgi
- Collie
- German Shepherd Dog
- Old English Sheepdog
- Pembroke Welsh Corgi
- Puli
- Shetland Sheepdog

The Pembroke Welsh Corgi and the German Shepherd are shown in Figures 5-15 and 5-16.

If you live in the city, providing the Herding dogs with a flock of sheep or herd of cattle isn't going to be easy. Whether it's obedience training, playing with a flying disk, or bringing in the morning newspaper, give the Herders something to do! The herders have all the drive in the world to do it right. Life as a couch potato or confined to a small room day in and day out could easily make the Herding breeds neurotic and difficult to get along with.

Figure 5-15:
Smallest member of the herding group is the chipper Pembroke Welsh Corgi. Pictured is Ch. Nebriowa Paper Maché.

Photo courtesy of Cunha.

Figure 5-16:
Beauty and brains typify this striking member of the herding group. Few breeds surpass the German Shepherd in intelligence and trainability.

Ch. Altana's Mystique; photo courtesy of Vicky Cook.

Part III
Breeding Stock

In this part . . .

Consistently producing top-notch stock generation after generation is difficult. A good breeder's goal of always improving upon the previous generation adds another degree of difficulty. Handicapping yourself by starting off at the bottom of the quality scale — and aspiring to reach the top from there — presents you with odds that only the most naive person would want to work against.

All kinds of people have dogs, and plenty of them want to think of themselves as breeders. Only a handful of them, however, actually qualify. Far too many breeder wannabes started off on the wrong foot, and the most well-intentioned among them have yet to reach the point where they really should have begun.

This part helps you avoid making the same mistakes. You find out how to start off with stock that has come from a line that gives you a better-than-average chance of succeeding.

Chapter 6

Selecting Your Breeding Stock

- -

In This Chapter

▶ Why "well bred" is important

▶ How to interpret a pedigree

▶ Where to go to get the best

▶ What to look for in breeding stock

- -

*T*here are few real assurances when it comes to breeding animals of any kind, and dogs are no exception. As a dog breeder, you will be dealing with Ma Nature. I assure you that no matter how clever you might like to think you are, she who must be obeyed will have the last word! However, if she were to speak to you, I feel quite certain that her advice would indicate that it will be very hard (impossible?) for you to get anywhere in dog breeding if you don't know where you're going when you start off.

You may be familiar with the great old Broadway show *Damn Yankees*. It's a musical comedy based around baseball that has been revived many times and that even enjoyed great success as a movie. The show's signature song's refrain is "you've got to have heart." And while you too as a breeder must have heart (there are all those disappointments to deal with!) your refrain will have to be "you've got to have goals." This chapter helps you set those goals so that you don't spend the first years of your breeding program floundering around, wondering what to do next.

If you don't have realistic and attainable goals, you'll get nowhere as a dog breeder. Far too many variables are in this endeavor for you to ride off in all directions at once. Talk to your mentors and get serious about what you can hope to accomplish considering the time, space, and financial considerations you live with.

I know a good many individuals who have operated on an extremely small scale and have made great contributions to their breed. I also know of others who have had seemingly unlimited resources and who have not even made so much as a footnote on the pages of their breed's history.

As in all sound ventures, it's not how much is invested but how well it's invested that matters. I'm convinced those ancient Romans were a smart bunch in this respect. Why do I think that? Well, because they coined a phrase that not only applied way back but still does every time we shell out our hard-earned cash. The Romans said it in Latin: *caveat emptor.* No matter what language it's translated into, the meaning remains the same: Let the buyer beware!

This applies to anything offered for sale and especially to that ominous sign or advertisement we see in far too many places — "Pedigree Dogs for Sale." For some reason unknown to me, the word *pedigree* implies a whole lot more than it should. It makes people think there's something especially good about the dogs who have one. Therefore, it entitles the seller to charge a big price for the dog that pedigree is attached to.

A pedigree is just a line or list of ancestors; in humans it's usually known as a family tree. And just like in humans there can be all kinds of apples on that tree: some good, some bad, and some nobody wants to talk about (you know, great uncle Marvin who liked to wear the lamp shade and Auntie Minerva's high heels at the family reunion — that kind).

When you go out to plunk down your hard-earned cash for what will represent the foundation of your entire breeding program, I can only assume that you will want the best your money can buy. The stock should provide a firm foundation and not some rickety base that you will have to take all kinds of heroic measures to shore up.

This means educating yourself as best you can so that, if nothing else, you are able to determine who is doing a good job of breeding and who isn't. You owe it to yourself to know as much about the breed that you're going to specialize in as possible, but when push comes to shove there's no substitute for putting yourself into the hands of a veteran, respected, and successful breeder of well-bred dogs of the breed you have chosen.

That person is the one who can help you put all that book learning into practice so that you can find what it is you're looking for or what you need (not always the same thing!). In selecting your all-important foundation stock, there are many things that you will be able to see but a whole lot of others that are just as important that you can't see or that take a lot of experience to really appreciate — for instance, the nuances of what is referred to as breed type.

What Does "Well Bred" Mean?

"Blue blood," "royally bred," "crème de la crème," and maybe even "the cat's meow." All terms that remind us there are choices that can be made in all walks of life and of all the choices available, there is that one unique group called the best.

There's an old saying among dog fanciers that goes "breed the best to the best and hope for the best." Those who have had a lot of experience in breeding animals — and that's breeding anything from beef cattle to Chihuahuas — know that even when they use that breeding principle as a guideline, the chances of coming up with top-notch quality all the time are slim. They also know that great results are impossible when working with stock that is any less the best.

Is that to say that one of those magical flyers you read about as a child that comes out of two plow horses and winds up winning the Kentucky Derby isn't possible? I guess anything is possible, but I assure you in this instance it's highly improbable.

Even if something like that were to occur, how likely do you think it would be that your plow-horse winner would produce anything of consequence? The likelihood of smart horse breeders taking leave of their senses and sending their best brood mares to your miracle horse is less than remote!

Breeders of thoroughbred horses are too smart and have too much invested in their breeding programs to ever consider using anything but well-bred animals who come from an unquestioned line of well-bred animals. The cost is too considerable and the long-term damage that comes from breeding to flukes is beyond measure.

Dog breeding is no different, and since you've set out to produce a line of quality rather than an accidental acceptable one, starting at the bottom and hoping lady luck will do your work for you is being somewhat naive, if not entirely foolish. Since the choice of breeding stock is yours to make, doesn't it make sense to stack the odds in your own favor?

Looking at the stock's background

What you want to launch your breeding program with is stock that is as well bred as possible. Stock that comes from an entire family that registers at the high end of the quality scale.

Be careful of the stock that comes from what I call "shored up" backgrounds. That is, offspring produced by a female of mediocre quality who has been bred to an outstanding male. This is also called "breeding up" and is resorted to frequently by those who have no other choice but to begin low and hope to breed their way to the top.

You are just beginning. Trust me when I say that you will be infinitely wiser to wait until you can afford to start as near the top as possible. Your foundation should come from a line that has been dedicated to eliminating mediocrity for generations. Don't spend the years and the money breeding up and attempting to compensate from someone else's shortcomings.

Even with a marked improvement in the resulting offspring from these shored up breedings, you still have resulting stock that is poorly bred. What you've got to remember is that even if one or more of the puppies from such a breeding turns out to be of better-than-average quality to the naked eye, that poor quality ancestor is not erased from the gene pool. The influence lives on genetically for many, many generations beyond what you might expect.

In Chapter 9, I write considerably more about why what you see in a dog (phenotype) does not always reveal the dog's genetic makeup (genotype). In respect to breeding, suffice to say that what you see is never all of what you get.

Identifying well-bred dogs

The well-bred animal comes from a line that has been carefully culled through generations to remove not only mediocre or faulty specimens but the dogs that produce them as well. Each succeeding generation of a breeding program conducted in this manner will be progressively less apt to produce individuals who harbor the problems you are trying to eliminate.

Don't get me wrong. I am not implying that well-bred animals are incapable of producing anything less than perfection. To the contrary. Success in breeding, or the lack of it, is measured by how well the stock from your breeding program measures up against the respective breed standard. *How well your stock measures up.* Breed standards describe perfection, and I hope I've convinced you by this time that Mom Nature simply doesn't comply to that order very readily, if at all.

For example, your top-quality male or female from a well-bred line may have many outstanding virtues that are difficult to achieve in the breed — but the dog's eye color may be too light. Light eye color, therefore, is the flaw that must be dealt with when that individual is bred. With some good luck and a well-thought-out breeding, you might be able to keep the quality you have achieved and also correct that flaw in at least some of the offspring.

However, if the dog you're breeding (even if she's a better-than-average example of the breed) came from a breeding program that not only had light eyes amongst its faults but poor color, bad feet, and not enough size, then think of the many variables that would have to be considered in that breeding and how many variables would be lurking around in the genetic makeup of whatever is produce — even if none of these faults are visible.

What's in a Pedigree?

The pedigree is your dog's family tree. The breeder of every AKC-registered dog is required to supply the buyer with a copy of this document. The pedigree lists the dog's ancestors back to at least the third generation by giving each of the registered names and registered numbers.

WARNING!

All purebred dogs have a pedigree. The pedigree does not imply that a dog is of show quality. It is just a chronological list of ancestors — nothing more, nothing less. Some unscrupulous dog sellers, who are attempting to gouge a higher price out of an unsuspecting buyer, indicate a pedigree has some special significance — that it indicates show or championship potential in some way. This is not true.

A pedigree simply lists ancestors and indicates that all the dogs listed are purebred. All the dogs in that pedigree could easily have been from the shallow end of the gene pool — mediocre or worse in quality.

Reading a pedigree

A pedigree is read from left to right. The first two names in the first column on the left are the puppy's sire and dam (dog talk for mom and dad). The sire's ancestry, reading left to right, occupies the top half of the pedigree. The dam's ancestors appear on the bottom half.

In most cases, pedigrees are hand written or typed by the breeder. These unofficial documents give you your puppy's ancestry, but like any document prepared by a human, they can contain spelling errors and other assorted mistakes.

Titles

If there's anything that indicates one pedigree is better than another, it is the titles that the individual dogs in the pedigree have earned. Most of these titles are indicated on the pedigree, often via abbreviations and often in red ink. The titles can be earned for excellence of conformation on through to basic and advanced obedience accomplishments, tracking, guard work, herding, and a myriad of other activities.

Kennel prefixes and names

In reading pedigrees, you will notice that in many cases the first part of a dog's name is repeated in several other names on the pedigree. This part of the name is what is referred to as a *kennel prefix*. A kennel prefix is usually a coined word that identifies the dogs from a certain breeding program.

For instance, all my dogs were registered under the Beau Monde prefix. The pedigree of Beau Monde The Beauhemian tells you that the female Jacquets-Beaus-Red-Valentine was bred to the male, Tonatron Latin Lover. Five kennel names are involved: Jacquet, Tonatron, Goldfields, Angel, and my own, Beau Monde. If you go further back, you see that Latin Lover is the result of two generations of Tonatron dogs. Red Valentine, on the other hand, has dogs from both Angel (see Angel Angelli) and Goldfields (see Goldfield's Onyx De Jacquet) kennels behind her.

These kennel prefixes tell us several things. Primarily, they're a means of quickly identifying all the dogs that come from one kennel. As you become more and more familiar with the breed you've chosen, you will begin to realize that there are some kennel names that have become famous and highly respected because of the outstanding quality of the dogs bred there. Thus, a preponderance of dogs from that famous kennel would, if nothing else, add luster to the dog whose pedigree it is.

In movies, Merchant Ivory is a production company. To many, the name "Merchant Ivory" indicates excellence within a certain genre of film. Thus, the Merchant Ivory movie *A Room With a View* comes preapproved for excellence in some people's minds. This is no less the case in purebred dogs. Using the kennel prefix associates the individual dog with a specific person or kennel.

No two dogs may be registered using exactly the same name. Any attempt to register a dog with a name that has been used by any dog of any breed in the past will be rejected. The kennel name or prefix helps to make a duplication of names less likely.

In other words, there may well have been any number of dogs named White Lightning registered by the AKC in the past, but there would only be one registered as Beau Monde White Lightning. In certain rare cases, the AKC might permit a name to be used again, but a Roman numeral suffix would be attached to the name — in other words, the name then would be Beau Monde White Lightning II.

Note: The official, AKC-registered name is seldom what the owner actually calls the dog. My dog's official name is Beau Monde the Beauhemian, but I call him Raif!

The AKC likes breeders to create coined words or contractions as kennel names. This reduces the possibility of kennel name duplications. There are many people breeding dogs whose last name is Smith or Jones. If the Smith's wanted to register their Dalmatian as Smith's Spot, it's very likely that somewhere, sometime back in the American history of the breed, someone else by the name of Smith might well have been clever enough to think up a name as original as Spot. The Smiths would be far better off to coin a distinctive kennel name based on their own surname — for instance, Smithstar or Hysmith.

For a fee, you can apply to the AKC to have your kennel prefix registered so that you're the only person registering dogs with the AKC who can use that name as a prefix. Once the name has been approved as not in common usage, the prefix is published in the *AKC Gazette,* the AKC's monthly publication. If there are no legitimate reasons against its being used, you are given exclusive use of the name.

Identifying kennel names do not always precede the dog's name. Some breeders prefer to use their kennel name at the end of the dog's name; for instance, Sammy of Hysmith rather than Hysmith's Sammy. It's really of no consequence how it's done, unless you're interested in registering your kennel name with the AKC. Kennel names may only be registered as prefixes, but that does not always protect you from having someone else use your prefix as a suffix.

Breeding method

Pedigrees can also tell you the method of breeding used to produce the dog whose pedigree it is: linebred, inbred, or outcrossed. You can discover the details about these methods of breeding in Chapter 8. Here's the rapid-fire explanation: On the pedigree of Beau Monde Beauhemian, Tonatron Comanchero sired Tonatron Latin Lover. Latin Lover's dam was Tonatron Solo Glory. The sire of both Comanchero and Solo Glory was Tonatron True Glory, but also note that they have different mothers (Prize Doll and Belladora).

Thus Comanchero and Glory are half-brother and half-sister. Breedings of this kind are considered *linebred.* If Comanchero and Glory had the same parents, they would be full brother and sister and the type of breeding that they produced would be called *inbred.* If there is no relationship between the two dogs who are being mated (other than the fact that they're of the same breed) in, let us say, at least three or four generations, it's considered an *outcross* pedigree.

Obtaining an official pedigree

If you want to obtain an *official* pedigree — one that is certified to be correct by the AKC, you can call the AKC at 919-233-9767 or visit the AKC online at www.akc.org. The information contained in a certified pedigree is taken from AKC's computerized files, as is the actual registration certificate.

Registration applications also contain a box you can check off if you want to order an official pedigree, which costs $17 in addition to the $10 registration fee. For the sake of your own breeding records as well as the records of those who will be buying stock from you, you should obtain and file a certified pedigree for any dog you intend to use for breeding.

The breeder's pedigree

Nigel Aubrey-Jones unquestionably stands among the world's most successful dog breeders and connoisseurs. His St. Aubrey-Elsdon line of Pekingese, bred in partnership with R. William Taylor, is legendary for its quality and its achievements. Aubrey-Jones is also one of our best dog writers. Countless statements he has made are worth quoting, but none are so profound as one that relates to the subject at hand. "The most important name on a pedigree," he wrote, "is the breeder's."

Getting Help from a Mentor

In Chapter 1, I write about the great advantage potential breeders have if they put themselves in the hands of an experienced and successful breeder. Having a mentor helps you avoid all those trial-and-error steps that so many people take because they don't know that what they're attempting to do has been tried over and over and experience has proven that it just doesn't work.

I'm not trying to downplay the value of experimental breedings or going "where no man has gone before." At the same time, there's a time and place for that and I can assure you that the time is not before you know what you're doing and the place is not in the beginner's home or kennel.

What a mentor can offer

In a good many cases, mentors are actively breeding and showing their dogs. You may be able to purchase your foundation stock directly from that person. If this holds true for your mentor, you are a giant step ahead of those who don't have this advantage. Just a few of the reasons:

- It's highly likely that you will have become personally familiar with the individual dogs who stand behind the breeding stock you begin with.

- You not only have experienced opinions to guide you, you also have someone who has a personal interest in seeing that you start off with the best. You are, in fact, the mentor's protégé.

- You've been schooled in what is important in your breed by your mentor: The dog that you get from the mentor will most likely excel in those areas that you have been taught are essential.

- You will have first-hand knowledge of the environment that has proven most suitable for your breed.

✔ The breeder-mentor knows a great deal about both the virtues and faults of the dogs in his pedigrees and is able to discuss any of the problems that could conceivably exist. He also explains what kind of testing he does to avoid those problems.

Even though your mentor may no longer be actively breeding, he or she probably knows where the stock being bred from his or her line may be found. Perhaps a student who came along before you is carrying on your mentor's line.

If your mentor is unable to provide you with selections from within his or her own line, he or she may be willing to recommend a breeder who you can put your confidence in. Respected breeders who test their stock for genetic problems and who place mental and physical soundness above all else usually associate with other breeders whose standards are equally high. You will find they aren't apt to recommend anyone whose standards do not live up to their own.

I'm sure you can you see what a great advantage all this is over shooting in the dark and buying stock that looks good but whose history is a mystery.

If you can't find a mentor

Not everyone is going to have the advantage of a guardian angel to watch over his or her every move. Then it becomes a case of "eyes and ears open — mouth closed." Nothing makes experienced dog fanciers step back and become silent more quickly than the novice who is an instant expert. This is not to say that questions are out of line. I've never met an experienced breeder who minds answering a sincerely asked question of any kind, but no self-respecting breeder will waste time trying to convince a novice to do the right thing.

There is a great deal to be learned just by listening to people who have themselves been successful. Good listeners are also able to separate talkers from achievers. There are many of the former, few of the latter!

Eventually the clever novice begins to recognize the difference between what appears to be taking place and what is actually happening. Dazzling advertisements and the numbers games (numbers of awards won, numbers of champions produced, and so on) do not always tell the complete story or lead the student to what is best in a breed. Genuine knowledge of one's breed and the ability to recognize excellence in it will assist the sincere student through all the hype.

My role as mentor

I'm always more than happy to recommend someone who has taken dogs from my bloodline and gone on to do well with them. I'm also able to give a more experienced and qualified opinion when someone asks me to evaluate a litter or select a puppy for them when the stock I am evaluating is down from my own bloodline.

While I can't claim infallibility, even when a puppy or a litter has all my breeding behind it, I at least have seen many puppies of the bloodline mature and develop and my opinion is enhanced by that experience. I know what little shortcomings in a youngster usually improve

with age and I am aware of the problems that don't seem to go away with time or that may even grow worse as the dog matures.

Am I always right? Emphatically no! But I've been fairly accurate in dealing with puppies and young stock from my own line. When it comes to making selections from bloodlines with which I have had no experience, the most I will ever venture to say is what I see at the moment. What may or may not happen later is not within my domain. I can make general assumptions based on trends of development within the breed, but I can make no claims for accuracy.

What to Look for in Breeding Stock

Testing for health and temperament is, of course, extremely important to everyone concerned with dog breeding and ownership. That the experienced breeder you've located has not been testing every generation is highly unlikely.

The vast majority of all breeders' dogs go into homes as companions, and temperament and longevity are the most important considerations of those pet owners who expect to live with their pet for many, many years. And in the end, of what consequence is any line that produces beautiful animals of foul temperament or short lives?

Dr. Jacklyn Hungerland, breeder of the consequential de Russy Poodles and an AKC judge of many breeds, speaks with authority when she says, "Breeders striving for mental and physical health in their dogs will usually avoid the extreme exaggerations in their breeding and show stock that are seen by some others as flash and glamour. While the attractiveness of the latter are certainly not to be underestimated," she says, "they should never be regarded at the expense of health."

Carefully studying winning and producing bloodlines is important. Do note that I say winning *bloodlines* and not just winning *dogs*. A good bloodline can and will produce many winners; a winning dog does not necessarily come from a good bloodline nor will she necessarily produce winners.

Structure and style

You can find out more about the standard of perfection of a breed in Chapter 2. Familiarity with the standard reveals how a given breed should be constructed. That is, how characteristics like height, weight, proportions, and the manner in which the various parts of the anatomy are joined together produce a good specimen of that breed. If a dog has most of these characteristics in the proper amount and relationship, an experienced dog fancier would be inclined to say that the dog is *well made*. The dogs you select as your foundation stock must be, at the very least, well made.

As beginners progress along their way to understanding more and more about a breed, it's inevitable that they will begin to develop likes and dislikes of their own. Within the framework of any standard, some latitude exists for one's own individual prejudices and interpretation. This does not mean, however, that any and all interpretations of a breed standard are valid.

An example of this latitude may be found in the definition of a short back, which is a characteristic that many breed standards call for. What we are referring to here in dog parlance is the distance from the highest point of a dog's shoulders to the set on of the tail.

The question that has to be asked here is, "How short is a short back?" Often, standards do not offer specific proportionate measurements, so characteristics like this one can be interpreted to a certain degree by the observer.

This does not give anyone the liberty to dodge the confines of the breed standard, however. The Honorable David Merriam, Chairman of the Board of Directors of the AKC and a successful breeder and judge, addressed standard interpretation quite well in an article he wrote for *Kennel Review* magazine. "While verbal communication and the printed word describing type is less than explicit," Merriam wrote, "it isn't a matter of 'anything goes' either. The experienced and educated eye will not mistake a long, sagging back for the short sturdy one required by a well-written standard."

Experience and common sense usually govern the extent to which a standard can be interpreted. It should be understood, though, that even within the confines of entirely correct interpretation, there are minor variations. The way in which an experienced and knowledgeable breeder interprets the standard determines the style of dog that he or she desires.

Coming to terms with breed standards sounds simple enough, right? Unfortunately it's not quite as simple as it appears, because of a very important factor that I haven't yet introduced. You will hear it discussed the first time you talk to someone about breeding and you will hear it repeatedly on through the rest of your life in dogs. It's like one of those weather things that everyone talks about all the time and seemingly does nothing about. In this case, however, everyone is doing (or probably better stated as "trying to do") something about it. That mysterious, illusive factor is *breed type*.

Breed type

Two words, only nine little letters. Yet, if I were going to compile a list of buzz words for the entire realm of dogs and dog breeding, *breed type* would most certainly have to head that list.

It makes no difference where one falls on the dog fancy scale of involvement or what is being discussed. Sooner or later, the conversation will turn to these two words that describe the most important term in the dog fancier's vocabulary. You will also find the term launches more prolonged discourses and pontificating than any other we might use.

In themselves, the words are simple and straightforward. Standing alone, they aren't the least bit complex or ambiguous. But once put together and tossed out into the dog breeder's arena, you would think they were expressed in Egyptian hieroglyphics.

Breed type describes characteristics that are most certainly there but can't really be verbalized. Nor can breed type even be pictured in a manner that is effective for anyone other than those who have already developed the ability to recognize it.

A person's picture of ideal type is constantly honed and refined by having that picture compared to many dogs. Seeing a good specimen of the breed once will not do the trick. Comparisons over the years help the eye become aware of deviations of the ideal, no matter how subtle those deviations may be.

Achieving any great success in breeding dogs without an understanding of breed type is impossible. Because it's so important to the breeder, I chip away at this mystery in the next few sections.

Not all dogs have it

To begin with, every purebred breed of dog that exists has a correct and distinguishing type. But this is not to say that every dog in a given breed, as regally blue as its blood may be, has breed type or even that those having it have it in the same degree. Some dogs may score very heavily in type; others may border very closely on having none at all.

Pictured in Figure 6-1 are two purebred Labrador Retrievers. Dog A is registered and has an official pedigree from the AKC. You don't even have to read the Labrador Retriever's breed standard to recognize the fact that there is a tremendous difference between Dog A and Dog B. Dog A, as purebred as he might be, just barely has enough breed type to make him identifiable as a Labrador Retriever (although those specializing in the breed might argue that!).

The picture of Dog B, on the other hand, makes it clear that this is a dog who has the balance and proportions and the other special Labrador Retriever breed characteristics that are stated and implied by the breed standard. Even to the untrained eye, the striking difference between these two purebred dogs is easily discernible.

Figure 6-1:
The dog in the top photo (A) has barely enough breed type to distinguish him from most any kind of mixed breed black dog. Ch. Weathertop Storm Cloud, the dog shown in the bottom photo (B), exhibits the type characteristics described in the Breed Standard to such a high degree that he is an AKC champion.

Photos courtesy of Linda Anderson and John Cook.

The responsibility of real dog breeders then, is to determine the correct type of the breed of their choice, and then do everything possible to breed close to that ideal. Understanding what the correct type in a breed is, however, is more difficult that what you would expect. Probably the main reason for the difficulty is that people are inclined to see the various interpretations of the standard as different breed types. It is important to realize that there is only one correct breed type — that which is described in the standard of the breed and/or in the breed's history and origin.

Breeder's attempts to produce correct type in the manner in which they understand the correct type, even when they might emphasize certain characteristics, are simply producing a style within the correct type. When an emphasis extends well beyond the confines of the standard, the result is, actually, a caricature of what is desirable in the standard.

Why breed type matters to you

A clear understanding of breed type is absolutely critical to a breeder's success. Therefore, I strongly suggest that anyone who looks to expand their knowledge of type go back to the origins of the breed — back to when, where, and why the standard was written. It's there that you find the reasons for which the breed was created. In the origins of the breed, you can find what the creators of the breed were trying to set to make their dogs a separate and distinct breed. The dog having a preponderance of these characteristics was and is correct type.

As time has passed, there has been less opportunity for dogs to be observed serving in the capacity for which many of them were created. Thus, having the characteristics that, in theory, best prepare the dog to function as intended becomes increasingly relied upon. For example, few German Shepherd Dogs actually herd Germans (or whatever they herded back in the day.) However, the breed standard calls for dogs that have the same attributes as their herding ancestors, dogs that, in theory, would be good working dogs. Every single breed of domesticated dog known to man has a valid and specific purpose, whether that purpose is to assist or simply to please.

Often, referring back to the breed's original purpose reveals that what is now considered a point of beauty was originally meant to enhance performance. Through time, achieving this quality in a breeding program or in an individual dog became an element of breeding success and a source of pride — thus a point of beauty. The dog lacking these important characteristics today may well be sound of limb but would be unsuited for the particular purpose of the breed and therefore would be considered to be lacking in type.

For instance, the long ears of the Bloodhound were developed to enhance the breed's trailing and scenting ability. When the dog put his head to the ground, the long ears helped channel the scent of what was being trailed to his nose. Few Bloodhounds are called upon to put their ears to use today but

the breed's long ears are considered a part of what creates the ideal specimen of the breed and no Bloodhound with short ears could be considered to
have correct breed type.

How much is too much?

I spoke of dogs becoming caricatures. This comes about through the penchant
for believing that if a characteristic is called for at all, then the more of it a
dog has the better. In reality, a dog can have too much — too narrow a head,
too long a back, too small a nose. Breeders, in their attempts to enhance a
desired quality, can emphasize it to the degree that what was once desirable
becomes a deformity — a caricature of what the breed was intended to be.

No breed should have to endure that. This applies to deformities of any kind,
physical or cosmetic, that we intentionally breed into or exaggerate in our
breeds.

Therefore, a dog having type is not the final element of success. The dog
must have the characteristics called for in appropriate amounts and in balance
with each and every other part of the dog's anatomy.

Determining this, of course, takes time and study. But without some consistent basis for evaluation of breed type, breed students can sit and study a
breed until hell freezes over and in the end will know little more than what they
knew when they began. Even the most knowledgeable person in a breed will
not be of help to the student unless there can be some mutual agreement as to
what the components of breed type in the breed — any breed — really are.

Having an eye

Through the years, the innate ability to assess breed type has become known
as *having an eye*. Some consider it a gift, and quite frankly I do believe this is
so. Having an eye is simply an inherent appreciation for line, balance, and
symmetry. All good artists have this gift, as do many people whose only
association with art is pure enjoyment.

Even with this gift, however you want to refer to it, fathoming all the subtleties
of breed type still takes time. Good mentors can provide the proper clues
that enable students to find their way to correct type, but it's entirely up
to the student to take that information and create an accurate picture.
Evaluating dogs is an art, and like any artistic endeavor it takes time, trial,
and error to hone one's expertise.

No one, myself included, can teach you to recognize type, but it is possible to
provide you with the information that can send you along the path that leads
to its recognition. If you're ever going to recognize type, you must first understand what the components included in the word actually are. Otherwise,
you'll wade through your life in dogs never really understanding what it is
you're looking for or recognizing it when it appears.

Not everyone who chooses to breed dogs will do so at the highest level. Still, anyone who is dedicated and willing to invest the time to study and understand correct type in his or her breed can enjoy at least some measure of success. The best way to understand type is to first learn to recognize what the components of breed type include. They are the bottom-line basics that you must have if you hope to progress and understand. They are the building blocks upon which the structure of the ideal dog is based.

All representative purebred dogs have these elements, but it is the degree to which a dog excels in them that determines where the dog ranks on the scale of breed type excellence. No one should ever attempt to breed dogs until he or she is able to recognize the degree to which a given dog succeeds in these areas.

The five elements of breed type

After long and careful consideration, I came up with a list of the characteristics with which I evaluate dogs and on which the great dogs I have known have scored very heavily. These are, in my opinion, the components of breed type:

- ✔ Breed character
- ✔ Silhouette
- ✔ Head/expression
- ✔ Movement
- ✔ Coat

Breed character

The most obvious thing about any dog is whether or not she carries herself and acts in a manner that's appropriate for that specific breed. Character is probably best described as the sum total of all those mental and physical characteristics that define not only what the breed should look like, but also how it should act.

For instance, a standard's description of the breed's head really means little or nothing if, in the end, the dog's expression doesn't say, "I am a Boxer" or an Afghan or a Bull Terrier. So it is with the whole dog. If you can't look at a dog and instantly recognize, by its general look and attitude, that it has the style and bearing appropriate to that breed, then it's really not a true representative of the breed. That is in spite of what a pedigree and registration certificate might say.

We have breeds whose history and origin tell us they were intended to be stalwart, brave, and protective. Others have origins that call for a calm, retiring, and affectionate character. And there are still other breeds that by their very nature are aloof or wary of strangers. Dogs who behave contrary to what is correct for their breed lack a very important part of their breed's essence.

Silhouette

As I drive down the street, what catches my eye and makes me look is the overall silhouette of a dog. What my eye tells my brain is whether or not the animal I'm looking at is a particular breed. Closer examination will undoubtedly reveal how good a specimen of the breed the dog is, but the closer the dog's silhouette comes to the ideal, the more quickly I will be able to identify the breed and the more apt that dog is to be a quality individual. It's the whole that classifies the breed and the details within that framework that tell me how closely the dog conforms to the ideal.

Correct proportions create the proper silhouette. A good example is shown in Figure 6-2. Proportions are something concrete. A neck that is one-third the length of the body is something you can see. One-third of anything is exactly that. There's no mystery about it. And so it goes for the entire dog. Once you've taught yourself what the correct proportions are, you'll be able to recognize correct dogs by their silhouettes — because what it took to make those silhouettes was the sum of all the correct parts!

Figure 6-2:
The silhouette of Miniature Poodle, Ch. Cutter's Ebony Wisteria, leads the viewer to anticipate lots of quality contained within her outline.

Photo courtesy of Sprung.

In order for the overall silhouette to be accurate, the parts that created it must themselves be pretty close to being correct: the height-to-length balance must be there, muzzle-to-skull proportions must be in the right balance, the neck must be of the proper length and set. Hopefully, the dog that you observe as correct when standing still will also be correct when moving about. If that silhouette is also held in movement, the parts are not only there but they are also working correctly.

Head

Without its unmistakable face and its particular expression, even the dog whose character and silhouette tells you that it's a member of a particular breed would be a disappointment.

Would it be a Borzoi without that stiletto head and lordly expression? If a Border Collie's gaze puts you in mind of a Basset Hound, can it truly be a Border Collie? That head is part of the parcel that gives us a breed, as Figure 6-3 demonstrates. Notice though, I say head is part of — not all. Do not make the mistake so many people do and think that the head is all that distinguishes a breed. Breed type extends far beyond a dog's head. At the same time, few breeders fail to appreciate the dog whose head and expression vividly portray what is recognized as the breed's ideal.

Figure 6-3: Few breeders fail to appreciate the dog whose head and expression portray what we have come to recognize as a breed's ideal. Such is the case in this Dale Gourlie painting of the Springer Spaniel icon, Ch. Salilyn's Aristocrat.

Movement

Many standards are quite precise in their description of movement. If a dog moves poorly, it is usually due to the dog's construction. I'm talking about what the legs do or do not do — whether or not the movement is actually correct for the breed. A dog can only move properly for its breed if it is constructed properly *for its breed* (see Figure 6-4).

Here, I must digress a bit. You'll note that I've italicized the words "for its breed." All breeds are not constructed the same and therefore all dogs will not and should not move the same. It's important that a breeder clearly understands the correct construction of a given breed so that he will also understand what kind of movement that construction demands.

When you change movement, you change construction. When you change construction, you are tampering with breed type. It's not always acceptable for one breed to move like another. A draught dog is not to cover ground like a Sporting dog. A Spaniel does not move as fast as an Afghan Hound, nor should it. Nor, on the other hand, is a Spaniel as slow and rolling as a Bulldog.

If all breeds were allowed to move in the same way, we would soon have a whole race of dogs differing only in size and color and the amount of hair they carry. They would, quite simply, be generic dogs.

Figure 6-4:
All breeds are not constructed in the same manner and therefore do not move in the same way. The construction of this Whippet, Ch. Sporting Field's Luke Kinsman, allows him to move in a free and athletic manner.

Photo courtesy of Michelle Perlmutter.

Coat

In the case of most breeds, you should be concerned with both the color and texture of the coat. Most standards for the utility breeds describe a coat that assisted the dogs in performing the task for which the breed was created. An Alaskan Malamute, for example, with a long silky coat would have a hard time working in the snow. Likewise, a retriever should never have a coat that absorbs and holds water.

It's not just in the breeds that have a job to do that coat is important. The silky coats called for in the Yorkshire Terrier and Maltese Standards are every bit as critical in defining type as are the protective coats of the breeds that work for a living.

Chapter 7

Keeping Track of Type

· ·

In This Chapter

▶ Setting up the basic type tracker chart
▶ Who to include in your type tracker
▶ Solving breeding problems
▶ Variations of the system

· ·

After you've come to understand what the characteristics are that constitute correct type in your breed and you've got them all carefully studied and notated, you should be ready to set the world on its ear with all the spiffy dogs you'll be breeding. All the dogs that you breed will have the best of what it takes to qualify as a great dog, and then you and your breeding program will exist in happy-ever-afterville. Indeed, it's falling off a log from here on in.

Think again my friend. We who have been through the mill a few times just wish it were all that easy!

Keeping track of what characteristics your dogs have, what it is you want, and, as you breed along, what the next generation has and doesn't have is a major undertaking in itself. All those details are more than the average person (or even better-than-average person!) can hope to keep neatly stored in the memory box.

All this information is extremely important, particularly when you follow all the directions, "breed the best to the best," and it doesn't work out. I can assure you that all of us who breed dogs have made more than one breeding that should have been terrific but absolutely did not work out the way we planned!

Was it simply bad luck? Perhaps, but more often than not, the characteristics you didn't expect and didn't want were lurking somewhere in one, if not both, of the parents' backgrounds.

I go into the genetics of breeding in Chapter 9. What I cover there gives you a better understanding of why and how desirable and undesirable traits are passed along from one generation to the next. For the time being, however, I'll stick to the basics and keep things simple.

Acquiring Knowledge

You need to know what you want in your foundation stock and what you will be looking for in the litters that are subsequently produced. You'll also need to know where all those surprises — and there will be many — come from. Knowing where both the good surprises and the not-so-good surprises are coming from is about half the battle in producing top-quality dogs.

As the puppies start growing and faults become apparent, you'll need to know if the faults are permanent or temporary. There are faults that disappear as the puppy develops. Likewise, there are qualities that aren't fully achieved until the dog reaches maturity. These things vary from breed to breed, and just as often from line to line within a breed.

An experienced breeder learns through trial and error that there are some faults that an otherwise happy, healthy pup exhibits that make the pup ineligible for showing and breeding. The breeder realizes that the pup may as well be neutered and get on to enjoying life as a family companion rather than spend its entire puppyhood there at the kennel waiting for the fault to go away.

I find that breeders (and I admittedly include myself here) are inclined to resort to selective memory when it comes to dogs of the past. As years and generations go by, objectivity blurs and the dogs we have fond memories of seem to shed any of the faults they may have had. The dogs that had faults we didn't find acceptable are all too often recalled as having no redeeming features whatsoever.

This chapter shows you a nearly foolproof method of keeping track of all these characteristics that your pups will exhibit. (I say "nearly foolproof" because it's we humans who are doing this, and the only person that can't be fooled is, you guessed it, Ma Nature! She'll have it her way, regardless of how smart we think we are.)

What's especially good about this system is that it not only helps you keep track of the information you need, it assists you in developing an accurate assessment of your entire breeding program while you're doing it. It's an easy do-as-you-go kind of thing that may well help you avoid making serious breeding mistakes and will be enormously helpful in making breeding decisions.

Setting Up the Basic Type Tracker Chart

All you need to set up the basic type tracker chart is a sheet from a three-hole bookkeeper's analysis pad. I use a sheet that has 12 vertical columns. It gives me all the space I need to record both specifics and any general notes I may have on any dog in my breeding program. Once you've created your master chart, you can simply photocopy it for each additional dog that requires a chart.

The pads are obtainable at any office supply or stationery store. While you're at it, you may as well get yourself a three-ring, standard-size, loose-leaf notebook. The 12-column sheet is 16⅜ inches wide. Folded in half, it fits nicely into a standard three-ring loose-leaf folder.

I file the sheets in alphabetical order by the dog's name. In order to facilitate easy location of the individual dogs, I print the name (A) in bold letters at the top right-hand corner of the folded sheet. Place the dog's individual registration number (B) below the name.

A sheet should be created for every dog you are considering as possible breeding stock. I begin entering data at six to eight weeks which, depending on the breed, corresponds to my first evaluation of the individual puppies in the litter. If the puppy does not meet expectations and is to be neutered and sold as a companion, the file is closed. Otherwise, I make periodic notes on development until the dog reaches maturity. There is more on keeping ongoing records in Chapter 16.

Reading the columns from left to right across the top of the page: The first column (C) is for notes regarding the individual. This space is for recording any data that may prove to be of value later in the dog's life, like the number of living puppies in the same litter as the dog, health problems, and unusual traits or habits.

The next column (D) is where you record your assessment of how well the individual dog succeeds in regard to the five elements of breed type. Columns (E) and (F) are where you record the name and numbers of the sire and dam of the individual dog. You don't need to put anything in column (G) if you are the breeder or owner of the sire or dam. If you do not or have not owned the sire or dam, this is a good place to note any significant data you may have observed about either one of them.

Using the type tracker as a spreadsheet

I am just barely computer literate. Word processing is about as far as I've progressed to date (extremely embarrassing in that my nine-year-old nephew is an absolute whiz!). The manner I suggest for creating your type tracker is for those of us who still haven't worked our way through *For Dummies* computer books and graduated to paperless record keeping. I've been told that the type tracker can very easily be set up on a computer spreadsheet. I certainly don't fail to realize the value in doing so, but when I'm doing anything on a computer, I live in constant terror of pressing the wrong button and having my, or my dogs', entire life history vanish into cyberspace. I'm sure any of you who trust these infernal machines will be able to adapt my simple directions to more modern methods!

A word of caution here regarding notes on sires and dams. I would be inclined to include only information you have gathered firsthand yourself or that was passed on to you by a reliable expert. Unconfirmed hearsay is not the kind of information you want recorded in a type tracker. Some people are extremely critical of stock other than their own, and unfortunately there are some dog breeders who find it extremely difficult — often impossible — to admit that their own dogs have serious faults or are capable of passing faults on. Recording misinformation can have a disastrous effect on your breeding program.

Entering Your Notes on Type

Every breed has its own characteristics that need charting. As you become more and more familiar with the information that is included under each of the five elements of breed type, your charts will become ever more meaningful. Chapter 6 has more information on these five elements.

I'll just use a hypothetical breed here to give you an idea of what it is that you may want to include on the chart for the dogs of your breed that have been retained to use for future breeding. What you include depends entirely on what is important to your breed. The only mistake you can make in recording information is including too little rather than too much.

Breed character

The dog I am setting up this chart for is of a companion/watchdog breed. The breed serves as a watchdog through a willingness to sound the alarm vocally when doing so is important. Therefore, a high level of alertness is an important characteristic and that becomes the first entry under character.

Since alertness is such an important characteristic of this breed, the level of alertness can be given a numerical value of 1 to 10, 10 being best. Another measurable characteristic is responsiveness — to name and to commands. This might be evaluated in the same 1-to-10 manner.

In the case of this particular breed, moderate size and medium bone (substance) are considered important elements of type and, in fact, the breed standard includes a disqualification for any member of the breed that is over 14 inches at shoulder. I have chosen to include size under breed character because it's such an important part of what creates the right look in this breed.

Give plenty of time to those characteristics that really count in defining your breed's character. Read what I write about breed character in Chapter 6 and review your breed standard. Unfortunately, some of the breed parent clubs chose not to reformat their standards when the AKC requested they do so in the late 1980s. Therefore, not all standards include details on this important element of breed type. If your breed's standard is lacking, research into the origin and purpose of your breed will provide a good part of the information you need. List those characteristics that are important to your breed and those that help distinguish it from other breeds.

Silhouette

The detail included under silhouette can be very detailed or less so, depending on the importance of silhouette to the breed. Our sample breed is one in which the standard provides significant detail: Height — no more than 14 inches at the withers. Body length (sternum to buttocks) is ¼ longer that height at shoulder. Body depth (withers to lowest point of chest) — ½ of the distance from the withers to the ground. Length of leg (elbow to ground) — ½ of the distance from the withers to the ground. Neck — (back of skull to withers) ⅓ of the body length.

In some breeds, a straight or sloping topline or a rise over the loin are significant to the silhouette and should be included under silhouette. The amount of forechest that extends ahead of where the legs are set can also have a significant effect on the silhouette. The degree of rear quarter angulation has great effect on a dog's silhouette.

Suggesting all the characteristics here that might be significant to each and every breed isn't practical. As you study and put in time, your knowledge will increase and you'll have a better feel for the amount of important detail to be included. Your being aware of what's important to your breed helps you to become increasingly accurate in evaluating the dog you are creating a chart for.

Head

Head proportions comprise a part of a dog's silhouette, but since a breed's head is such an important element of breed type, its details are included under a separate heading. A correct head is a virtue comprised of elements that make up the whole. What these elements are vary from breed to breed. For instance, most breeds muzzle-to-skull proportions are significant. Eye shape and eye size significantly affect the desired expression in some breeds.

Ear size and ear placement can be significant factors. Improper alignment of teeth is a disqualification in many breeds.

The characteristics that most affect what's desirable in your breed's head are what should be listed here. The degree to which they approach or vary from the ideal is what you should record.

Movement

Many standards describe and request movement that includes "good reach and drive." Reach is simply a reference to the distance covered with each stride — that is, a dog that is said to have plenty of reach is one that has maximal stride length. Drive is the term used to describe hindquarter propulsion. Dogs who have powerful hindquarter propulsion are referred to as having "good drive."

There are other breeds in which some unique characteristics of movement take precedence. For instance, the Miniature Pinscher's hackney motion in the forequarters and the Bulldog's roll are highly distinctive and extremely significant in defining breed type.

Our sample breed has a standard that calls for ground covering reach and drive in profile. Moving away and coming back, the standard dictates that the legs should converge toward a center line (single tracking). There are many breeds that have common faults of construction that interfere with desirable movement. For instance, a short upper arm that restricts forward reach plagues many breeds, and undoubtedly should be included here as a factor to be considered in movement. The amount of detail that is included here should be in proportion to how important movement is to your breed.

Coat

Each breed's standard determines what the important considerations are for the breed's coat. Serviceability, growth pattern, color, trim, and amount differ from breed to breed. Since pigment is closely aligned with color in many cases, it should also be included here.

In some breeds, color is a minor consideration with the standard reading "any color allowed" or "a good dog can't be a bad color." In other standards, not just the color but the *shade* of color is a key element of type. For instance, the Sussex Spaniel's standard reads, "Color — rich golden liver is the only acceptable color and is a certain sign of the purity of the breed. Dark liver or puce is a major fault."

The standard of our sample breed allows only one color — white. Further, the standard faults shadings of any kind. A flat single coat (no undercoat) is called for and waves or curls are faulted to the degree of their departure from the ideal. Pigment of the eye rims, nose, and lips must be jet black. Faded pigment or breaks in the pigment are considered severe faults.

Solving Breeding Problems

A beginning breeder might look at all the recording of detail involved in keeping a type tracker as an exercise in futility. After all, why write down everything about a dog that is standing there in front of you? "Just look. It's all there!"

This is true and would remain so if all one had to contend with in a breeding program was a single dog. However, depending upon a breeder's facilities and his or her time involved in the breed, the one foundation bitch could conceivably lead to dozens and dozens of descendants over the ensuing years. Granted, breeding dogs is hardly like breeding rabbits, but think about those little traits and characteristics one dog is capable of having and then multiply that by 20 dogs and 5 or 10 years. Get the point?

How the type tracker system helps

If you feel capable of trusting all the specific details of each and every dog to memory, I give you all the credit in the world. The rest of us, on the other hand, need some accurate method of finding out where all those faults and elusive qualities came from that we will be forced to deal with for as long as we continue breeding.

The real value of this system is that it not only provides a detailed account of where the qualities and faults come from in your line, but it also tells you what direction you should or should not go with subsequent generations. Breeders are often called upon to make uneducated guesses or play hunches. However, any breeder you talk to will be quick to tell you that being able to eliminate the need to do so saves time, money, and disappointment.

A real-world example

Early on in my Bichon Frise breeding program, I purchased a female puppy from a litter sired by top-producing stud dog, Ch. Chaminade Mr. Beau Monde. The female had no common ancestors to my stud dog in at least four generations, if not more. Mr. Beau Monde dog was particularly noted for his beautiful head, dark eyes, and the jet black pigment of his eye rims, nose, and lips. The daughter I purchased duplicated her sire in head properties, but her pigment was best described as very dark brown. However, since this was equally allowable by the standard, I thought little of it at the time.

The daughter, let's call her Ami, became a champion and later produced two litters of healthy puppies for us. A good number of the puppies went on to become champions as well. The line down from Ami was just one of several successful ones that I was working with at the time.

A good number of years and generations of breeding passed, and then, to my surprise, I began to notice that in a number of instances females from my line were no longer exhibiting the inky black pigment that was considered a hallmark of the line. In fact individual females were being produced (albeit rarely) whose pigment was best described as very weak.

Fortunately, I had devised and begun to use my type tracker system with the first Bichon litter I had bred. I'd completed a page for every male and female that I had bred or owned. Thus, I was able to trace quite a few generations back from the weak-pigmented individuals who were appearing in my litters.

Invariably, my search took me back to Ami, who had been sired by Mr. Beau Monde out of an outcross female. Still, some of my best-pigmented stock had also descended from Ami. It seemed like a mystery until I discovered that, without exception, the weak-pigmented offspring traced back to Ami on the one hand and also to an outside male (I'll call him Snow) that I had bred one of my females to. Further research determined that the male I had used was a descendant of the same line that stood behind Ami's dam. When I looked into Snow's descendants, there was an occasional weak-pigmented offspring recorded. Not often enough or faulty enough to set up an alarm, but there nonetheless.

When both Ami and Snow appeared within four generations of the same pedigree, there were invariably weak-pigmented offspring, even though the pedigrees bore a preponderance of individuals of my own line. Had I not included the brown pigment factor in Ami's type tracker and several of Snow's offspring, I might never have uncovered the cause of my pigment problem.

This example, of course, deals with a fault. I found the type tracker just as useful in determining which individuals I needed to have up close in my pedigrees to sustain certain desirable qualities.

Variations of the system

A number of breeders who I've helped set up the tracking system have gone on to use it in a variety of ways. The primary purpose for which it was developed was to record the significant type characteristics of any male or female that was about to be included in my own breeding program.

There's no reason not to include outside dogs if you're using them in your breeding program, but I would confine this information to that based upon your own personal observance or that which might be provided by the dog's owner or by an extremely reliable source who has first-hand, educated information on the dog.

Other breeders have used the tracking system in developmental stages. That is, recording some or all the data at progressive ages. Some breeds have height and/or weight disqualifications, and breeders have developed the ability to fairly accurately predict the height and weight of an adult dog based upon recording these characteristics at regular intervals over several generations and in a significant number of offspring.

Part IV
Getting Your Breeding Program Started

The 5th Wave   By Rich Tennant

"I got him a bowl, a collar, and since he's a dalmatian puppy, a small fire extinguisher to make him feel right at home."

In this part . . .

To produce worthy dogs of any breed, you need to know what constitutes a top specimen. Nailing down that knowledge leads to the next phase of breeding, which is to figure out the best way to get all that background to work in your favor. In this part, you discover proven methods to achieve the quality that you strive for. You also find out how breeders' experiences and scientific discoveries can help pave the way to your success, determine the ways to increase your chances of producing dogs that live up to the standard of their breed, and discover how to avoid the pitfalls that nearly every breed is susceptible to.

Is mastering these established methods a guarantee of any kind? Not at all. These methods are only the best known methods — and they seem to work when intelligently applied. The only guarantee involved is that a person who embarks on a breeding program without sound knowledge is bound to meet with more failure than success. If failure were the worst of it, you'd have only yourself to blame. Remember, however, that in breeding dogs, you perpetrate your mistakes on an unknowing and unsuspecting public.

Chapter 8

Establishing a Breeding Program

*W*hat *Breeding Dogs For Dummies* has dealt with so far is what I call the prep-steps: the things that come long before an aspiring breeder should even be thinking about that first breeding. If you've absorbed all the material contained in the preceding chapters by reading this book or through direct observation over the years, give yourself a resounding pat on the back. Having the patience to do first things first makes you far better equipped to breed intelligently and achieve some degree of success than the fellow who gets underway somewhere in the middle and then finds himself riding off in all directions.

Granted, we learn by our mistakes. But having to continually backtrack and restart over and over again does nothing but waste time unnecessarily. Lady luck may enter the picture and give the "seat of the pants" kind of breeder a win or two but don't ask someone who's come up that way to repeat what they've done. Chances are they'll not have a clue how they got from point A to point B.

Pilots don't jump into the cockpit and fly off into the wild blue yonder before they've completed all the requisite courses and passed all the tests that prove how much of what they've studied has been absorbed. Nor does the surgeon learn what's required by hacking away at a patient's liver. No one is allowed to assume those responsible positions without the extensive study that prepares them to do so. The day pilots and surgeons are no longer required to be as prepared as they are now is the same day I'll stop traveling by air and begin exploring the possibility of alternate therapies to cure my ills!

Unfortunately, there are no courses of study or tests of knowledge required of people who breed dogs. They just buy a female and bang, they're out of the starting gate! Unlike pilots and surgeons of the world, disreputable dog breeders aren't forced to live with or suffer the consequences of their mistakes.

Uneducated and irresponsible breeders sell, give away, or simply abandon their mistakes with no thought given to what the result of their carelessness will be. Unsuspecting dog lovers like the young couple with the Rottweiler in Chapter 1 are saddled with thousands of dollars in veterinary bills and a chronically ill dog because the people who bred the dog had absolutely no idea of what they were doing nor, obviously, did they care.

If an investigation were done, I feel fairly certain that very few instances of dogs maliciously attacking children can be attributed to dogs coming from responsible breeders. Some dogs have a more aggressive nature than others and breeders who own and appreciate these dogs go to great lengths to make sure their dogs go only to homes where they will be properly trained and supervised.

Let's face it, you're not going to be able to produce worthy dogs of any breed unless you know what it is that constitutes a top specimen. And even when you've mastered that part of your education, it's only the beginning. Look at this groundwork in the same light as you would view the medical student's undergraduate work. Necessary? Without a doubt. However, that far from qualifies the individual for certification as an M.D.

All the preparatory work that I've recommended qualifies you to begin the next phase of a breeder: figuring out the best way to get all that background to work in your favor. Keeping all that your breed should be in mind and examining the tried and true ways to make that come about is your next major step. It is also what this section is all about. This chapter gives you an opportunity to look at what the breeder's experience and scientist's discoveries have proven are the best avenues of getting what you want.

Is mastering these tried-and-true methods a guarantee of any kind? Not at all. They are only the *best known* methods, and they seem to work when intelligently applied. The only guarantee involved is that a person who embarks on a breeding program without sound knowledge is bound to meet with more failure than success. And if failure were the worst of it, one would only have themselves to blame, but in breeding dogs we are perpetrating our mistakes on an unknowing and unsuspecting public.

There are ways to increase our chances of producing dogs that live up to the standard of their breed and there are methods of avoiding the pitfalls which nearly every breed is susceptible to. This chapter gives you some good insight on how to go about taking advantage of them.

Start with the Bitches

I go into greater detail on the countless factors that support the value of having a female in your breeding program in Chapter 11, but for now, I'll unequivocally state that, as far as I'm concerned, there is absolutely nothing more important to your breeding program than starting with a well-bred female of representative quality.

Perhaps this is a good place to start using the term *bitch* instead of female. Everyone you deal with in dogs refers to the two canine sexes as dogs (males) and bitches (females). Since you've worked your way through elementary levels of your education in dog breeding, you may as well start using the terminology the big guys use.

Why you don't need to keep males

The hobby breeder who's only interested in establishing a breeding program and setting a distinctive, yet representative, style, needs only to house bitches. It's absolutely pointless — in fact, counterproductive — for any beginning breeder to house males.

The male will seldom, if ever, be used on the mother who produced him or on his sisters or his daughters. (You'll find that on a rare occasion a very experienced breeder will resort to this kind of mating, but only in very special, well-thought-out circumstances.) If you can't use him on any of the dogs in your own breeding program, what would be the reason for keeping him there?

If it's for those thousands of dollars you think you'll make on stud services — think again! Chapter 12, which is devoted to that possibility, will get you over that pipe dream in nothing flat!

In order to properly use a male, you will have to go out and purchase the right female to breed to him. This puts you right back to square one, with nothing to do but repeat the breeding over and over again. That will give you lots of offspring but nothing to help you carry on a breeding program. All the dogs will be bred exactly the same — too closely to breed to each other.

The pointlessness of keeping a male becomes even more obvious when you stop to realize that you have access to any top-producing male in the country. And you can use a different male with each breeding.

The importance of the foundation bitch (or bitches)

I have spoken to scores of highly successful breeders around the world. Regardless of breed, these highly respected breeders have agreed on two things: First, as I have already pointed out, beginners must go to a successful breeder for their foundation stock. Second, it's critical that the beginning breeder buys the best possible daughter that they can afford of the breed's best producing dam.

You might ask why these knowledgeable people have advised buying *a daughter* of a top producing dam rather than the dam herself. To quote Norma Hamilton, a dear friend and the world-renowned breeder of the Quailmoor Irish Setters of Australia: "Only the person who has taken total leave of their senses would ever part with the great producing bitch herself! It would be like giving away your sails and then showing up to compete in the America's Cup."

Without a doubt, your bitch is the cornerstone, the very foundation, of everything you will do as a breeder. Don't even *think* of economizing in this respect!

Successful breeders also seem to be pretty much in agreement that the foundation bitch doesn't have to be what could be described as a glamour girl — one who has won yards of blue ribbons. Records seem to indicate that as long as her bloodline credentials are impeccable and she's well-made and sound in all respects, her chances of being a noteworthy producer are very good.

Would I add anything to the advice of these breeders? Just one thing: If you could possibly arrange to do so, I would purchase *two* daughters of the producing bitch. They could be litter sisters or even half-sisters with different sires. In Chapter 11 I write about all the possibilities that sister bitches provide, but for the present suffice it to say that there's no better way to assure yourself of establishing a tidy little producing nucleus than through obtaining high-quality sisters. The possibilities of breeding them out and then returning to your own line with the offspring are endless. That process is given ample coverage in Chapter 11.

Having both quality male and female offspring emerge from even your earliest breedings isn't entirely unusual. But again, it's not necessary or advisable to keep any of the males in-house, no matter how good they are.

When you breed a fine male

When and if you do breed that great male, have no fear, you'll be able to make all sorts of breeding arrangements so that you will have access to him down the line when and if you have a bitch who's appropriate to breed to him. Don't sit up nights worrying about what to do if that one-in-a-million male comes along. That's what the chances are of your producing him in your first litters — one in a million, if that high.

But believe me when I tell you that there will be a line from here to Yonkers (or Timbuktu, if you're already in Yonkers) waiting at your door if you have a top, show-quality male to place. Now, mind you, I said *top* as in the very best. Trying to place the average just-good-enough-to-become-a-champion male is not so easy. The reason for this is that average is easy to come by; tops is not. Further, a male of only average quality is not one that will be sought out for breeding, nor should he be. Remember, we're aiming for the bull's-eye!

Moving Outward: Making Partnerships

Working with bloodlines that seem to click, after a time you may find that you are coming up with a considerable percentage of high quality, intelligently line-bred bitches. In fact, you may be coming up with a few more than you can house properly but are afraid to let go entirely.

This creates the small-breeder's dilemma: deciding which should be kept, the females who have proven they can produce for you or the females who have been produced and are one step further along in your quest for improvement.

Solution? A partnership. Even the most limited breeder, working closely with a partner, can create miracles. Naturally, it's important that the partners have basically similar goals in mind and are in agreement as to what constitutes the essence of the breed. Both partners must also be dedicated to setting type and maintaining it. And neither should be unduly influenced by win records or fads and fancies. The partnership is, in fact, a marriage of kind. Be sure to pick someone with whom you're compatible!

Breeding partnerships in Russia

No greater proof exists of the value of breeding partnerships than what I observed among breeders in Russia. Restricted by 70 years of communist domination, purebred dog breeders networked their breeding programs between partnerships of sometimes five, six, and seven breeders. Almost all the people I knew there were living in apartment complexes. All of them were severely handicapped by the lack of funds and the lack of nutritional supplements for their dogs. Even at that, when the iron curtain was lifted, quality sprang forth as if from an underground stream!

I find it very interesting that a good many, if not *most* of Great Britain's great, show-winning dog exports to America were dogs whelped in the most modest of homes — in the kitchen behind the stove, so to speak. The dogs shared living quarters with their owners and their exercise came from being put out in the garden several times a day and from walks around the block with dad or the kids.

I can't repeat it often enough: It isn't how many or how elaborately the dogs are kept, it's how good they are that counts!

So is establishing and maintaining type in this day and age when breeders have greater limitations easy? No, I can't say it is. But then, it never really was, except perhaps for the few breeders blessed with the means to maintain those super kennels of the past. Can it be done today? Of course it can.

Small hobby breeders all over the world limit themselves to one litter a year, often less. These small but important breeders are counted among the most influential in their respective breeds. Their influence didn't come about in a day, a week, or a year. It took time, but it happened.

The Principals of Breeding Dogs

Every foundation animal you buy, whether male or female, toy breed or giant, is the result of some kind of a breeding program. Breeding programs run the gamut from intelligent and conscientious to haphazard and irresponsible. I can only hope that your stock is a result of the former, and that by this time you understand why stock from a quality program is so important.

Every good breeder approaches his or her mission in a slightly different manner. You'll find that, more often than not, experienced and successful breeders are adamantly dedicated to their own method. It shouldn't come as any surprise that their dedication to a particular approach is a result of its having worked for them over the years.

Interestingly, when all the various theories and breeding strategies are analyzed, they can be categorized into the basic few into which all controlled breeding programs of animals fall: *inbreeding*, *linebreeding*, and *outcrossing*. These breeding methods derive their names from the degree of relationship of the two dogs mated: within the immediate family, among more remotely related family members, and of the same breed but with no common ancestors within five generations.

Inbreeding

I begin with inbreeding, not because it's the most popular or most successful kind of breeding, but because it is, as many geneticists have proclaimed, a powerful two-edged sword.

Inbreeding should never be attempted by anyone who doesn't have in-depth knowledge of all the good and bad points of the individuals who stand behind the two animals being mated. Inbreeding can intensify desirable characteristics to the degree that the resulting offspring are highly dependable for producing the desirable qualities. However, inbreedings can also call forth catastrophic consequences.

Inbreeding increases the chance that a gene obtained from the one parent will duplicate (match) one obtained from the other. This is the case for what is desirable and what is not desirable. Often harmful, sometimes lethal, genes float around in the pedigrees of dogs within a breed.

Knowledgeable breeders are apt to know if and where these genes exist. They use the utmost care in bringing animals together in any mating that might reproduce these abnormalities. In some circumstances, experienced breeders intentionally make breedings that risk such results, but there are specific reasons for their doing so. Only carefully selected individuals from those matings are retained for breeding and all others are neutered and eliminated from the gene pool.

Inbreeding can be scientifically defined as the mating of individuals more closely related than the average of the population that they come from. In other words, what might be considered inbreeding in a new breed with a small gene pool might not be considered inbreeding in a long-established breed that has hundreds, if not thousands, of dogs in the gene pool to draw upon.

In layman's terms, and for our purposes here, inbreeding is best explained as the mating of two *directly* related animals. Most dog breeders consider the following as inbreeding:

- ✔ Father bred to daughter
- ✔ Son bred to mother
- ✔ Full brother bred to full sister

One frequently hears those who are not familiar with intelligent breeding practices blame inbreeding for producing the health or temperament problems that exist in popular breeds. This is seldom, if ever, the case. Inbreeding isn't the main cause of a preponderance of health problems in a breed. People who lack knowledge of what exists in a breed's background create problems of this nature. If two dogs, closely related or not who have a debilitating problem, are mated, the chances of all the offspring having the problem are obviously going to be very high.

Quite frankly, I do not believe that anyone would intentionally breed two animals who are both afflicted with the same serious health problem. However, if the two animals who are mated are themselves free of the problem, but the problem runs rampant in the genetic makeup of their immediate ancestors, the chances of their passing it along are, for all intents and purposes, just as high as if they were afflicted themselves. I write about all this in more detail in Chapter 9.

Linebreeding

Scientifically speaking, linebreeding and inbreeding are the same. The intensity is all that differs. In other words, if inbreeding increases the chance that a gene obtained from the one parent will duplicate (match) one obtained from the other, linebreeding reduces but does not eliminate those chances.

Although inbreeding is not to be attempted by anyone who isn't very experienced, intelligent breeders are also aware that a helter pedigree made up of dogs who are related only by breed isn't going to ever provide any consistency or lock in any of the good traits that are necessary to maintain. Further, it's doubtful that even the accidental outstanding individuals can be relied upon to reproduce themselves.

Linebreeding then, is the best way to concentrate the qualities possessed by certain outstanding animals in the pedigree without running the risks of inbreeding. The certainty of getting what is desired is not as great through linebreeding as it is through inbreeding, but neither is the risk of intensifying highly undesirable traits.

Outcrossing

When there are no common ancestors within five generations of the two individuals being mated, the breeding is generally considered an outcross. True outcrosses are somewhat unlikely if breeders are working within popular bloodlines. By *popular* I mean the bloodlines that are producing the kinds of dogs who are winning at the dog shows.

Outcrossing is the opposite of inbreeding. This method of breeding mates individuals of the same breed who, for all intents and purposes, are not related. This approach is less likely to fix faults in the offspring, but neither can it concentrate specific qualities with any certainty.

A certain look or style within a breed will become popular because it does well at the shows. Usually, this style will emanate from a successful breeder's line or be stamped by an especially dominant stud dog. Other breeders will invariably attempt to incorporate that winning look into their own line. They do this either by dipping lightly into the winning line by making a single breeding to it or by heavily reshaping their breeding program around the line that is producing the winning look. As a consequence, the breed as it is popularly seen becomes influenced to a greater or lesser degree by a few dogs from the source that began the trend. Eventually, there's hardly a dog in sight who doesn't have at least a touch of the popular line somewhere, thereby making a true outcross breeding very rare.

Making a choice

So which is the best way to go: linebreeding, inbreeding, or outcrossing? The following sections offer some thoughts.

The conservative breeder

Some breeders have a very clear-cut interpretation of the standard and stay within the lines that will produce that look and temperament, regardless of trends. Fads will come and go, but these breeders stand by their linebreeding program that produces what they believe is correct and refuse to change hats even when that refusal creates a lull in accumulating those coveted blue ribbons.

Sticking by your line isn't always an easy thing to do. The trends can become so all encompassing that your dog becomes what you might call odd man out — the only dog in the lineup that looks different. It takes the knowledgeable judge who has the courage of his or her own convictions to decide which style is really right for the breed and to reward it accordingly. I've found, however, that these diehard breeders weather the storms of popularity and are there waiting when the winds of change calm down. In a good many cases, these kennels prove to be where newer breeders find the foundation stock that sets them in the right direction.

An eye on the prize

Other breeders keep abreast of trends within a breed and adapt their lines to keep pace. They are attracted to the qualities of the dog of the hour and use him or the bloodline that produced him in their own breeding program. These same individuals often have an eye for those winning qualities and are able to pick the dog most likely to succeed from their own litters. Soon, they are out and winning with dogs sporting the new look.

Usually, a significant amount of outcrossing is involved in breeding programs of this kind. Reliability is not the long suit of the line. Outcrossing can be a hit-and-miss affair, but those who subscribe to this approach seem entirely satisfied with those occasional hits that come along because often they're big hits and account for highly successful win records.

Outcrossing for elusive qualities

Outcross breeding isn't done only to follow a fad or trend. When properly employed, outcrosses can bring qualities to a breeder's line that he or she sorely needs. Many intelligent breeders resort to occasional outcross breedings for very sound reasons. At times, a breeder's line will generally satisfy the breed standard in all respects but one or two — say, for instance, pigment and eye color. The breeder finds that try as he or she might, those qualities remain elusive within their line.

The logical thing to do, then, is to seek out another line (one known to consistently produce good pigment and eye color) and make a breeding, sometimes two, into that line. Often this requires outcrossing into another line that doesn't bear a close relationship to one's own. The method is more apt to be successful if the outcross line is closely linebred because the chances of it being dominant for the desired qualities are higher. The dog whose appearance (phenotype) is not backed up by a concentration of the genes for that quality (genotype) may not be strong enough to pass along that quality to another, stronger line. I go into the details in Chapter 9.

Finding the formula

In addition to inbreeding, linebreeding, and outcrossing, breeders have to factor in another approach. In some cases, the sexes of the individual dogs who are used have a great bearing on what characteristics are passed along. These are referred to as *sex linked* characteristics.

In some cases, the male will be best at bringing in the quality you need from another line. In other instances, the female will be more apt to give you what you want. It's almost as if Mom Nature is taunting us by giving us part but not all of the equation. Then it's up to us to find the missing piece and come up with the right answers.

Breeders who set out to improve their line or correct faults rather than simply accepting

them as part of the territory may need generations of dogs to do so. In the end, however, the persevering breeder usually accomplishes his or her goal.

Getting an animal good enough to show is one thing. Getting one good enough to carry on your breeding program or to take the breed one step further along the line of progress takes time, perseverance, and often great disappointment. However, the dogs who carry our breeds to greater heights in the show ring, in competitive events, and as producers are usually the result of someone's being willing to deal with all these setbacks.

Chapter 9

Bare Bones Genetics

· ·

In This Chapter

▶ Mendel's first pair of genes

▶ Practical application

▶ Breeder's sense and sensible breeders

▶ Genotype and phenotype

· ·

*I*n Chapter 8, I write about each of the three standard approaches to establishing and maintaining a breeding program. Inbreeding, linebreeding, and outcrossing each have their pluses and minuses — elements about them that increase or decrease the chances of your getting what it is you're after or what it is you're trying to avoid.

Predicting the outcome of any breeding is based upon a tried-and-true science called genetics. Genetics is from the Greek word *gene* meaning *race*. Genes are the way that all characteristics owned by living things are inherited or passed along.

You're blonde, blue-eyed, and short or dark-skinned, brown-eyed, and tall because of the genes you inherited from your parents. Your children look or will look a certain way because of the way the genes you inherited got together with those of your mate at the moment of conception.

This chapter is about just how all this takes place. Don't panic. I'm not going to send you off on a scientific expedition into the intricacies of genetics. I'll try and keep this as simple as I possibly can so that you will have a clear understanding that in dog breeding (in just about *any* breeding) what you see is seldom exactly what you'll get.

This is simply the bare bones of it all. If you want to pursue the field and become an expert on genetics — and it is a most fascinating field, I assure you — the pursuit can become a lifelong study. There are books by the carload on the subject and enough courses available at universities across the country to maintain your student status until you're called on to the big dog show in the sky.

A Little Bit of History: The Work of Gregor Mendel

Relatively speaking, the field of genetics isn't all that old. But once scientists realized its importance, advancements have been nothing short of astounding. When you stop to think that not much over 100 years ago, the answer our ancestors might have given their children to why living things look as they do was probably something like "because," "dunno," or "God wanted it that way."

While it may well be true that "He" does want it that way, a master plan is involved. Today, depending upon the extent to which parents have studied genetics, they not only could tell little Mary why her hair is curly, but some parents could make a living, breathing, and exact duplicate of Mary's little 4-H project! We've advanced from "because" and "dunno" to cloning. And this is how it all began.

Back about the mid 1800s, an Austrian monk by the name of Gregor Mendel started keeping careful notes on some experiments he was doing with peas that were growing out in the backyard of the monastery. Some of the flowers produced by the pea plants were red and some were white.

While the rest of the monks were content to split the peas for soup or mix them with their carrots for dinner, good old Mendel had bigger plans for his pea patch. He cross-pollinated (mated) the red peas with the white peas. The flowers produced by the plants resulting from these matings were all red — nary a white one or even candy-striped flower in the bunch. "Odd!" Mendel no doubt thought. Apparently, the white-flowered parents of the new plants didn't have any clout.

Mendel didn't stop there. When he mated two of the red flower children (flower children of the pre–Haight Asbury variety, that is) from these first generation plants, he was astounded to find that although most of the plants bore red flowers, every once in a while a plant had white flowers.

Calculating the odds

Now Mendel, not being one to leave well enough alone, made thousands of these red-to-red crosses. After awhile, he discovered that the results always had an exact ratio. One out of four plants had white flowers and three out of four had red flowers. "Eureka!" he shouted to himself. (All the other monks were busy praying — probably for Brother Mendel, who they were sure had taken leave of his faculties, to say nothing of his kitchen duties.) But Mendel knew he was onto something. He wasn't sure of exactly what, but something indeed.

Brother Mendel then took some of those one-out-of-four whites and mated them together. What resulted were plants that produced *only* white flowers. No matter how many times he crossed the whites, they produced just that — *white*. The red color had been completely eliminated. But when he mated the three-out-of-four reds from this same generation together, he was in for another big surprise.

Although all the reds were just that — red — when Mendel checked all those records he was keeping he found that only one out of three of these reds could be relied upon to produce only red flowers. The other two-out-of-three reds, when bred together, produced both red and white flowers.

Dominants and recessives

Mendel was hooked! Did these ratios stay good for other characteristics? The good monk made controlled pea plant breedings in every available nook and cranny of the monastery's grounds — tall to short, big-leaved to small-leaved, yellow-seeded to green-seeded. What he found was that in every instance one characteristic (like white flowers or big leaves) was always dominant over the other, and in his first generation crosses the results always looked just like the dominant parent.

Even more interesting was that the other characteristic — the recessive one (for instance, small leaves) — would reappear in the same 1-out-of-3 ratio as had the white flowers when the first generation crosses were mated. Not only that, the characteristic reappeared in the *exact* form of the original, and this happened generation after generation.

Well, old Mendel was beside himself! "Who would have thunk!" he thought. When he rushed in to tell his fellow monks about his amazing discoveries, they looked at him with blank faces and said, "So, can you get back to cleaning the kitchen now?" Nobody in the monastery gave a hoot nor, as Mendel would find, did anyone else in or out of the monastery.

So, a sadder but wiser Mendel cooked all his peas, shelved all his notes, and returned to his kitchen. He, like everyone else, forgot all about the great pea caper and all his hard work stood stagnating on the shelves for years.

Practical application

When Mendel's work was rediscovered, the world had already entered the twentieth century. Suddenly old Brother Mendel (who had since gone on to his just rewards) was hailed as revolutionary. The old boy was considered a genius and far ahead of his time. Even the monks who had joined up after the old ones had moved heavenward agreed that Mendel must have been pretty doggone smart to figure all that out. *"But,"* they were quick to add, "he did have help from a Higher Source!"

Mendel's discoveries and theories provide the foundation upon which all genetic studies are built. Mendelian genetics initiated a chain of events that have changed the world we live in. Although genetic inheritance has proven far more complex than what Mendel originally assumed, the basic theory still holds true. Had it not been for Mendel, who knows how long it would have taken us to figure out how to cross our peas?

Genes, chromosomes, and characteristics

Mendel's discovery led scientists to eventually understand that all living creatures are made up of microscopic cells. Each of these cells has a membrane-bound nucleus that contains thread-like structures called chromosomes, and every living species has a definite number of these chromosomes. Humans have 46 pairs. All dogs, regardless of breed or breeds, have 39 pairs. Basically the chromosomes are paired, two of each kind in the cell.

In animal reproduction when the reproductive cells are formed, the pairs separate so that every single one of the male's sperm or the female's eggs contains only one of each pair of chromosomes. The male's sperm containing 39 chromosomes fertilizes the female's egg also containing 39 chromosomes. A new cell is formed and thus the number of chromosomes is restored to 78 — one of each pair from each parent.

During normal growth, the fertile cells divide and multiply in such a way that one cell becomes two and two become four. Each cell is an exact duplicate of the one from which it derived. Therefore, the essential form of the cell is unchanged and the chromosomes remain the same.

The individual characteristics living things inherit are carried by what Mendel had named genes. There are probably many thousands of these genes, but each of them is found in a specific place on a specific chromosome. A gene always influences the same specific feature. It's passed on, for all intents and purposes, generation after generation without change.

Each parent contributes one gene of the pair to its offspring. When one gene in the pair differs in its effects from the other, one dominates the other. Thus there are *dominant* and *recessive* genes.

Take a look at Figure 9-1. Here, we have a pair of theoretical dogs, one black and one yellow. A black coat is caused by the dominant gene B. A yellow coat is caused by the recessive gene Y. If these two dogs mate, they produce offspring with B and Y genes, but since the B gene is dominant, all the offspring are black. Now if the dogs with both B and Y genes mate, there's a 1-in-4 chance that they will produce a yellow (YY) dog.

It should be understood, however, that very few aspects of inheritance are influenced by only one gene or one pair of genes and that one gene can influence more than one characteristic

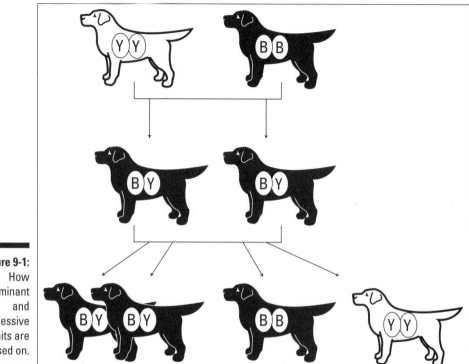

Figure 9-1:
How
dominant
and
recessive
traits are
passed on.

A single characteristic can actually be influenced by dozens of pairs of genes. When you stop to consider that one gene of the characteristic comes from dad and the other comes from mom, the combination possibilities affecting a characteristic are — well, let's just say far greater than finger counting will determine.

Applying genetics to dog breeding

Does this all sound too complicated? Don't give up on your plans to breed good dogs because the details of genetics sound beyond your comprehension. For the time being, just remember that each pair of genes works *exactly* how Mendel said it did. Which genes and how many influence what can come later. The fact that so many genes are involved and that the possibilities and influences are so complex really isn't as important as understanding your breed and knowing what a good specimen looks like. Once you get that and know there's more to breeding than meets the eye, you'll be heading in the right direction.

Because all breeds of dogs have exactly the same number of chromosomes, all can be compatibly bred. This means that even the tiniest male from the

---

Old wives tales

There are old myths that you think would have disappeared by now, but I guess as long as people believe that bad luck comes from black cats and broken mirrors and that politicians "work for us," why wouldn't they continue to believe tales that had to have been handed down to us from the Dark Ages?

It was once believed that strolling your female past a male of the color you desired for her puppies would insure your success. Or if your purebred female were to be "caught," as they used to say, by the local cur, she would be ruined forever in respect to producing purebred offspring. Even today, some longtime breeders believe that matings of opposites (large to small, light cream to red, fast to slow) result in a halfway point between the two extremes. That is, large

to small would produce a dog of medium size, light cream to red would produce a medium tan, and the slow to fast mating would give a dog who moves along at a moderate pace. This is entirely incorrect. Even the most basic knowledge of genetics clearly illustrates that an animal can only receive its parents' genes (one from each) for the characteristic. Genes do not *blend*. The dominant gene prevails.

If the small parent's genes for size are both for small size, those genes are all that parent can contribute. Suppose that large size is the dominant factor in this instance. The large parent could carry a gene for smallness from one of her parents, and even though she's large, she's capable of contributing that gene for small in any of her matings.

---

smallest breed in the world could be successfully bred to a female of any giant breed. If you're going to be mad enough to try such a dingbat experiment, I would seriously suggest assisting the little fellow with as many Manhattan telephone directories as you can get your hands on. Either that, or talk to your local vet about artificial insemination. Were it me (and in this case it wouldn't be, I assure you) I would certainly opt for the latter.

Environment versus Heredity

Remembering that genetic inheritance only contributes the *potential* for a characteristic is important. For example, environment can contribute heavily to growth. Nutrition, as well as freedom from disease and parasites, is a strong factor in a dog's ability to achieve his or her potential in regard to maximum growth. Nor would all the genetic potential in the world result in a luxurious coat if the dog were poorly fed and infested with fleas and worms.

At the same time, even the best environmental conditions only allow a dog to achieve his or her genetic potential — *nothing more*. All the food and vitamin supplements in the world are not going to make your Chihuahua grow to the size of a Great Dane.

There are artificial growth hormones that humans have resorted to for their own use — with dubious results. But here again, use of such products does not affect what an animal has inherited genetically. It's undoubtedly possible to artificially force an animal beyond what the animal was intended to be, but experience continually seems to prove that resorting to such tactics is dangerous, at best.

Breeder's Sense

I'm the first to admit that my understanding of genetic principles is elementary. Most of my success as a breeder has come from what graduates of the old school of stockmanship might well refer to as a very strong *breeder's sense*. Breeder's sense is an ability to quickly evaluate what's right and wrong for a breeding animal and what combinations seem likely to work.

Common sense and breeding

I attended an excellent seminar recently in which the lecturer had devised some very impressive formulas and equations to help a dog breeder be successful. The formulas were based on genetic research and scientific principles. As the gentleman worked out the formulas on the blackboard, I heard little gasps of delight as those in attendance began to understand what the formulas meant. I personally was delighted to find that science's formulas confirmed that the practices employed by many longtime breeders like myself were sound and that the projected results of the formulas pretty much confirmed what I had experienced.

The disappointing part came at the seminar's conclusion. I couldn't help but overhear the conversations of some of the day's participants. Evidently, our lecturer had made the points he set forth very well and had convinced his audience of the value of his formulas. Unfortunately, the point that he didn't stress nearly enough was that the formulas' success was entirely dependent upon the user's thorough understanding of correct type in his or her breed. Then and only then would the user be able to effectively bring together the right elements of those equations.

I heard the participants marvel at how much time they had wasted doing this, that, and the other thing in order to breed good dogs. Their take was that successful dog breeding was much simpler than they had made it and was easily achievable by using the magic formulas.

As I walked off to my car, I couldn't help but think "only in their dreams." Obviously my fellow students were under the mistaken assumption that the ends were exclusively the result of the means — that the formulas did the work and not the dogs brought together according to the formula. Science is an adjunct to a breeding program. It's generous to those who use it in conjunction with a crystal-clear picture of what is needed to make what is wanted. It's called using common sense!

Breeder's sense isn't anything magical. I believe it comes from the same place that gives a person the eye for a fine animal. It's accompanied by an innate ability to recognize the animals who have an ability to pass something along to succeeding generations.

At the same time, there's no doubt in my mind that even the most highly developed breeder's sense is facilitated by a basic understanding of genetics. I know for certain that what I strive for in any breeding program I've undertaken is achieved by putting the animals with the right genetic makeup together and eliminating any and all whose inheritance brings in characteristics I do not want. Breeder's sense allows me to recognize what is of essence to a breed. Knowledge of genetics keeps me from having to make endless experimental breedings to get it. It provides some shortcuts for me. I haven't had to go all the way to ground zero in order to get myself going in the right direction.

Genotype and Phenotype

Every dog you use in your breeding program comes fully equipped with two distinguishing characteristics that set him or her uniquely apart from every other member of the breed. One you can see and one you can't. Genetically speaking, they're the dog's genotype (pronounced GEENO-type) and phenotype (FEENO-type). *Phenotype* is determined at first sight. It's what the individual looks like to the naked eye. It's the result of how the environment has dealt with what the dog was born with. *Genotype,* on the other hand, is the dog's genetic makeup — what you see isn't necessarily what the dog is capable of producing.

Phenotype: The things you see

In order to get that dog who looks like the picture you have in your mind, you have to use animals that look like what you want. This is phenotype stuff. Chapter 6 goes into a lot of detail about the importance of selecting representative dogs to start off with. If you haven't read that part yet, jump back there now and read through it. If it doesn't convince you that Kentucky Derby winners aren't about to be the offspring of retired plow horses, I strongly suggest that you think about gardening instead of dog breeding.

A good number of breeders make their breeding decisions based almost entirely on phenotype. That is, they breed like to like. They have a crystal-clear picture in mind of what they are after and they use the dogs who most closely resemble that picture.

Is this behavior caused by a total disregard for genetics? Not really. The respective dogs in use look as they do because of what they've inherited genetically. A Curly Coated Retriever like the one shown in Figure 9-2 has a curly coat because his genetic makeup allows him to have that kind of coat. You can breed Boxers from now 'til Doomsday and you won't get a curly coat, no matter what. (Well, you could if a genetic mutation occurs, but you'll probably win the lottery three or four times before that happens.)

An experienced breeder knows that if the individuals in use are linebred, the likelihood of their reproducing themselves is very high. However, if you use an individual from an outcross breeding or one whose pedigree is primarily the result of outcross breedings, chances of retaining any continuity become increasing less likely. The chances of unknown and unanticipated characteristics — those things I call the X factors — appearing also increase.

Scientific explanations and definitions aside, I've never been able to convince myself that an animal who doesn't look like what I'm after is one I want to use in my breeding program. Nor does an animal who doesn't have the look or the characteristic in great enough strength to appear as though he or she could give it away really inspire me to add him or her to my breeding program.

Figure 9-2: It's not likely that you'll ever be able to develop the coat of this Curly Coated Retriever into a breed such as Boxers.

Ch. Karakul; photo courtesy of Leslie Puppo.

> # Breeding around phenotype
>
> In order to bring a desired characteristic into my line, I have on occasion purchased a son or daughter of a dog who is not phenotypically my ideal. However, I do my best to find offspring who come as close to the look I'm after as possible. I'm very cautious about bringing anything directly into my line that is significantly outside of my overall picture of the breed. I make it a point to have a very clear mental idea of what I consider correct for the breed and I do my best to use only those animals who maintain that image. I make changes within that framework,
>
> but I do it one step at a time without giving away the overall balance and proportion that creates the framework.
>
> Were I trying to improve heads in my line, I would consider bringing a dog into my breeding program that had bad eye color but an otherwise beautiful headpiece. However, regardless of how correct the dog's headpiece was I would never consider him if his body proportions were entirely out of the range that I consider acceptable.

With that said, there have been exceptions. On occasion, I've seen very ordinary animals produce qualities that you wouldn't think them capable of based on their outward appearance (their phenotype). Would I breed to that kind of a dog? Only if no other way existed to get what I wanted. After carefully observing how dominant that individual dog might be in producing what I'm after and seeing how effectively he or she might combine with my own line would I allow him or her to enter my line.

Does this mean that the dog or bitch who has the look that satisfies you carries a guarantee that he or she will be able to produce what you want? Absolutely not. But your chances are certainly better than they would be otherwise. Here again, your formula will only work if you use the right components.

Genotype: What you don't see

The best way to put the odds in your favor is to maintain a breeding program in which the stock you use not only *look like* what you want, but whose *genetic background* reflects that picture as well. They are the dogs who are most likely to transmit their own characteristics to their offspring. Their genotype is relatively consistent with their phenotype. Since a dog's genotype is what you can't see, it can be a very tricky thing to deal with, particularly in dealing with dogs who have unknowns in their past.

Zinger, your very athletic and sound black dog who's blessed with a wonderful temperament, may carry the genes to produce white puppies with crippling diseases and nasty temperaments. Bred correctly, good old Zinger may never produce offspring that manifest those undesirable characteristics.

Bred without careful study and consideration, Zinger could produce offspring with more problems than you could conceivably imagine.

The dog whose appearance doesn't meet a breeder's specifications is normally out of the picture, so its genotype is of no consequence. But the dog who is seen as acceptable, even outstanding, may carry characteristics in his or her genetic makeup that could create havoc in a breeding program. Dogs who are less than top class in the looks department could be produced, but the situation is much worse when those unknowns result in offspring with chronic health problems or who are temperamentally unsound.

A point I make throughout this book is that you should devote as much time and study as possible to purchasing foundation stock. Reputable breeders know the conformation flaws and genetically reproduced health problems that exist in their breed. They have dealt with them in their own line and know where the pitfalls lie in other lines as well.

You absolutely can't afford to begin your breeding program with stock that doesn't come from someone who knows both the faults and virtues of the line. I would much rather have a dog of slightly less quality whose pedigree carries a *known* fault than the dog who might be more attractive to the eye but whose pedigree is made up of dogs that I know nothing about. Faults I'm aware of can be worked with. It's those that I'm not aware of that will pop up when I least expect them.

Recessive traits can be passed on undetected for generations. Two black dogs carrying recessive genes for tan could produce several litters before the first tan offspring appears.

If you were to breed the pair ad infinitum, Mendel's ratios would eventually work themselves out, but few breeder's females produce more than a litter or two in their lifetime — it's unusual to hear that one has been bred more than three or four times.

Even with the best of pedigrees, no breeder is able to *guarantee* a dog is genetically free of problems. The complex variations of genetic inheritance make it impossible to breed any animal with absolute certainty. However, science has made breedings less and less a gamble. In Chapter 10, I discuss some of these scientific advances.

Perpetuating Faults

No breed, in fact, no line of dogs, is free of defects — defects in the sense of characteristics that are undesirable. These undesirable characteristics can run the gamut from something minor like eye color that's lighter than desirable to a propensity for chronic illness.

Contrary to popular belief, genetic undesirables are not confined to purebred animals. Granted that in the wild any genetically transmitted infirmity that interferes with a newborn animal's ability to nurse, or an adult's ability to capture food or escape from a predator, is for all intents and purposes quickly eliminated from the gene. The likelihood of the factor running rampant through the breed is, if nothing else, greatly reduced. Again, understanding that the genetic basis for a problem can be carried on indefinitely, even though a problem doesn't manifest itself, is important.

Obviously, genetic inheritance works in the positive sense as well. If speed is a prerequisite of the species' survival, as it is in the great cats, the fastest cats have the best chance of catching dinner and therefore have the best chance of surviving. These fast cats tend to produce offspring that will reflect their parents' ability. The slowpokes would probably become extinct over a period of time especially if a scarcity of game were to develop.

If there are two cat families, and one's fast and one's slow, common sense tells you that the cats most apt to survive are the speed demons. Because of what we know about genetics, we know that even the cat family blessed with lightening speed has no insurance that a real slowpoke (or at least a slower poke) will not be born within their ranks. Anomalies of this kind exist in nature, but they seldom survive.

In the breeding of domestic animals, particularly dogs, the scenario is much different both in general and in particular. For humanitarian reasons, dog breeders strive to insure the life of all the puppies who are born. In many cases, this is contrary to what Mom Nature might do left to her own devices. Feeling responsible for bringing a little life into the world, a breeder may artificially feed and make heroic efforts to save the whelp who a mother dog would reject on her own and push out of the nest.

Does the mother of the puppy know more than her humans do? Do her instincts tell her that the puppy is unsuitable for carrying on the race and should not be saved? These are questions that have been and will be debated among dog breeders until science can probe the mysteries of nature and provide factual answers.

Dog breeding involves selecting for a vast number of characteristics beyond just the ability to survive. In fact, most breeders assume that breed survival is insured by merit of their interest, so there's no need to be concerned about it. However, consistently incorporating constitutionally weak individuals in our breeding programs can eventually have devastating results.

In too many cases, survival of the breed has taken a back seat, if it has a seat at all, to marks of beauty. For some breeds, rigid selection for conformation characteristics has taken precedence over longevity. Genetic disorders run rampant and cause early death. Science is looking toward means by which these disorders can be detected but, until that time, breeders must remain conscientious in tracking and doing their best to eliminate these problems from their breeding program.

Estimating Heritability

Those of a more scientific bent are inclined to scoff at terms like "breeder's sense," regardless of how the ability has served those who have it. Our doubting Thomases need physical evidence to be convinced of anything, particularly in the areas of breeding and modes of inheritance.

For those who are dedicated to the belief that science has all the answers we need, fairly reliable methods exist of predicting what one can anticipate in a breeding program. One such systematic approach is commonly known as *estimating heritability.* This technique has been used by livestock breeders for what is now approaching half a century. The system is based upon a complicated mathematical formula far beyond the scope of this book to fully explain and not entirely unlike those I mention in the sidebar "Common sense and breeding." It provides livestock breeders with a measuring system that enables them to determine how likely it is that particular traits will appear in the following generation.

A particular value of the system, as I understand it, is that it would assist the scientifically planned dog breeding program by telling the breeder how much genetic change might be expected through selective breeding from one generation to the next. The system can also help the breeder determine if the likelihood of the offspring inheriting a particular characteristic is high or low. A low heritability factor for a particular characteristic may indicate that the characteristic needs to be emphasized throughout the entire breeding program (in other words, that it needs to be possessed by all the animals in the program). A high heritability factor for the characteristic may allow the breeder to assume that the characteristic is more easily transmitted by a single dog and that the dog's phenotype is a strong indicator for that characteristic.

Adapting this system to the breeding of purebred dogs is significantly trickier than using it for livestock. Although dog breeders breed for a good number of characteristics that are similar to those that livestock breeders seek, dog breeders also require some other traits. Both the dog breeder and the livestock breeder want sound conformation and good health. Both want their animals to conform to a certain ideal: The Hereford breeder wants all his stock to look like outstanding Herefords, just as much as the Doberman breeder wants his dogs to conform to the Doberman standard.

But a Hereford breeder couldn't care less if his prize heifer has a dazzling personality or is smart as a whip. Dog breeders have some very complex characteristics they breed for: charismatic personality for the show dog, compatibility for the companion, a good nose for the hunting dog. There are some breeds that require all three of these and more. This says nothing of their conformation, which could be equally complex. Temperament and adaptability are governed by a complex set of genetic variables that, even if present at birth, may be overshadowed by environmental conditions. All of which is to say that science is a useful tool — but only as an adjunct to common sense.

Chapter 10

Recording Genotype Characteristics

*A*s a breeder, it's important that you track the results of your breeding program and record how well the individual dogs in it rate. The details of how to go about doing so are in Chapter 7. When you've discovered what it is you're after and how your breed should look, you can fairly easily give a numerical score to how close (or how far!) any dog you breed or breed to conforms to that ideal. But then there's that next step.

Anyone who has had any breeding experience at all knows that what can be seen is not all a breeder has to contend with. All kinds of closeted stuff has to be dealt with: those things that lurk around in a dog's genetic makeup that you know nothing about until *wham,* there they are in that new litter.

When those "whams" are for the goodies, you can pat yourself on the back and brag that you knew it all the time! But it's not the goodies that set you off in the wrong direction or produce faults that come as a total surprise. It's all the rest — the hidden recessives that you knew nothing about and that destroy all the wonderful plans you've made for the current crop of youngsters. Without a doubt, in dog breeding far more tears are shed over what can't see be seen than what can.

Recessive genes carry mental and physical characteristics, positive and negative, that need a breeder's attention but seldom get that attention until after the fact. The breeder isn't being neglectful; he or she just doesn't have any advanced warning. When the recessive carries positive qualities, the breeder is in fine shape, but breeders are seldom that lucky. The X factors are all too often the things that you didn't want.

So how do you go about keeping track of what you don't know is there? This is a question that breeders have been wrestling with since they began controlled breeding. Now, however, science has stepped in and is making ever-advancing progress toward finding an answer to the question.

Some breeders can have a certain amount of reluctance to abandon those good, old, time-tested breeding methods. After all, how can you argue with success that's been earned through those tried and true ways of doing things? Why fix something that's not broken?

In reality, what science provides us with is not an either/or situation. Science and stockmanship can be combined. These new developments may appear to look like just so much alphabet soup at first, but in reality there are some amazing advances in the field of genetic testing and DNA. This chapter takes a good look at how these advances can assist breeders in their quest for perfection.

Genetic Testing and DNA Results

Breeders who have been around a while look back a few decades and shake their heads at some of the devastating blows dealt certain breeds in the name of scientific progress. A few decades back, there was an ill-advised rush to eliminate every dog and bitch that came from a pedigree suspected of producing any kind of genetic disorder — hip dysplasia, to name just one. If the dog had a pedigree, every individual in it was suspect and a candidate for neutering.

Dog breeding was approached as though it were nothing more than a laboratory experiment — a laboratory experiment in the hands of someone who had taken Genetics 101 and knew all the answers. The approach was a part of the movement that laughed at an eye for a dog and breeder's sense. It was the time of genetics, plain and simple. Dominants and recessives were so oversimplified that genetics practically destroyed some breeds it was applied to.

Sadly, and often too late, those who were too hasty in scrapping what they had accomplished in their pedigree-cleansing fervor found they had tossed out the baby with the bath water. There was nothing of quality left in their line to make progress with. If anything positive came out of this rush to judgment, it was more proof that witch hunts do not provide solutions.

A well-developed breeder's sense can do a pretty fair job of directing the process of inheritance without the person knowing exactly what it is that's taking place on a scientific basis. But now science is in the process of eliminating a good part of the guesswork that was always involved in dog breeding. Science can help breeders achieve some of their goals much more quickly and on a less costly basis.

DNA research, genetic testing, and the manner in which they point out where things happen within a dog's genetic makeup may not be the easiest things in the world to understand. Fully understood or not, the answers they bring us make placing our trust in their validity well worthwhile.

Science for Greenhorns

In order to have a better understanding of what all this genetic testing and DNA tells you and how you can put it to use in breeding dogs, you need to know what DNA really is.

Each microscopic cell that all living creatures are made up of has a membrane-bound nucleus that contains thread-like structures called chromosomes. Basically the chromosomes are paired, two of each kind in the cell. Dogs, regardless of breed or breeds, have 39 pairs.

In animal reproduction, when the reproductive cells are formed, the pairs separate so that every single one of the male's sperm or the female's eggs contains only one of each pair of chromosomes. The male's sperm containing 39 chromosomes fertilizes the female's egg also containing 39 chromosomes. A new cell is formed and thus the number of chromosomes is restored to 78 — one of each pair from each parent.

Chromosomes in each living cell are made up of proteins and two kinds of nucleic acid — ribonucleic acid (RNA) and deoxyribonucleic acid (DNA). It's the DNA part of all this that you're primarily interested in here. (You don't have to remember those names or how to pronounce them — no one else does. Just remember the letters and the fact that the two are acids.)

A DNA molecule looks like a tiny spiral ladder. Genes are the sequences of DNA on a chromosome that initiate the production of proteins. The proteins, in turn, cause a body to function in a particular way. Between these body-function genes are long strings of what are generally referred to as junk DNA. This is the DNA that is precisely copied and passed down from one generation to the next. Since this material isn't of the active gene sort, it was looked at as non-functional in the past but this is no longer the case.

If an active gene is defective because of a mutation, the loss of the body function that results from the mutation often leads to the death of the organism, so these mutations are not generally passed on. Mutations in that junk DNA, on the other hand, have no significance — *except to geneticists.*

These super-smart guys use those long lineups of junk material to track family inheritance and mark where things are happening on active genes.

These genetic markers are very distinctive and allow scientists to see their way around our dogs' 78 chromosomes (and the something like 100,000 genes controlling the chromosomes). Scientists are in the process now of trying to mark where all the genes controlling human and canine traits are located.

Got it? Who'd of thought you were going to become a geneticist? Actually, this book just scrapes a little off the surface *of the surface* of what DNA does and how it does it. A full understanding and appreciation for the field will take as much time as you are willing to give it. At this point though, just give little Trixie an extra thank-you biscuit — after all, if it wasn't for her, you probably wouldn't know half as much as you now do about genetic testing and DNA.

Comparing where scientists are now with DNA to the potential of their work actually puts the field in its infancy. As work progresses, new discoveries are permitting breeders to locate which genes are responsible for chronic illnesses and degenerative diseases. The potential for the use of DNA is limited only by what humanity wants to know.

Working Toward Improvement in Breeding Records and Registry

The dog registries of the world are very much aware of the value of the work being done in the field of DNA and are implementing DNA testing to insure the accuracy of their breeding records. These breeding records, called *stud books,* are where the parentage of any registered dog can be traced.

Stud books

All the dogs that are registered with a particular kennel club are entered into that clubs stud book. However, when the records are published, only the individuals, male and female, who have produced offspring are listed. The first dog entered in the AKC's stud book was an English Setter named Adonis. The entry was made in 1878.

Prior to DNA testing, the authenticity of these records depended entirely upon the honesty and accurate record keeping of the person submitting the information. It goes without saying that a single incorrect entry in these important records would remain there forever and result in false readings for all generations to follow.

DNA testing: It's easy as 1-2-3

The United Kennel Club, based in Kalamazoo, Michigan, was the first registry to employ the use of DNA testing to ensure positive identity and the integrity of its stud book. Shortly after, the American Kennel club started its program.

Both organizations offer a number of additional services, beyond just stud book verification, based on DNA testing. The cost varies depending upon the information desired and available. Information regarding what services the AKC and UKC offer and the steps necessary to comply can be obtained by contacting the respective organization directly. (You can make contact via the Web at www.akc.org and www.ukcdogs.com.)

Understanding just how DNA tells us what it does is a lot harder than finding out what it has to say. The AKC and UKC have arranged a simple process that allows you to participate in their programs:

1. **Contact the UKC or AKC and order a DNA test kit.**

2. **Follow the instructions included in the kit by gently swabbing inside the dog's cheek with the small bristle brush that's included in the kit.**

3. **Place the sample in the envelope provided and send it, along with the required fee, to the organization from which you obtained the kit.**

The dog's name is entered in the registry's database and a laboratory processes the test results.

A certificate is returned to the applicant designating the genotype of the dog, with information as to what additional services may be used in conjunction with the testing.

Scientists have determined that testing 10 gene pairs distributed randomly across the 39 chromosome pairs is sufficient to establish a unique identity. If each dog of a mating pair has been tested, their offspring can be identified with absolute certainty.

Currently, the only information the test provides for dog breeders is verification of the individual and of parentage if the parents have been tested. Dogs whose parents are not as reported can be identified and dogs whose parentage has been questioned can have their pedigrees proven.

Although DNA testing provides positive identification, the identification takes some time because laboratory tests have to be completed. Therefore, DNA testing should always be backed up with tattooing or microchip implants for immediate identification.

TECHNICAL STUFF

Only 10 markers?

The reason the voluntary DNA certification programs currently only analyze the 10 markers they do is twofold:

✔ Examining 10 markers is sufficient to provide absolute certainty for individual identification.

✔ Because each of the 39 chromosome pairs contains 50,000 to 100,000 gene pairs, it is prohibitively expensive to test thousands.

Both the AKC and the UKC are increasing the number of markers obtained through individual profiling in order to establish a data bank for each breed. This gives breeders the opportunity to find just where in their breed's genetic makeup degenerative diseases and chronic illnesses are located.

The UKC and AKC have already seen that the benefits of DNA testing can extend far beyond what they are now. There can be little doubt that at some point in the future this process will cease to be a matter of choice and will become mandatory.

AKC compliance audit program

In Chapter 2, I explained that the AKC reserves the right to visit your home or kennel for the purpose of inspecting the registration records it requires you to keep. These inspections are a part of the AKC's Compliance Audit Program. DNA genotyping is a tool that AKC Inspectors may use as a part of a routine kennel inspection. These AKC inspectors review litter and dog records, check dog identification, examine the conditions of kennels, and collect DNA samples from litters and their sires and/or dams. These DNA samples are collected and processed at the AKC's expense.

If errors are found through the DNA testing — for instance, that puppies are not actually the result of the mating of a particular sire and dam — the litter registrations are canceled or corrected. Kennels with more than one litter that has been excluded within a three-year period are referred to the management disciplinary committee of the AKC for appropriate action.

AKC frequently used sires program

This program requires every sire producing seven or more litters in a lifetime or more than three litters in a calendar year to be DNA certified by the AKC. These profiles are then recorded to be used for parentage verification.

Is the guesswork gone?

What's the margin of error in all this DNA-identification stuff? Bob Slay, assistant vice-president of DNA operations at the AKC, has been quoted as saying that the possibility of error is less than 1 percent. So certain are the results that the laboratory handling the testing is contractually guaranteed to defend the validity of the DNA results in court.

So then, has genetic testing taken all the guesswork out of breeding? That's highly unlikely, at least in the lifetime of anyone reading this book. Stop to consider that every dog has somewhere between 50,000 and 100,00 gene pairs and that 50 percent of a dog's genes come from its sire and 50 percent from its dam.

This means that 50 percent of a sire or dam's genes are *not* present in their offspring. Half of what you hope to see from any great sire or influential dam is discarded at the moment of conception! Which half will you get and of what? Genetic testing and DNA helps tremendously, and will do so to an even greater extent in the future, but if you or your mentor are blessed with breeder's sense, I would advise you not to forsake it just yet.

Inherited Health Problems and Diseases

Work undertaken to identify the genes that are responsible for producing the health problems many of our breeds are subject to is still in its early stages. Even at this point, however, it has proven that there's absolutely no substitute for screening and accurate record keeping. This is why I stress throughout this book the importance of obtaining foundation stock from a reputable breeder. Reputable breeders set you years ahead in your breeding program because their stock is test bred.

Creating a list of the countless possible disorders and birth defects that the many recognized breeds are subject to would be almost impossible. In many cases, the parent clubs of the various breeds and the experienced breeders who make up the clubs have done extensive work to eliminate some of these hereditary defects and chronic illnesses.

In some instances, a dog afflicted with one of these hereditary problems can be treated so that he or she can go on to lead a happy, normal life. But remember, just because the fault is no longer apparent doesn't mean it's gone away nor does it mean that it has been removed from the dog's genetic makeup. It's your responsibility to know when a dog involved in the transmission of a health problem may or may not be used in a breeding program. What follows is a list of some of the genetic disorders found in the popular dog breeds. Discussions with experienced individuals in your breed and your veterinarian will help you determine whether or not individuals afflicted with or carrying genes for these health problems can be used in a breeding program.

Bloat

Bloat (gastric torsion) occurs in many deep-chested breeds. The condition causes the stomach to rotate so that both ends are closed off. The food contained in the stomach ferments and the gasses can't escape, thereby causing the stomach to swell. This pressures the entire diaphragm and leads to extreme cardiac and respiratory complications. Affected dogs are in extreme pain, and death can follow quickly unless the gas is released through surgery.

Bone disorders

Many large and giant breeds are susceptible to bone and joint diseases that can be traced to a nutritional, environmental, and/or hereditary causes. Still other bone and joint disorders are brought about by physical stress or accident.

Because these disorders can stem from such a wide range of causes, pay close attention if your dog is limping or in pain. If the problem persists, confine your dog and consult your veterinarian at once. A veterinarian's diagnosis is critical here, in that treatment ranging from prescribed medication to physical therapy could prevent permanent damage.

From puppyhood on, it's wise to balance the large and heavy-bodied dog's caloric intake against the amount of daily exercise the dog is accustomed to (sound familiar?). Although puppies need to be suitably plump, they should never be sloppy fat. Some breeds live to eat, and reducing exercise seldom makes a dent in the amount of food they might like to have. You are not being cruel by controlling the amount of food you give your dogs. Excess poundage weighs very heavily on the muscles and skeleton of the heavy-bodied breeds and can exacerbate bone and joint conditions that these breeds are prone to.

The following are bone disorders occurring in a number of breeds:

✔ **Canine elbow dysplasia:** The elbow joint is made up of three bones: the radius, ulna, and humerus. These three bones must join together when a puppy is growing to form a tight hinge joint. If this does not happen it can lead to three different conditions: united anconeal process, fragmented coronoid process, and osteochondritis dissecans. An affected dog may suffer from one, two, or all three in one or both elbows. The exact causes are not yet known, although heredity is a factor in breeds that grow rapidly. Trauma to the joint is also a factor.

Radiographic evaluation of the elbows is required by most breeders, as some affected dogs never show observable signs. Depending on the degree of ED, lameness varying from an occasional limp to a chronic condition develops. If any elbow disorder is suspected, it's extremely important to seek advice from a veterinarian who has had experience in dealing with ED so that the correct diagnosis can be made.

- Ununited anconeal process: In a young dog, cartilage gradually turns to bone and unites with the rest of the ulna (one of the two bones of the forearm). This occurs at approximately four to six months. When this union fails, the resulting condition is called ununited anconeal process (UAP). UAP leads to degenerative joint disease (DJO) due to the instability of the joint.

- Fragmented coronoid process: The coronoid process is a small piece of bone on the ulna. If it chips off or cracks it is referred to as a fragmented coronoid process. It's different from a fracture in that it is more apt to be the result of wear and tear from repeated trauma incurred in day to day activity. The normal elbow can handle the normal trauma but fragmented coronoid process could easily be an inherited perhaps design flaw in the elbow

- Osteochondritis dissecans (OCD): A condition in which the cartilage lining the bone surfaces in the shoulder joint, elbow, or stifle, and the hock joint is weakened to the point where it cracks. This allows the bone beneath it to become exposed and painful. The degree to which it takes place causes lameness varying from an occasional limp to a chronic condition.

✔ **Hip dysplasia (HD):** This disorder, simply put, is a failure of the head of the femur to fit snugly into the hip socket with resulting degrees of lameness and faulty movement. The inheritance of the defect is polygenic — having more than one source or origin, which means there is no simple answer to the elimination of the problem. Breeders routinely X-ray their breeding stock and breed only from superior animals who have received a grade deemed acceptable for breeding.

Although it's important that both the sire and dam have been X-rayed and cleared for breeding, it's just as important that their litter mates, grandparents, and so on have been X-rayed and their history known. Family selection is at least as important as individual selection in the case of polygenic diseases. Asking a breeder the hip status of the parents of the litter and about the incident of hip dysplasia in his or her line is important.

✔ **Osteosarcoma:** Osteosarcoma is the most common bone cancer in dogs and is most apt to develop in the large and giant breeds of dogs weighing over 50 pounds. Bone cancer commonly manifests itself in persistent lameness of a leg, and a malignant tumor often develops. Long term prognosis is not good but amputation and chemotherapy allow dogs to lead a good qualify of life for a relatively short period of time. Because the disease occurs only in large breeds, a genetic predisposition is suspected.

✔ **Patella luxation:** This condition is commonly referred to as slipping stifles. It's an abnormality of the stifle (the knee joint) that leads to dislocation of the kneecap. The problem is particularly prevalent among the small breeds. Normally the kneecap is located in a groove at the lower end of the thighbone. It's held in this position by strong elastic ligaments. If the groove is insufficiently developed, the kneecap leaves its normal position and slips to one side or the other of the track in which it is normally held. The dog may exhibit an intermittent but persistent limp or have difficulty straightening out the knee. In some cases, the dog may experience pain. Treatment may require surgery.

Cancerous and benign tumors

Cancerous tumors can spread into adjacent areas of the body or they may release cells to form secondary tumors in other organs. Possible treatment includes removal through surgery, chemotherapy, and radiotherapy.

Benign tumors appear at random on the body but do not spread by invading healthy organs. They do increase in size within themselves. In some cases, where rapid growth is anticipated, they should be removed surgically.

Cardiomyopathy

Cardiomyopathy is progressive deterioration of the heart. It's frequently undetected because dogs may remain without symptoms for years. The condition causes the affected dog to have arrhythmia (an irregular heart beat). Although many dogs are without symptoms, some may have episodes of fainting or collapse, weakness, and occasionally heart failure. Death often occurs from an inability to control irregular heart rhythms and is usually sudden. The recommended method of diagnosis is through the use of the holter monitor — a 24-hour electrocardiogram.

Cleft palate

Growth failure in the palate of an unborn puppy can result in incomplete fusion of the left and right halves of the roof of the mouth. In an extreme form, the division can continue right on up into the nostrils. Corrective surgery can be performed, but most breeders agree that any puppy born with this defect should be euthanized.

Deafness

Deafness in the geriatric dog is not uncommon. However, there are hereditary forms of deafness that are often found in all-white breeds or in breeds in which the blue merle color is present. Testing of all breeding stock of breeds of these colors is strongly recommended.

Demodectic and sarcoptic mange

Two distinctively different types of mange exist: demodectic and sarcoptic. Both can only be diagnosed by microscopic examination of a skin scraping. Demodectic mange is caused by a reaction to the demodex parasite, and the skin infection it causes is known as demodecosis. The parasite burrows into hair follicles and sebaceous glands.

The parasite is carried on the skin of most dogs in a localized form, but a suppressed immune system (often at puberty) can allow the mite to multiply and spread through the skin. An inherited defect in the immune system's response to the mite is suspected of some breeds. The lack of resistance can lead to extreme cases, and the dog becomes far more susceptible to infection. The common form may require intensive treatment and long-term antibiotic use. There is a slightly rarer and more severe form of demodectic mange, but only your vet can determine the difference.

Sarcoptic mange, which is also caused by a parasite, is not thought to have any hereditary basis. It's easier to recognize in that it's extremely irritating to the dog and usually causes severe scratching. Sarcoptic mange is extremely contagious to both animals and humans and must be treated with medicated baths. Orally administered medications or injections may also be prescribed.

Hypothyroidism

Hypothyroidism is a condition in which the thyroid gland malfunctions and its output is reduced. This happens when insufficient hormone is produced by an underactive gland. It appears in a good many of the large-sized breeds. The existence of the condition can be determined by blood test.

Poor hair growth is often one of the first signs of this disease. Overall lethargy and weakness are typical. Though appetite may decrease, weight gain continues. Thyroid hormone administered daily can control the disease, but medication may be necessary for the dog's remaining life.

Hernias

Hernias can be of several kinds, but all are soft swellings that appear in the general abdominal area.

- ✔ **Umbilical hernia:** The most common hernia is the umbilical hernia seen in puppies. A lump or swelling comes through the abdominal wall at the navel where the umbilical cord was once attached. The propensity for weakness in this area is hereditary. Depending upon the extent to which the navel protrudes, surgery may or may not be required.

✔ **Inguinal hernia:** An inguinal hernia is the result of a tear in the abdomen. It occurs through a structural defect that allows the intestines, and often the bladder and uterus, to pass into the inguinal region (sometimes called the groin). This hereditary defect seems to occur more frequently, but not exclusively, with the bitch.

Eye problems

Many breeds encounter hereditary defects and diseases of the eye. Many of these problems are of a complicated genetic nature and warrant examination by a board-certified veterinary ophthalmologist. The canine eye registration foundation (CERF) has established standards that all breeding stock from lines or breeds even suspected of having hereditary eye problems should meet.

The following is a list of common eye conditions and diseases found in dogs:

✔ **Entropion and Ectropion:** Entropion is a condition where the eyelids turn inward, causing the eyelashes to rub on the surface of the eyeball. Ectropion is a condition where the lower eyelids droop and turn outwards, creating a pocket in which debris can accumulate.

Both these conditions are best dealt with by corrective eye surgery. Veterinarians experienced in dealing surgically with these problems can entirely eliminate the condition, but you should understand that surgery to correct these problems eliminates the recipient from being shown in AKC conformation dog shows because the surgery is classified as cosmetic. If any dog with either of these problems is intended for the show ring, talk to an experienced breeder about the advisability of this surgery. However, there's no question that a humane owner would choose corrective surgery over a show career. The AKC's stipulation applies only to conformation show events and does not restrict the dog as far as competing in any AKC performance events.

✔ **Cataracts:** Cataracts are a degenerating condition of the part of the eye directly behind the pupil. The pupil becomes fully or partially opaque, giving it a milky or blue color. The condition is not at all uncommon among older dogs, and it can also be caused by an injury to the eye. In advanced cases, the condition can cause blindness.

Cataracts normally progress very slowly, so that if they first appear in an elderly dog the dog may live out its entire life with only a minimal loss of vision. There's a form called juvenile cataracts, which is hereditary. When juvenile cataracts are present, the problem can be observed in puppies, often immediately after the eyes first open. Little can be done for cataracts, other than expensive surgery.

✔ **Progressive retinal atrophy (PRA):** This condition, commonly referred to as PRA, is a degenerative disease of the light receptors of the eye. It progresses to blindness. Many breeds do not show signs of PRA until the dogs are adults. Therefore, a minimum of three years of age is required before a board-certified ophthalmologist can determine if a dog is certifiable as clear of this problem.

Von Willebrand's Disease

Von Willebrand's Disease, referred to as VWD, is an abnormal condition of the blood-clotting system that is similar to, but in most cases not as severe as, hemophilia in human beings. Many breeds are reported to be afflicted with this disease. It's seldom fatal in itself, but can present a serious problem if surgery of any kind becomes necessary as uncontrolled bleeding can occur. Stress can bring on this condition and it's evidenced by mild bleeding from the nose and gums and occasionally bloody stools or urine. Research has revealed some evidence that severity of VWD decreases with age.

Chapter 11

The Brood Bitch

*O*f all the animals man has attempted to produce with controlled breeding techniques there are none in which perfection is so elusive as it is in purebred dogs with the possible exception of the Thoroughbred horse.

And if you don't have the right bitch, as they're apt to say on *The Sopranos*, "forgeddaboudit!" Just ask any breeder and you're bound to get the same answer: Without a good, strong foundation bitch, your future as a breeder will hold more disappointments than it will successes.

Although this chapter deals with the nuts and bolts of the distaff (female) side of the pedigree — the science of it all — I also include a great deal about what successful breeders have learned through their experience. Understand, I'm not foolish enough to attempt to undermine the great contributions science has made to man's attempts to control nature — not by a long shot! Science has helped us make great strides in animal husbandry. At the same time, until the day arrives that the genes for those illusive characteristics like heart, breed character, and charisma are isolated, I'll continue to rely heavily on the foundation bitch for keeping a breeding program on course.

Not only does that cornerstone bitch have to be a worthy representative of the breed (her phenotype has to be superb), she must also have the ancestral background of quality to draw upon (her genotype must also be strong). The ability to pass on all the right stuff to her offspring (prepotency) is the most important trait of a foundation bitch. I've included the formal scientific names for these characteristics for you in case you have a scientific bent.

What is a Thoroughbred?

The word *Thoroughbred* is incorrectly used when referring to a dog of pure breeding. A Thoroughbred is a specific breed of horse, just as Arabians, Morgans, and English Saddlebreds are specific breeds of horses. Thoroughbreds are bred specifically for the track. Those big fellows you bet on at the Kentucky Derby or Hollywood Park are Thoroughbreds. The romance that surrounds these valiant racing horses has created a tendency to apply their name to greats in other areas as well, even to humans. However, as great as a person or a dog may be, a Thoroughbred remains a specific breed of horse. A dog of pure breeding is a *purebred.* A great human being? Well, there are any number of terms that might be applied there. I guess all of them might be valid, depending on just how objective you're being in your evaluation.

Health Issues for the Foundation Bitch

In this section, I get down to the nitty-gritty — what your foundation bitch should be physically. Figure 11-1 shows the anatomy of the female dog.

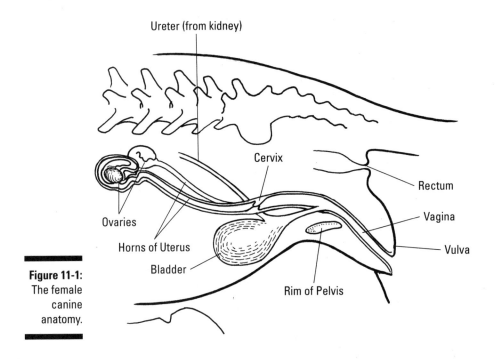

Figure 11-1:
The female canine anatomy.

Ureter (from kidney)

Cervix

Rectum

Vagina

Vulva

Ovaries

Horns of Uterus

Bladder

Rim of Pelvis

The basics

Your bitch should be healthy, of course, and from a long line of good "doers" — that is they are vigorous from birth and go on to maturity with a minimum of health problems. Some people I know have to really struggle to keep puppies alive in every litter that they breed. The mothers are poor whelpers, indifferent to raising and nursing their puppies, and the puppies themselves are weaklings. The resulting stock might be pretty, but one generation to the next, they are simply unthrifty. This is not where and how you want to begin.

In addition to having correct breed type, the bitch you start with must have a strong constitution and come from a line noted for it. You also want her to come from a maternal line known to be easy whelpers, that is, a line that experiences few complications in the birth process.

 There are some breeds, the bull breeds in particular (Bulldogs, French Bulldogs, and Boston Terriers) that by the very nature of their construction need caesarean sections in order to give birth to their offspring. This requirement is something that breeders of those breeds must contend with. However, in most other cases, natural whelpers are the norm. You should expect to start with nothing less.

Feel the heat: The estrual cycle

A part of a healthy female line is regular seasons (or heats), meaning estrual cycles. Females of different breeds have their first seasons at various ages, but most occur between 6 and 10 or 11 months of age. The larger breeds are often slower coming into heat their first season.

The frequency of female estrual cycles can vary from breed to breed and to some degree in individual dogs within the breeds. Most females have two seasons per year — six months apart. Some can be counted on like clockwork to come in every six months; others can be less dependable. Basenjis are known to have only one season a year, and I've had Cocker Spaniel females that have come in fairly regularly every four months. You'll have to depend on your own watchful eye to know when your female is in season.

Recognizing the signs

 The first sign of an impending heat cycle, as far as the females I've owned have been concerned, is a change in behavior. Even the tomboys suddenly become possessed of a very fragile nature. They react to simple requests like Sit and Come as though I had just hurled history's worst insult at them! Right then, I know what's coming and that the dog will be emotionally delicate for the next 21 days.

The first physical sign is a swelling around the vulva. Depending upon the breed, there can be just a little swelling — or *swelling!* Next comes *spotting,* a bloody discharge. Every breed and every female within each breed has a unique way of passing through this stage. Some barely spot, although with others (a particular Boxer bitch I owned comes to mind here) you would think that an axe-wielding Lizzie Borden was on the loose!

No female should ever be bred until she is fully mature. This normally means that she has had at least two full seasons. A female who has not reached maturity herself is not a good candidate for motherhood. Either she or the puppies will suffer for it. When she's bred too young, an important part of the nutrition that a female needs for her own development is channeled to her unborn puppies. Shortchanging her development certainly can't have a beneficial effect on her, her litter, or on her future litters, for that matter.

Determining the right time to breed

The best time for conception is something that varies from breed to breed and female to female. Somewhere around the tenth day after you've first noticed the bloody discharge is generally optimal. At that point, the discharge has diminished in color to a very light pink, or in some cases it is almost colorless. Some females reach the ready stage at the end of the first week of their season, and others who you would be almost sure were completely out of season pick their own boyfriends as late as the 25th or 26th day and, surprise, become pregnant!

Staying in close contact with your veterinarian if you suspect your female is coming in season is a good idea if you plan to breed. With a vaginal smear, a vet can microscopically determine just when your bitch is ovulating and the day on which she is most apt to conceive. An experienced stud dog is another reliable evaluator of when the time is right — some know *exactly* the right day, regardless of what anyone else may think.

You can't always (make that, you can seldom) rely on the female as to her readiness. Some females I've owned, ovulating or not, will scream bloody murder at the mere sight of a male dog from the 1st to the 21st day. Others have been absolute trollops, who I swear would have gladly stood for the stud dog the whole year-round!

The Intangibles of Being a Great Bitch

An experienced breeder knows that health issues are not something that begin or stop with the individual female. More often than not, erratic seasons, poor whelpers, and indifferent mothers are strong indicators of what was and what will be. And you won't want to contend with any of these problems generation after generation.

Your foundation bitch is responsible for all the above — *plus*. She also has to provide the puppies' nutrition while they are in the womb and while they are nursing. Equally important, she contributes her emotional stability, or lack of it, as the puppies are nursing and growing up. Do not underestimate the importance of a nursing dam's stability. The mother who becomes hysterical at the sound of a doorbell or some other unanticipated sound, one who flies into an uncontrollable rage or runs away and cowers when a stranger arrives, can have a serious adverse effect on nursing puppies.

I've seen entire litters panic without knowing why, other than their mother was overreacting to some unexpected noise or occurrence. Stability is both inherited and environmental. Poor temperament is not something that should be tolerated in either the sire or the dam of a litter, but you can easily see how a genetically shy or hysterical female can have twice the negative affect upon the character of her offspring than a sire cursed with the same fault would have.

What a Good Bitch Looks Like

I find it interesting that even though a stud dog has had his fun, deposited his half of the gene pool with the mom-to-be, and is off livin' la vida loca some-where else when the puppies arrive, most people ask, "Who are they *by*?" Dogs are referred to as being *by* a sire and *out of* a dam. Like the stud did it all, right? As an afterthought, inquiries are made about the dam, but even then it's usually done by asking, "Who's she *by*?"

Although conformation (again, phenotype) is only one factor in determining the influence that your foundation bitch and the puppies she will eventually produce will have on your breeding program, I'll deal with it first because it's the most immediately observable characteristic. Then too, I think you'll find that a good many long-time breeders seem to believe the quality bitch has the advantage of more closely embodying that which might be referred to as ideal breed type in their breed.

Although the female duplicates the male in general make, shape, and col-oration, she is also afforded the luxury of having the more delicate lines and nuances of a breed standard, those delicate lines and curves that on a male might seem out of place. In other words she's feminine, commonly referred to as *bitchy*. The male must be stronger and more robust in most breeds. This in itself, although no fault, strays a bit from the picture of classic beauty that many find easier to see in the female.

Leaping the gender gap

"A woman's place is in the home!" If I heard that once growing up, I heard it a thousand times. My father wasn't alone in his chauvinism; it was typical of the day. Actually, it was typical well on through a good part of the twentieth century!

That I grew up in a world in which sexual equality had not yet arrived is obvious. America saw a female's role in society as secondary, or if not secondary, certainly not on a par with that of a male. That limited view existed in the dog world as well. Not at all complicated — males were the show dogs; females stayed home and had puppies. It took just as long for the dog game to get past its flawed philosophy as it did in the real world.

Until the last quarter-century, a bitch who was shown extensively was apt to be somewhat of an exception to the rule. It was thought that any prolonged show career interfered with the female's maternal duties, which were her only purpose. Therefore, greater emphasis was placed on producing quality males. A lesser male was apt to defeat a better female at the run-of-the-mill show simply because he was the male.

Today, far less discrimination exists and a good female's chances in the ring are equal to that of a good male's. This is as it should be, but the result has had consequences far beyond the dispersal of blue ribbons. The smart hobby breeder has always realized the value of keeping his females, but had to forego ring success. Now the picture is much different, and even the small hobby breeder can enjoy ring success *and* puppies with his golden girls.

Goal models

A show campaign might temporarily delay an outstanding female's contribution as a producer, but many believe these show girls make an enormous contribution in the interim by serving as what might be referred to as *goal models.* The comparatively brief delay in their maternal duties is overshadowed by the contribution they make by bringing their exceptional quality to the attention of competitors and judges.

A perfect example of all this is the win-record holding Bichon Frise bitch, Ch. Devon Puff And Stuff. Although she was certainly not the first Bichon Frise with correct make, shape, and balance, she was the one who, through her incredible style and attitude, brought the proper look to the attention of not only the dyed-in-the-wool dog fancier, but also to the general dog-owning public. As the Bichon breed has continued to progress, better and better specimens will undoubtedly come along, but they will all have to pay homage to the little female who manifested her breed standard so well.

None of the foregoing is meant to diminish a bitch's importance when it comes to breeding. Obviously, from what I have already said, I think the female is of the utmost importance. Rather, it's offered as encouragement to get the top bitches into the ring for as many fanciers as possible to see.

All too often, males will be campaigned, photographed, advertised, and otherwise given every opportunity to become a permanent visual part of a breed's history. In many cases the bitches, whose only place to shine was in the whelping box, are destined for anonymity, other than having their name on a pedigree. Those who place as much, if not more, emphasis on the contributions of the distaff side of a pedigree are often left to guess what key the bitches are playing in the pedigrees that stand behind breeding stock.

Although the acceptance of quality bitches in the ring has certainly been a huge plus for the breeder, don't think that campaigning a bitch is simply a bed of roses. I would say, overall, it is considerably more problematic than exhibiting a male.

Doping in show bitches?

I have a theory regarding those über-females who rack up show victories. It's not based on scientific fact of any kind, but on my own observations and conversations I've had with other breeders. It leads me to wonder if the more masculine traits that many great show bitches possess are hormone induced, or probably better stated, are due to an imbalance of hormones. These imbalances shift some of the female's characteristics *in the direction of* masculinity, and as a result make these dogs just a bit more competitive than some of their sisters.

As I said, there is no scientific fact on which to base my theory, but it is interesting to note how the producing impact of many of the big-winning females falls far short of their records in the show ring. A good many have never produced puppies at all. There are exceptions, of course, but thinking back over the years, there are enough examples to make one at least wonder if there isn't some truth to this pet theory of mine.

Another possibility to explain the difficulty encountered in getting some of these major winners to conceive, or even have normal estrual cycles, is that medications are often used to keep them from experiencing normal cycles while being shown. Bypassing the natural feminine rhythms eliminates having to cope with those difficult days and keeps the females from experiencing estrual cycle coat loss and false pregnancies. Many bitches who are put on this medication never have a normal season again, or require a few years before they regain anything resembling regularity in this respect.

Both handlers and owners, who aspire to show a female champion through an extended campaign, often resort to these medications. In many cases, the dog has no adverse reactions to these drugs, but there have been enough reports of barren or difficult to impregnate bitches as a result of their use to warrant caution. Any drug administered to a dog, but particularly one with such consequential effects, should really be under the supervision of a veterinarian. Breeders who send their females to professional handlers to be shown should be very clear in regard to their wishes regarding this kind of medication. The future of a breeding program may depend upon it.

In many breeds, the female suffers a significant loss of coat when she comes in season. That time of the year itself creates a set of problems all its own, not the least of which is that fragile emotional state some females experience or, worse yet, a false pregnancy. Certainly those delicate feelings can be worked with, but when they come into play moments before the judge is ready to point for a Best in Show award, they can prove to be more than a little unnerving for the handler!

There are some unique bitches, however, who never seem bothered by anything. They are every bit as tough as their male counterparts, and in many cases have only a shade less stature, coat, and muscularity. Many of these females have become the all-time record holders in their respective breeds. But some believe their futures as producers are hexed because of the very characteristics that made them great show winners. See the sidebar, "Doping in show bitches?" for more information.

Breeders' Thoughts on the Foundation Bitch

When my partner and I were at the height of our Bichon Frise breeding program, we made sure that we did not lose control of the good bitches that our line produced. In order to not have this happen, I decided to employ the basic principles of a system a Cocker Spaniel breeder I had known many years earlier had successfully put to use. Accordingly, we never sold our top show-quality female puppies without retaining co-ownership until they were shown to their championships and had produced a litter. Even at that, we were extremely discerning about where our best bitches were placed. There were few important breeding decisions left to new owners, unless they were experienced and successful breeders themselves.

After the bitch we sold in coownership had gained her title, my partner and I decided which stud the bitch would be bred to for her first litter. The choice puppy from the litter, usually a bitch, came back to us. This not only gave us control over our line's best bitches, it kept our entire breeding program moving in the direction we wished it to go without us having to house an inordinate number of dogs.

Further, and by no means less important, the system provided us with a fail-safe testing ground for the producing abilities of any young male we may have decided to keep. Not only was the prospective stud dog given access to these bitches of outstanding phenotype and genotype, the bitches had pedigrees which were, in most cases, perfectly orchestrated to complement the male's own genetic makeup.

Stiff terms for the buyer? No argument there. However, we felt our first responsibility was to the breed and to our line. The number of truly outstanding

Group and Best in Show winners that were produced during this period attests to the success of the plan.

We made it very clear to prospective buyers that they were in no way obligated to accept our terms if they felt the terms were unreasonable. In fact, we were always ready to offer them females who were not in that can't-entirely-let-go category. We often referred buyers to other breeders. There were always plenty of young Bichons offered for sale throughout the country, but if the terms were weighed against the results of the arrangement, most prospective breeders felt they could only benefit from working with us.

The buyer not only wound up with a top class champion, their bitch was bred in the proper way and, more often than not, produced a high-quality litter. Equally important, the owner was also automatically enrolled in a network that more often than not would continue producing top quality for generations to come.

Influencing the future

It seems generally agreed upon in most breeders' circles that the quality present in the bitch classes of the day determines the quality of the entire breed in the next generation. It was important to us as Bichon breeders, particularly so in those early days of the breed, that we kept the level of quality in our bitches as high as possible.

Even the best stud dog needs the help of good bitches in order to keep a breed moving in a forward direction. There are very few stud dogs that are able to compensate entirely for their mate's lack of quality. The few that are able to do so are seldom able to extend that influence beyond the first generation. It should always be remembered that a poor or mediocre bitch remains in a pedigree *forever.*

If one agrees with the premise that the bitch contributes far more than just 50 percent of her genetic makeup to a litter's success, what chance does a breeding out of a poor or mediocre bitch have? Accidents (throwbacks) can and do happen. On the other hand, a great dog can occasionally appear in just about any litter that boasts at least a few decent ancestors. It would be foolhardy though to expect that flyer to ever fully escape the influence of the poorest animals in its pedigree.

It's not all about glamour

Norma Warner, an extremely successful Cocker Spaniel mentor of mine, had a little sign posted in her puppy room that read, "A beautiful female is something to behold. A beautiful bitch is something to hold on to. *So don't ask me to sell you my best one!*"

Few breeders are going to be in a hurry to sell the best females they've bred — much less to a novice. But a top-flight show bitch is not the only launching pad for one's breeding program. You may have to spend several years before you find that superstar who is for sale. But just between me and thee, it isn't always the award winner who is the best producer.

Cam Millard, Australia's master breeder of the Grenpark Smooth Fox Terriers, gave some interesting advice to the beginner in an interview I conducted with him for *Kennel Review* magazine. The following portion of that interview is particularly significant:

"I have always advised new breeders that the tap root of their line should be the best bitch they can afford to buy and this should be their first task in the plan. The beginner might not find this the easiest mission in the world in that no breeder is anxious to sell his best, for top breeders love and cherish their bitches, value their genetic potential, and know how quickly this can be wasted in the wrong hands. But the newcomer must try his best — if you cannot get the bitch you wanted, you may be able to buy a sister — but above all, make sure you get a sound foundation bitch, one from a reputable breeder that has consistently produced good winners and producers, one that has the potential to help you attain your plan."

Some time later and halfway across the world, I interviewed Kathy and Jim Corbett, nationally acclaimed breeders of the Wyeast Bloodhounds in the Pacific Northwest of the United States. They not only shared Milward's beliefs, but added:

". . . and if you can't buy a top brood bitch, lease one. Maybe you won't be able to get her outright, but you could get your hands on her for a litter. And I would tell you that no matter who you got her from, if she was really good, the person who bred her must know something. Please let that person guide you as to how she should be bred. Go to a breeder you can trust, and then for heaven's sake, listen to her or him. They know what's behind their stock and they can say, 'There's a little problem with the sire (in a particular respect) but there's nothing like that behind this bitch so don't worry about it,' or 'Darn, I haven't seen that (problem) for five generations; I thought I got rid of it, but it is back there so be sure you don't double up on it next time.'"

The Corbetts went on to caution, "On your own, you might look at this (fault) as a little problem — only to find out later that it's something that has mushroomed out of control. Or on the other hand, you might never see it again. Why not save yourself a lot of heartache and listen to what the people who really know have to say in the first place?"

Here we have two different breeders from two distant parts of the world who have never spoken to each other and who have breeds that are about as dissimilar as can be. Yet, they offer exactly the same advice. Only the very foolish would choose to ignore it.

You should also note that neither of these accomplished breeders said anything about trying to obtain a glamour bitch. Rather, they both indicate what you are really looking for is a rock-solid foundation. The great Dachshund breeder Peggy Westphal, whose Von Westphalen bitches have left such an indelible mark on the breed, was the first person I ever heard refer to the not terribly glamorous females as *peasant bitches*. Peasant bitches are the ones that exhibitors with aspirations of, say, winning Best in Show at Madison Square Garden are apt to ignore in pursuit of obtaining their flashy litter sisters.

That peasant bitch is essentially very well-made, with all the right angles in the right places, and she comes from the right line of producers. She just lacks the essential glamour of her bound-for-Best-in-Show sister. She's not the kind that makes spectators stop you on the way out of the ring, with lust in their eyes and checkbooks in hand. She may not even have the sparkle, which is usually an integral part of the winning showgirl's makeup. *But,* because she is so well constructed, all you need do is find the fancy dog within her line to breed her to. Success could easily be yours as soon as the next generation!

Sally Stewart Bishop, successful breeder of the Fox Meadows Pembroke Welsh Corgis, described her early dogs by saying, "My earliest dogs admittedly weren't as pretty as they could have been, but sound they were and as I look back, it was a perfect foundation. And I guess a real step in the right direction was the purchase of Am.Can.Ch.Nebriowa's Jordache Fox Meadow, who has produced 18 champions (out of those bitches) for us thus far. Jordache brought a whole lot of pretty to the line."

My own mistake

A perfect example of the value of that not-the-pretty-sister type is clearly illustrated in the story of two Bichon Frise bitches and an error in judgment that I made in my breeding program.

The mistake I made was in a pair of bitches I had purchased from a litter bred by another and sired by one of our stud dogs. Not that there was anything wrong with the bitches. On the contrary, the pair was from a breeding combination that, in the course of three litters, produced 13 champions. And not just champions, *champions.*

Both bitches finished their championships easily and the one, Sunbeam, was the first bitch of her breed to win an all-breed Best in Show. Sunny's sister, Sunflower, had all the parts, good angles, and a front that was near textbook perfect. She showed well enough to attain her championship — *just* well enough! She was good, but not glamorous, and dog shows were not at the top of her fun-things-to-do list.

A long-time friend in England, who was then a breeder of Poodles, called and asked me to send her a really good mature Bichon bitch to get the breed started in Great Britain. At the time, the only bitches I had who were good enough to send her were the Sun Sisters — Sunbeam and Sunflower. I certainly was not going to let her have Sunbeam!

So off went Sunflower, who had been linebred to her champion nephew who we had been showing. The resulting litter was whelped in England and became one of the most highly influential Bichon litters in British, if not world, history.

Sunflower was subsequently sold to Australia, where she continued to produce great quality. Her descendants are now scattered to the four corners of the world and still, many generations later, Sunflower's correct construction is evidenced in a good many of them.

Several years after Sunflower had journeyed first to England and then on to Australia, I was invited to judge in Sydney. Not to anyone's surprise, I had been assigned to judge Bichons and they were my first breed of the morning. A young woman came into the ring with a dog who caught my eye instantly. The dog moved around the ring with the ground-covering ease that was what we in America had set as a goal for the breed but were rarely able to achieve.

The dog was put on the table. As I went over him, my hands met parts that I knew could only have come from dogs I had owned or bred. This dog was so much a product of all I had tried to combine in my breeding program that all I could do was wonder how, *when,* the dog could have ever slipped through my fingers and come here to Australia!

The dog won his class, was Best of Breed. After the judging, my suspicions were confirmed. The dog *was* of my breeding! Fortunately (or unfortunately, depending on how you look at it) he had not "escaped" from me but was a son of that little peasant female, Sunflower.

I learned the dog's name was Leander Snow Star and that he had already enjoyed a brilliant show career in Australia. He later emigrated — what was really full circle — back to the United States, where he proved to be a sire of great merit.

Sunflower's glamorous sister Sunbeam stayed home, enjoyed the aforementioned show career, and produced two champions. And though Sunflower had escaped us, one of Sunbeam's daughters produced a total of 17 champions and remains to this day the top-producing dam in Bichon history. However, nothing produced by Sunbeam could rival the profound effect her plain-Jane sister had upon the breed. For all intents and purposes, Sunbeam's greatest impact on the breed was through her show record. Sunflower, however, was to help the breed take a great stride forward. Both are shown in Figure 11-2.

Figure 11-2: Ch. C&D Beau Monde Sunbeam (left) and her sister Ch. C&D Beau Monde Sunflower (right) had great impact on the breed but for different reasons: Sunbeam as a show dog and Sunflower as a producer.

Photo courtesy of Missy Yuhl.

Quite frankly, in my mind there is no higher compliment that can possibly be paid the distaff member of a canine family than to say she is good enough to be a brood bitch.

Genotype and the Foundation Bitch

Regardless of breed, the pedigrees on the dogs I have bred are linebred as often as possible, not on a male or males, but on *prepotent females* (females who have influenced the breed by producing quality offspring). A breed is extremely fortunate when two or three of these influential matriarchs exist within the span of a few generations. When this is so, the breeder is able to concentrate the blood of these producing bitches in the pedigrees of his or her dogs. This is what I call "pedigree building." Pedigree building is not the least bit unique but it is usually accomplished by line-breeding on dogs rather than bitches.

It is worth noting that a good number of our most successful breeders agree, without reservation, that the best built pedigrees are those that have a strong producing bitch foundation. These same breeders are inclined to use sons of the producing bitches as frequently as possible. I believe so strongly in this mother-son connection that I would have to think long and hard before I would ever consider using a dog at stud whose dam I did not like. Very often, my final decision to use a particular stud dog in my breeding program is made on the basis of who his dam is and who his sisters are.

Ch. Chaminade Mr. Beau Monde, the Bichon Frise I purchased from breeder Barbara Stubbs, was obtained because he was, in many respects, a male version of his mother, the extremely typey bitch Ch. Reenroy's Ami du Kilkanney. Probably the main reason I came home with a male rather than with nothing at all (there were no daughters to have) was that Mr. Beau Monde did resemble his dam Ami so much.

As a sire, Mr. Beau Monde had no equal. He had many top winning sons, but his best offspring were his daughters. What was so remarkable about them was that regardless of their own dams, Mr. Beau Monde's daughters all bore a striking resemblance to his dam, Ami.

Dolores Wolske was one of the pioneer Bichon breeders in the Midwest. She had become a major fan of Mr. Beau Monde when she saw him win at a show in the Midwest. It was then and there that she decided to breed her Ch. C & D's Countess Becky to Mr. Beau Monde. In three breedings, 13 champions of note were produced, including the famous Sun Sisters that I wrote about earlier in this chapter. Again, the bitches were the most outstanding of the champions, and in the end, many of them became the breed's top producers themselves.

If ever there was testimony for the value of concentrating the blood of outstanding bitches in a pedigree it most certainly lies in the story of this famous Bichon combination. Were it but an isolated case, the concept would be one well worth pursuing. But there are countless other examples to be found in so many breeds I have been associated with — Boxers, Cockers, and Irish Setters among them.

Does the reader find me biased in behalf of bitches? It is only because I am — totally and completely. Give me an outstanding bitch or two in *any* breed and, with any luck at all, in just a couple of generations I'll make you a bloodline you'd be proud to own.

The Ideal Breeding Program

Recently, a young breeder asked me to outline a breeding program that I would consider an ideal way to proceed if I were a young breeder like himself. I told him, of course, that we aren't always able to start off in exactly the way we would like, but that if given the good fortune of being able to obtain just what it was I wanted, I would begin as follows.

I would hope to find sister bitches, hopefully daughters of a great producing bitch, or at least the result of one of the breed's top bitch lines. I would then hunt for two sires that were sons of outstanding bitches. The two males could be, but don't have to be, related.

One of the sisters would be bred to the one male and the other sister to the second male. It is important to keep in mind that through this entire plan I am always speaking of individuals who are phenotypically compatible. This being the case, the possible choices of where to go from there are all but endless.

The offspring of one of the sisters could be crossed to a son of the other sister. A female from each breeding could be bred to the sire of their aunt's litter. Males from the one litter could be bred to their aunt. You could also breed the first generation puppies back to their own grandparents and the original sisters themselves could be bred to the opposite sire next time around. All this, with just the first generation! When you're working with all these possibilities, you almost have to hit upon the right combination some-where along the line.

If you choose to follow this sort of model, it's important to remember that as you move along in this line-breeding program you'll be concentrating your quality and your faults. That's why this program is effective only if you are working with the best — only the best. If the faults are there, you have to go about correcting them.

This program is about *blending* rather than crossing. The blending happens over the course of two or three generations, keeping the overall picture con-stant and working to improve the parts within the framework and within the line. You know what you're working with. There are few surprises — you can almost predict what the qualities and the faults are going to be.

If you stay within your carefully screened gene pool, you may well get to that point where you find that you may need an outcross. Although the program I've set up is an ideal one, another conscientious breeder who has been doing exactly what you've been doing, but with different set of dogs, would be readily available! After you've gone about as far as you can with your own linebred program, you could then start looking to other breeders' lines to see if they might have what your line is missing or be able to fix what your line needs to have corrected.

If so, you begin by taking two sister bitches from your line and mating them to two different dogs from the other breeder's line and . . . hey, isn't this where we began? Exactly!

Chapter 12

The Stud Dog

*1*f you ask the average guy at the dog show for his definition of a stud dog, you would probably get something simple, like "the male we use for breeding." Although you can't say the answer is wrong, that definition is like describing someone in the baseball hall of fame as somebody who played ball well.

For our purposes as dog breeders, being a stud dog has so many elements to it that being male and capable of breeding a bitch is just the very beginning.

If you've jumped through all the hoops required to get that rock-solid foundation bitch I've recommended in all the previous chapters, you certainly don't want to blow it now when you make your first breeding. So pay attention. What you do next will affect your entire breeding program.

After I cover the nuts and bolts of what your boy must have to even get off first base, I'll take a look at the profound effect a real *stud dog*, in the breeder's sense of the word, can have on a breeding program.

Checking the Nuts and Bolts

The stud dog has to be sound and complete — that is, he must have all his parts. Not only the parts he needs to walk, see, and eat with, but his reproductive parts as well (see Figure 12-1).

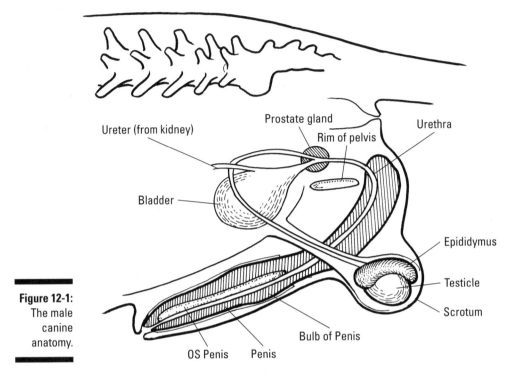

Prostate gland

Ureter (from kidney)

Rim of pelvis

Urethra

Bladder

Epididymus

Testicle

Scrotum

Bulb of Penis

OS Penis   Penis

Figure 12-1:
The male
canine
anatomy.

Those reproductive parts include the correctly formed penis he'll need to get the job of breeding done and functioning testicles to produce the sperm that will join with his partner's egg and create the puppies you want. He's also going to have to *want* to do the job.

The best way for a stud dog owner to make sure that all is as it should be is to seek a veterinarian's help. For what usually is under $100, your veterinarian can do what is called a breeding soundness evaluation. If this is your regular vet, he will thoroughly scrutinize your dog's medical history, paying close attention to the reasons for each and every visit your boy has made to the office.

TECHNICAL STUFF

Testicular development

Males who do not have two normally developed testicles descended into the scrotum are barred from being shown at AKC dog shows. A male who has only one testicle descended is referred to as being *monorchid*. When both testicles are missing, the male is called a *cryptorchid*. Monorchidism and cryptorchidism are definitely hereditary, and breeding into a line that consistently produces males who have problems in this area is extremely unwise.

The vet will record the number of times your stud dog has been bred (if he has been bred before), and the vet will also want to know how successful the breedings were in respect to the number of living puppies. Semen will be checked, and a thorough analysis will provide important information:

- ✔ **Whether or not live sperm is being produced:** Your boy may not yet be old enough to produce live sperm or, horror of horrors, he could be sterile.

- ✔ **Concentration of active sperm cells.** Although millions of sperm cells are emitted in a breeding, only the active ones are going to have a shot at creating a pregnancy.

- ✔ **Mobility of the cells.** Each well-formed sperm cell has a little tail that enables it to swim vigorously along and reach the female's egg and create pregnancy. Cells that are malformed or lack vigor will never reach their destination, and make breedings hit and miss affairs, at best.

All three of these factors are important in order to avoid *misses,* as breedings that don't produce puppies are called. A miss is not only disappointing, it can also be very costly, particularly when bitches are shipped in from different parts of the country. In order to minimize misses, regular checkups with the vet are important for both the popular and the infrequently used male.

By the time the evaluation is over, your vet will even have made notes on good old Rover's libido — yes, his sex drive!

Sex Education

Nature handles the desire part you say? Instinctive behavior, right? Think again! As sexually mature as you, or even your vet, may decide your dog is, many young males haven't a clue as to what this sex thing is all about. They have to be taught, step by step, how to go about accomplishing what Mom Nature intended. That's right: Sex Education 101 *for dogs!*

Most males eventually do get the message, and the natural process takes its course over time. However, when an important breeding is at stake, that natural process can make molasses in January seem like a riptide. You, the female, and the stud dog might all be sprouting gray hairs before everything falls into place.

Seeing is believing, in this case. If you are fortunate enough to have an older, experienced male who your youngster can observe at work (play?), watching other stud dogs do the act often lights the lights and toots the whistles in the sex department. Encouragement, with or without an older dog around, is very important as well. Call upon all your talents as a thespian and act like your youngster has just recited the alphabet — backwards and in Greek! — if he shows the least bit of interest.

Males of the different breeds mature sexually at different times, and some individuals within the breeds more slowly or more quickly than others. Normally speaking, puberty occurs between 6 and 12 months, depending upon mature body weight. The toy and small breeds reach their mature weight much earlier than the very large and giant breeds.

The joys of sex

Although the bitch is only receptive to the male on a given number of days during her heat cycle, a sexually sound male is receptive to breeding her, and any other female for that matter, on any and every day he feels there is the remotest chance of doing so. This is particularly true of some young males who have only recently discovered the joys of sex and are thoroughly convinced every female they meet is just as ready, willing, and able as they are to enjoy a romantic tryst. Older males have usually learned through experience that there is a time when it's possible to get the job done quickly and easily, and they seldom pester the visiting female much, if at all, until she reaches that point.

When is enough enough?

How often a male can be used at stud is an often-asked question. (Don't ask your male, because there will be a stock response of "*very* often," as far as he's concerned.) If the male is sexually mature and in perfect health and is a popular and active stud, he can be bred a couple of times a week for months on end with no ill effects. However, because he *can* be bred that often doesn't mean he should be.

WARNING!

Safe sex for dogs

Many breeders have their stud dogs checked before every breeding to make sure everything is in order and that the dog is not carrying any infectious diseases that might be transmitted during matings. The owner of any stud dog worth using is going to be extremely careful in regard to the dog's general health and, particularly, in respect to exposing him to infections that may be carried by a female he is being bred to. Both major and minor diseases can be contracted sexually, and a smart stud owner will always require veterinarian certification that visiting bitches are free of any signs of infection.

Canine brucellosis is a highly contagious venereal infection that can be spread through sexual contact. It can render both the male and female permanently sterile and can cause abortion in the female. It is incurable, so its detection should never be left to chance!

Using a stud a couple times a week would certainly have to give rise to questions about how many of those breedings are to worthwhile females. A female who is registered and of the same breed may or may not be a worthy candidate to be bred to a quality stud dog. In Chapter 10, I mention that when people ask about a puppy's breeding, they begin by saying, "Who is the puppy *by?*" meaning who is the *sire*. If the puppy is exceptionally beautiful, the stud gets the credit. If the pup is exceptionally ugly — dad gets the credit as well.

Stud dog owners, particularly owners of top-producing stud dogs, have to determine just how anxious they are to have mediocre females owned by others to be bred to their dog. Experienced breeders may do so in their own home or kennel to test their stud's dominance or to see if he is carrying a particular recessive. These people also know how to responsibly place the puppies that result from these breedings.

Stud dog owners have little control over what happens outside their home or kennel. Poor quality puppies can result from outside breedings to a mediocre female and all too often they find their way into the show ring. People in a breed seldom excuse the sire from responsibility. Poor quality offspring are always his fault!

Common sense and our old friend Padre Mendel have taught us that it takes two to complete the inheritance tango. Not everyone who breeds dogs wants to acknowledge the female's part of the dance, particularly if they are bitch owners and not the owner of the stud dog who fathered the ugly ducklings.

The stud dog must be sound of body, according to the standard of the breed, but sound also in the sense of being able to perform the sexual act. Some breeds are sound in respect to their standard, but because of their construction need significant assistance to perform sexually. Bulldogs and Chow Chows are but two examples. These, and a few other breeds, usually are bred by artificial means. I look into the various methods of artificial insemination in Chapter 13.

The Makings of a Good Stud Dog

So much for what's on the outside and what's swimming around on the inside of the prospective stud dog. Your study of the breed standard that governs your breed and the input of your mentors and veterinarian tell you if a male is capable of doing the job. What I'm going to look at next is what I consider the most critical factor involved in determining the value of a stud dog — his producing ability.

Despite the fact that most males are physically capable of siring puppies, only one kind of a male dog should ever be even considered worthy of being called a stud dog. The dog must be of superior quality and must have a pedigree that speaks — no, make that shouts — of quality. Although there are those fanciers who may want to disagree, I feel a breed is *extremely* fortunate to have more than a few dogs of this type at any given point in time.

Looking beyond the surface

I will devote a good number of pages to the discussion of stud dogs, but before I go on, here is my personal definition of what I believe a stud dog is and should be:

A stud dog is a dog who, by merit of his genetic prepotency, has proven he is able to sire offspring whose quality alters the course of the breed in a positive manner.

In dog parlance, *prepotency* just means having great positive influence on the offspring. It is extremely important to understand that a stud dog is *altering*, not *changing*, the course of his breed. *Alteration* is used here in the sense that one takes a coat to the tailor so that it will fit better — not to have it made into a shirt and a pair of pants. A true stud dog modifies or improves his breed; he does not reinvent it. As glamorous, exciting, and different as a dramatic new dog on the scene may appear to be, it is a part of our responsibility as breeders to honor the integrity — the essence, if you will — of our chosen breed.

Dog fanciers would be very upset at the thought of someone secretly cross-breeding their line with another breed or falsifying pedigrees. Yet, these same people would think nothing at all of breeding to a dog who, for all intents and purposes, defies the actual essence of the breed.

Dog breeds can also change or start moving in another direction subtly, slowly, and without anyone ever having a real intention to bring about radical change. Usually those involved aren't even aware that a change is taking place.

A change in course is most likely to happen when a dog comes along who is so glamorous and charismatic that, despite his failings in the area of character and conformation, he is able to accumulate an impressive record of wins. Winning dogs attract breedings and often set a fad or trend. Those lacking sufficient knowledge about the breed do their best to duplicate the winning dog. Retracing a breed's steps when this occurs can take generations. Often, many years pass before the breed is set right again.

Although many fanciers pay lip service to the definition of a stud dog as it's been given here, they are far more apt to breed to a dog who isn't a true stud dog because of several other reasons:

↙ They own him.

↙ He lives much closer than the dog who is really their first choice.

↙ He is a champion.

↙ He has a great show record.

↙ He is related (directly or even remotely) to a dog who *is* producing quality.

JUST FOR FUN

Good tracks do not a good breeder make

I was asked to participate on a breeder's panel somewhere off in the middle part of America. Each of us on the panel had selected a topic to speak on that had something to do with either soundness or type.

One of our panelists spoke at length about anatomy and how it affected movement. Pretty general stuff, but it obviously impressed one member of the audience who raised his hand and volunteered his own story about soundness.

It seems the gentleman had a male dog (to protect the innocent, let's say the dog was a Pointer). The dog showed no promise of ever winning in the ring and no one was remotely interested in buying the dog.

The dog, let's call him Percival, just hung around the kennel growing less and less attractive, from the standpoint of breed type, as time progressed. Summer passed into fall and fall into winter and yet Percival stayed on.

It seems a particularly heavy but short-lived snowstorm developed one morning. On that same morning, Percival decided to take a hike down the road. Fortunately, Percival's owner was very solicitous of the welfare of all his dogs and kept a close watch on them even when they were out exercising in their runs. In no time at all, he realized that Percival was missing.

In very hushed tones as he spoke from the podium, Percival's owner said, "As I took off down the road after Percival, I immediately found his tracks in the snow. As I followed the tracks, I came to a startling revelation.

"There in the snow were the most perfect set of tracks I had ever seen! The only thing I could think of was all the books I had read on movement and the little tracks I had seen in the diagrams. There they were in the snow — *perfection!* Percival had perfect tracks!"

Our speaker went on, "And to think I almost sold that dog as a pet and worse yet, that he had almost escaped. Well, I didn't sell him and he didn't escape and I wound up not only keeping him but I bred him to every single bitch in my kennel!"

I couldn't resist passing by the Pointer ring at the show on the following day. I just *had* to see what kind of mark old Percival was leaving on the Pointer world. Without a doubt, Percival had left his imprint on the breed. Unfortunately, the best part of that imprint was back in the snow!

Now mind you, there is certainly nothing wrong with leaving nice footprints in the snow. But if old Percival's descendants are any example, a lot of breedings are made without a whole lot of thought being put into them or how they can take the breed further on that winding road toward perfection.

These are just a few of the reasons why matings are actually made — but none of them is a legitimate basis for a breeding. And these are just the tip of the iceberg. Sometimes the rationale used for the selection of a stud dog can boggle the mind! See the sidebar "Good tracks do not a good breeder make" for more information.

Producing ability

Every stud dog was once young and unproven. Naturally, there is no possible way to know if the youngster will produce well or not until he has been successfully used at stud. But the young, unproven dog is not a toy for the unsophisticated breeder to experiment with. The young dog is for the seasoned breeder — one who knows the background of the youngster and what stands behind the bitches that he is being bred to.

The established breeder usually has firm ground on which to anticipate the producing potential of a young male. Any beginning breeder should attempt to use an unproven male only upon the recommendation of an experienced breeder. Now, by unproven I mean that the dog has not established an ability to produce superior quality. The fact that a dog can produce *puppies* proves only one thing: The dog is not sterile.

Champions may not be good studs

By this time, I am sure you can see that a stud dog is not simply a male dog. Nor does siring living puppies score a dog a lot of points. And although it may come as a surprise to some, neither show records nor championships have anything to do with a dog's producing ability.

Show records and producing ability are two entirely separate things. A dog can be a truly great show dog and a poor sire. It is just as simple as that. The biggest mistake a breeder, novice or veteran, can make is to confuse his show dogs with his breeding dogs. They can be the same. We *hope* they will be the same, but often they are not.

Many fanciers believe show wins are the indicator of a dog's value to the breed. In other words, if many judges agree that a particular dog is the current ideal in its breed, then this agreement, in effect, indicates that the dog should be bred to. This is not necessarily so. Any dog's value to a breeding program can be proven by only one thing: the quality of his offspring. Every judge in the country can be in complete agreement that the dog of the hour *is* the dog of the hour, but if the dog's potential isn't realized in the whelping box, all the wins in the world mean nothing.

There is no doubt that you will have an opportunity early on to see what a big winning dog is producing. More often than not there is a landslide rush to breed to the new big winner. Take a good look at the results. Is this what you

A misused stud

A good example of the misuse of a very important and very valuable dog is the scenario that surrounded the great winning Boxer, Ch. Bang Away of Sirrah Crest. The dog was a magnificent show dog. His elegance, bearing, and attitude brought an entire new look to the Boxer breed. He nicked with some bitches. He didn't nick with a lot of others.

Bang Away's 1951 Westminster Kennel Club Best in Show win made the American public Boxer crazy and created a Bang Away gold rush among Boxer fanciers and would-be breeders. For a period of time, there were comparatively few dogs and bitches in the U.S. who did not trace directly back to Bang Away within just a generation or two.

Whether or not these descendants were suitable for breeding at all seemed irrelevant. Bang

Away's name on a pedigree was enough. Bang-Away-bred Boxers sold like hot cakes.

There is no doubt that the dog was responsible for some great winners and producers. At the same time, however, many attribute the breed's post Bang Away downward spiral to the preponderance of mediocrity that resulted through incompatible breedings made to him.

His fault? Not really. The dog was not used carefully. Everyone wanted what he had, even if what he had (or didn't have) made him unsuitable for their bitch. Bang Away brought elegance and charisma to a breed that was not really known for these characteristics. Although his glamour brought eye appeal to the breed, in many cases there was far more eye appeal than there was real Boxer quality and substance.

want or what you need? He may not be suitable for your bitch. He may not be producing quality at all. The Best in Show rosettes he wins have no influence on his ability as a sire.

This is not to say a winning dog can't also be an outstanding producer. Records prove otherwise. But I cannot stress strongly enough that it is the producing ability that must be looked to and not the show record!

Bitch compatibility matters big time

Another thing that's important to remember is that even sires of quality can be and are misused. Most breeds have had those truly wonderful show dogs who develop records that become the envy of one and all. Unfortunately, they become the envy of too many people who feel that if a dog is good enough to win every award in sight, they must be good enough to breed every bitch in sight. Wrong, wrong, and if it hasn't sunk in — *wrong!*

Many of these fine dogs produce well only with certain kinds of bitches but not with any and all kinds of bitches. Indiscriminately used, these sires can be nearly as detrimental to a breed as a dog who has no producing ability at all. In some instances, they can be even more destructive.

When quality pups appear on the scene, produced by an outstanding dog out of compatible bitch lines, the parade all too often begins. Every bitch, regardless of her compatibility, joins the waiting line. Soon, there are puppies everywhere by the dog.

As I have stressed over and over, no dog is able to do it all. Some bitches are not well suited to a particular sire but are bred to that sire regardless. The offspring by the current top winner have great sales appeal. Thus, the market is soon flooded with the mediocre-at-best offspring, and soon they enter the breed's gene pool, diluting what quality may already be there.

Savvy breeders know where to draw the line and what to do with what they have, but as we all know there are seldom a great many breeders who can be classified as savvy at any given point in a breed's history. Dog breeding is far more apt to be plagued with the belief that "if a little bit is good, a whole lot more is even better." This is seldom the case.

Positive changes

Occasionally a breed is blessed with a dog who not only incorporates the essence of the breed but is also astoundingly prepotent in passing along these characteristics to his offspring. A perfect case in point is Ch. Ttarb The Brat, an unforgettable Smooth Fox Terrier owned by Ed Dalton. The Brat almost single-handedly brought his breed back to a level of quality it had not enjoyed for decades.

Sunny Shay's Afghan Hound, Ch. Shirkhan of Grandeur, gave his exotic countenance to sons and daughters who were able to pass along that unique beauty for many generations to come. Mrs. Julie Gasow's English Springer Spaniel, Ch. Salilyn's Aristocrat is another dog who undoubtedly deserves to be included in this rarefied group. I was fortunate enough to have owned one of these producing icons in my Bichon Frise, Ch. Chaminade Mr. Beau Monde.

Producing ability is not a numbers game. Some dogs may only produce a minimal number of champions during their time at stud, but those few champions become outstanding winners as well as noteworthy producers. You must look further than the numbers: A stud who has produced 100 champions may not have produced any truly significant offspring.

All this is not to discredit good sires — the ones whose siring abilities are somewhat limited — who are capable of producing quality only if used very carefully and on certain kinds of bitches. They have their place and if they are used with care, they too can make significant contributions.

Finding a Stud to Keep

So far in this chapter, I've primarily discussed the bitch owner's search for the ideal stud. Established breeders have no less a need for a dog to breed to and chances are their own line may produce a prospect that could just be the next important stud in the breeding program: One the breeder feels has most of what the line already excels in *plus* the quality or qualities that will carry the breeding program one step further up the ladder to that elusive perfect dog.

There is one thing that even the most successful breeder can't know before it is an accomplished fact. In the end, after all the preliminary questions about fitness have been satisfactorily answered, there is only one way to determine a dog's producing ability: The dog must be test bred. Test breeding a young stud is a long, time-consuming, and costly affair. It should begin as soon after he is matured as possible.

Keeping a prospective stud dog entails his being linebred, inbred, and out-crossed. Space and suitable placement opportunities allowing, he should be given the opportunity to test his prepotency on all levels of quality. Perhaps he even deserves a shot with a bitch who is merely adequate to see what he can do. But again, the latter is for the experienced breeder who has a very sound reason for doing so and will neuter and responsibly place the resulting puppies.

Keep records

Do everything you can to see as many of the puppies produced by your stud. It is important to take copious notes recording the common denominators that exist among the puppies he has produced. A number of litters are required before these records can pay off. You want to look for the similarities that exist through *all* the litters. What are the peculiarities when he is linebred, outcrossed, or inbred? Do not trust these characteristics to memory. Write them down. Keep a copy of each of the pedigrees of each dam that he is bred to. Compare what you see in the puppies with the progress and development chart you kept for the sire.

You are learning what this dog's genetic makeup makes him capable of producing. If your only concern is that he sires living puppies for those who plunk down a stud fee, you needn't bother with all this. Keeping abundant, accurate records is only for people who are serious about improving their line and making a contribution to the breed.

Remember that consistency counts — sometimes

Look for an overall consistency of quality in the young stud's progeny. There should be at least some quality puppies in most of the litters. If not, there's not much hope for the dog's future as a sire. Some dogs have the ability to sire quality. Others do not.

Hopefully, you can spot similarities in the puppies, whether they are from like pedigrees or not. Look for a general uniformity among the good ones. There will always be the odd big one, the small one, and the ugly one. Do not expect all the puppies in a litter to look alike. Do hope the good ones will have common characteristics.

Some breeders rave about how similar the puppies are in their litters, or say that they would rather have a consistent litter than one that contains just one or two top dogs. Beware! The no-fault litter can just as easily be a no-quality litter. Toads all look alike. (Please, no offense meant to the toad lovers of the world, but even they must admit we're not talking about beauty contest material there!)

Looking for Mr. (or Ms.) Goodpup

Look for the good ones. Don't worry about the lesser individuals in the litter. They won't be shown; they won't be bred from. They are of no consequence to the breeding program. Needless to say, that doesn't diminish your responsibility to find the lesser pups a good home and to make sure they are socialized every bit as well as your pick hits. They too have important roles as family pets.

Ringside spectators can spot the offspring of truly great sires without having to open the catalog to see what sire is listed. These are the sorts of animals you're looking for.

Love for Sale! Making the Most of Your Stud

So at long last you have your holy grail in your possession — the dog of a lifetime — the one who can really be called a *stud dog*. You've linebred him; you've outcrossed and inbred him, and he's had the opportunity to be bred

WARNING!

When a breed crashes

No doubt about it, I'll put my money on the distaff side of the breeding program any time. Everything I've written thus far makes it clear that I consider a producing bitch more valuable than gold. At the same time, those golden girls can't do it all on their own. They do have to be impregnated before they can make their contribution in the whelping box.

I've seen more than one breed crash for lack of good sires. Sometimes, a breed crashed simply because there weren't any prepotent sires in existence to make use of. I've also seen a breed languish because the males that could have done the job were withdrawn from service and kept only for private use. And, sadly, I've seen vicious gossip about "the other fellow's dog" completely destroy a potentially great sire's opportunity to contribute to the breed.

to the good, the bad, and (don't tell anyone) even the ugly! You've kept the notes, studied the pedigrees of the bitches, charted development, and he's passed all the tests. The task is complete. But now what?

Do you put Mr. Superstud in a glass case and take him out only when your own world-famous-never-been-a-better-one Best in Show bitch is ready to be bred? Or do you offer your dog at stud? Don't recoil in horror. The term *at stud* was highly respected until the past decade or so. Somehow, it has become fashionable to refuse the services of dogs to anyone who is not friend or family. Perhaps this is a reaction to the damning criticism that is heaped upon a dog whose less-than-perfect offspring find their way into the show rings of the country. This is not to say the dog won't produce less-than-perfect quality at home just as easily as he will at large. It only means that if you control who he is bred to, the public will only see the dog's hits and seldom, if ever, his misses.

My dogs were offered at stud. Perhaps not public stud, but rather in a by-private-treaty or to-approved-bitches-only arrangement. These arrangements give the stud owner an opportunity to accept or reject on a merit basis. Previous examples of how studs can be misused or even wasted should stand as proof of how necessary some selectivity is.

Nevertheless, even with restrictions, I personally found acting as the stud monitor for the dogs that were bred to outside bitches less than a joyous affair. Granted, I loved the thrill of evaluating the subsequent litters and finding budding superstars, but in retrospect I doubt I would jump at the chance of doing it again.

If you wonder why I wouldn't be terribly anxious to do it all again, I'll tell you why: There were too many midnight rides to the airport for late arriving bitches and too many all night waits for the ones that didn't make their connections. There was too much time spent on figuring out what to do with the snapping snarling bitches who absolutely *refused* to let anyone remove them from their shipping crates. There was all that to say nothing of all the bitches that came in way to early to be bred and just as many who came in way too late. *That's why!*

Promoting the stud dog

In this day and age, there are few of us who are able to house a sufficient number of brood matrons of the various kinds who might prove suitable for testing a particular stud dog. When housing is a problem, I strongly suggest entering into a partnership with someone who sees the breed as you do. The collaboration allows both parties to work separately toward a common goal and provides a greater nucleus of similarly bred breeding stock. An alliance of this nature also protects both parties in the event disease or forces of nature strike a fatal blow to one of the breeding programs.

Once the test breedings begin to show the results hoped for, the time has come to bring this success to the attention of others within your breed. You can't hope to influence the breed in a positive direction if you don't make what you have accomplished available to the breed at large.

The two best places to spread the news about your successful program are the breed's specialty magazine and your national breed club's annual National Specialty Show.

Breed magazines

In years past, dog magazines appealed to breeder and exhibitor — in that, for the most part, most fanciers were both. Through the years, the dog game has more and more divided itself into two relatively distinct groups: those who are primarily breeders and who show on a limited or low-key level, and those who are primarily exhibitors and who are more apt to buy their show dogs than they are to breed them.

Although the rare exception does exist, most all-breed magazines cater to the exhibitor, with only enough emphasis placed on breeding to satisfy those fanciers who operate on both levels.

Thus, the single-breed magazine has risen in importance for the breeder and stud owner. If stud dog promotion is the goal, there really isn't a better place to accomplish this than the well-edited and well-produced breed magazine.

Photos help tell the tale

Good pictures of a stud dog's young offspring are a great way of bringing a dog's producing ability to the attention of breeders. Attractive photos of quality puppies, even very young puppies, can be most impressive.

You can't say a whole lot about puppies, but good photographs speak for themselves. What you can give are particulars about the bitches that the puppies are out of. Nothing is more effective than running an attractive picture of a puppy or a litter and giving the breeding of the bitch that produced so successfully with your dog. If nothing else, doing so is a sure way to draw the interest of those who have a bitch whose pedigree might resemble that of the dam who produced the litter.

As the stud dog's puppies mature, photograph them in a manner that reveals their conformation. The conformation that the stud dog is dominant in producing is sure to attract even those breeders whose stock doesn't represent line breeding for the stud dog. Many breeders have bitches for whom they will occasionally select a mate on the basis of conformation, even though the breeding is a complete outcross.

When the sire's offspring hit show age and start winning their puppy classes, encourage the owners to get photographs taken. An advertisement doesn't have to go on and on about the dog's producing ability if you have good win pictures of his offspring. A good picture is, in fact, worth a thousand words. No promises need be made, as it's all said in the few words: "Winning youngsters sired by (insert name here)."

An ideal situation is one in which quality youngsters are shown in the classes where their sire is being shown in Best of Breed competition. This is particularly true at the National Specialty, where a good percentage of the people are shopping for the dog that might present an answer to their breeding problems. Seeing is believing!

Just the facts, ma'am, just the facts

One of the most effective advertisements for a stud dog that I've ever seen appeared in a popular single-breed magazine. A picture of the stud dog, along with his pedigree, headed the advertisement on the first page. On the following pages, there was a photographic list of all the dog's champion offspring, along with the dam's name and her sire and dam. No exaggerated claims or promises. Just simple, straightforward statements of fact. I spoke to the dog owner who had conceived the ad a few years later, and she told me the ad brought more of the right kind of bitches to the dog than she could ever have imagined.

Keeping tabs

Make a point of seeing as many of the litters sired by your dog and owned by other people as you possibly can. Your knowledge helps those who have not seen your stud's other litters. If you have been careful in charting the development of your stud, and possibly even his sire and dam, as outlined in Chapter 10, you have priceless information to contribute. Each new litter you assess gives you a more accurate picture of what your dog is capable of contributing to a breeding.

If you keep a puppy from a litter, remember that it may not be representative of the entire litter. The pup could be the litter's best, or its worst. He could look entirely different than his littermates. If a disappointing pup is the only one you see from the litter, a natural, but incorrect, assumption might be that the breeding did not produce what you had anticipated. In reality, all the other pups in the litter might be just what you thought they should be.

Seeing every litter your dog produces precludes the possibility of that one-in-a-million pup slipping through the cracks. Your dog may be capable of siring the greatest son or daughter the breed has ever seen, but if those high caliber offspring spend their lives sitting on someone's sofa and never see the inside of a show ring, no one will ever know what perfection has been achieved.

To make sure that I didn't miss any great offspring sired by my own stud dogs, I often bought the good puppies who the breeders were not planning on keeping. I was then able to direct the placement of these dogs. I had two purposes in doing so: I was making sure the dogs worthy of achieving their championships were given the opportunity to do so, and at the same time I was setting up my breeding program for the next generation.

My purchasing these promising offspring also proved to be a great way to have quality bitches of the right kind available for any promising new stud dog my breeding program produced. This is not to say I kept all the bitches I purchased in my own kennel, but even if they were sold to others, I did maintain control of how they were bred. Keeping every puppy you buy would be impossible, and doing so is not necessary. Placing puppies well allows new breeders to obtain better-than-average stock, and under your direction they will be able to breed top quality as well.

When placing quality offspring of a stud, I had a principle that followed that I felt really paid off: The longer the distance, the better the puppy. In other words, I made sure that any show puppy who was going into an area in which none of our stock had ever been shown before was absolutely the best I could come up with.

Sending the best offspring I could to new areas gave breeders who wouldn't normally see the individuals my studs were producing an opportunity to see something really special. I think that when you're sending your stock into foreign territory, the pups should be as good as what's already being shown there, if not better.

Determining worth

The time it takes to do the stud dog thing right? Immeasurable. The dollars invested in having it happen? Countless. Getting just what you bred for? *Priceless!*

Totaling costs

The testing and legwork involved in offering a dog at stud makes a breeding to him worth something. That something is the stud fee. Believe me, there's no money to be made in stud fees. Even if a dog is a whiz-bang of a sire and produces champions by the carload, a lot more money goes out than will ever come in.

If you've bred the dog, there's all that led up to his birth — keeping the proper bitches until they are old enough to be bred, showing, the money you've put out in stud fees, advertising, and endless veterinary bills. Also, you have to include the cost of things like buying the puppies sired by your dog who would have otherwise gone by the boards.

And all this is to say nothing of those puppies a stud owner might buy who show all the promise in the world and turn out to be nothing more than lovely pets. I've never known a stud owner who goes back to a breeder from whom he has purchased a show prospect sired by his dog and demands a refund or a replacement when the prospect doesn't work out.

When breeders buy a puppy, they look at it as their gamble. They hope it turns out, but very often it doesn't. Such is the name of the game. Some times nature smiles upon you, and at other times she simply laughs. It can be quite a different story when the situation is reversed. When a puppy is purchased from a breeder, and the puppy doesn't win everything the buyer thinks the puppy should, the buyer wants another dog.

Again, don't think for a minute that offering a dog at stud is some get-rich-quick idea. It just doesn't work that way. At the same time, however, breeding to a dog who produces well has to be worth something. A legitimate stud is certainly worth a good deal more than Fido down the block, who has never produced a quality puppy in his life.

Setting the stud fee

Practically every breeder you talk to has a different way of setting proper stud fees for their dogs. Personally, until I was sure a dog of mine had sired living puppies, there was no stud fee. Normally I'd have the dog sire pups with one of my own bitches, but there were occasions when the proper outside bitch was ready before any of my own bitches were.

Once the stud had produced living puppies, the fee was very moderate — after all, most any dog can sire living puppies. As we began to see what the dog was capable of producing, the stud fee was adjusted accordingly. At first, I'd make it commensurate with the amount a person would spend to buy a very well-bred and properly maintained pet-quality puppy. If a dog is worth breeding to at all, he's worth at least that much.

After a dog has established himself as a noteworthy sire, the picture changes. Because no stud fee adequately covers all the work involved in receiving and caring for outside bitches, regulating prices for significant sires is somewhat arbitrary.

In addition to the quality of the stud's offspring, things like the asking price for puppies, size of litters, popularity or rarity of the breed, and reputation of the stud owner all come into play. Here again, the advice of your mentor is well worth considering, as is the norm for your breed.

Some breeders give a sizable stud fee discount to champion or champion-producing dams. Some have even gone so far as to reduce the fee in half for bitches who previously produced champions by their dog. Certainly a wonderful gesture to those important producing matrons. If you are attempting to establish a producing reputation for your stud and hope to attract producing bitches, acknowledging their abilities by gestures of this kind can certainly do no harm!

Chapter 13

Putting the Act Together

. . . .

In This Chapter

▶ Timing is everything

▶ Lending a helping hand

▶ Putting it on ice!

▶ Figuring out why a breeding didn't work

. . . .

*E*verything in this book prior to this chapter has been aimed at helping you establish a mental picture of what constitutes the ideal in your breed, which is the goal to which you aspire in your breeding program. Each detail you add to the five elements of breed type, which are outlined in Chapter 6, assists you in bringing that picture into ever-sharpening focus. Clear vision is particularly important in this next step in your march along the road of progress. Clarity is so important here because the results express publicly your translation of the words that appear on the printed page of the breed standard into living, breathing flesh.

You are about to have that worth-her-weight-in-gold foundation bitch mated to that male you've found who, to the best of your knowledge, will help you straighten out the lines to make your next-generation living picture more accurate.

I find it surprising how many breeders have come to this critical juncture and still do not realize that the results of their breeding programs and what they take into the show ring are, in fact, pictures of how they view their breed. In some cases, the pictures are so erratic that the viewer would have no idea as to what is being said. Other attempts stray so far from the original intent and purpose of the breed that the resemblance is little more than coincidental.

We will always have dogs in our breeding program that fall slightly to the right or to the left of that ideal; however, the ideal remains in the center: It's the bull's-eye that we keep aiming for. Bull Terrier fanciers readily admit there are several styles or looks to their breed due to the breed's conglomerate origins. In some outstanding dogs, the traces of England's old Bulldog surface. In others, residuals of Terrier character prevail. There's been more than one quality Bullie who sports the contributions of his Dalmatian ancestry.

These variations are continually present in many breeds like the Bull Terrier and they are both legitimate and acceptable. At the same time, a Bullie aficionado would never advocate any single variation as perfection. If there were such a thing as a perfect Bull Terrier, he would be the dog who expresses the best qualities of all these styles: the dog in the center, the dog whose silhouette is the reflection of all the reasons the creators of the breed brought those disparate breeds together.

Proportions and Balance: Choosing the Right Combination

Far too many fanciers breed in such a willy-nilly fashion that there can never be any hope for consistency. If they come up with a top dog, it's purely by chance. They take a bitch that, let us say, is basically well put together with the right proportions and who needs improvement primarily in head characteristics. They find a dog that has an absolutely magnificent head, but ignore the fact that the dog is not only much too long in body for its standard but also has an incorrect coat.

The breeder is only interested in the prospective stud's beautiful head, and so the dog is bred to. Unless the bitch has already proven without question that she can hold her qualities against a breeding that challenges them, a breeding of this kind is doomed for failure. Even if she were to hold the best of what she has, the offspring represent a genetic hodgepodge.

A pup or two may be lucky enough to get all the right stuff in the right combination, but will the breeder have any certainty that the individual will then perpetuate only the desirable characteristics and not the faults that lie there in the gene pool?

Breeding a giant to a dwarf does not result in a following generation of moderate size. Breedings of this kind result in some large, some small, and worse yet, some offspring whose parts are made up of both large and small and therefore are completely out of balance.

Some breeding programs house and consistently breed two quality lines of opposing types. Champions and winners can and do emerge from breeding programs of this kind, but more often than not, there is little consistency of type among these winners. The outside person who goes to that line can be dismayed at how different the results are from what was anticipated.

Knowing exactly where you are heading and what you want helps you avoid the erratic results that are typical of the poorly organized breeding program.

Coming to Terms: Put It in Writing

After the sire of the forthcoming breeding is decided on, the conditions, outside of a guarantee of actual mating, should be discussed in advance. Stud arrangements and contracts can include anything the stud and bitch owners will agree to but whatever is agreed to should be clearly outlined in a stud contract or breeding agreement. This agreement should list the amount of the stud fee, when the fee is due, and any special conditions that apply.

For instance, there are times when the owner of the stud must resort to artificial means to insure a breeding. Will the owner of the bitch be notified in advance if this is the case? Who incurs any additional costs involved in artificial insemination procedures should also be made clear.

The contract should also indicate what charges or refunds, if any, will be applicable if an actual breeding can't be accomplished. That a stud fee pays for the mating only and that there is no refund if the bitch fails to produce living puppies are pretty well understood in the dog game. No stud dog owner can guarantee living puppies as a result of breeding to her stud dog. The most that can be guaranteed is a breeding of some kind.

Most stud dog owners provide a return service to the same bitch (meaning another breeding) if she should miss. Again, there is no guarantee of a return service unless you've got it in writing. Having all this set forth in a written agreement that is signed by the owners of both the bitch and the dog is a good idea, so that there are no misunderstandings or disappointments.

Determine how far in advance of the breeding day the stud owner wants the bitch to arrive if she is being shipped. If she is to remain on the premises of the stud owner while being bred, the contract should also state what additional costs, if any, are involved in keeping her there. The contract should state what the owner of the stud dog is and is not responsible for while the female is in residence.

Pick of the litter

On occasion, the owner of a stud dog will agree to have his or her dog mate your female in return for first choice of the resulting puppies. This can be a good arrangement for you if you do not plan on keeping a puppy from the litter for yourself. If you plan to keep a pup from the litter to show or to breed or for any other reason, think carefully before you agree to this sort of arrangement. Why? More often than not, the breeder of the litter and the stud dog owner wind up wanting the same puppy. Giving up a puppy that you or your family has grown attached to or one who is exactly what you had hoped for as a show prospect is extremely difficult.

Breeding reservation

The owner of the female should make a breeding reservation based upon the female's previous seasons. It is unwise to breed any female until she has successfully passed through one full season, indicating she is on the road to maturity.

After your female shows signs of coming into season, notifying the stud dog owner is important. Doing so gives the owner of a popular stud dog the opportunity to schedule other females who may be coming in to breed to the same dog you've chosen. Even the owner of a stud who is used only occasionally should have advance notice, in order to complete any health and fertility tests that he may want to have done.

The Scenario Heats Up

Most females come into heat, called *estrus*, for the first time at about nine to twelve months of age; however, the timing is breed sensitive. A good number of the Toy and small breeds experience their first season as early as six months, and the giant breeds not until past a year. That said, dogs do not read the rule books. Your female can come into heat exactly when you don't expect her to and when you are entirely unprepared.

In other words, do your best to determine when most females of your breed cycle first, and then watch her closely well before that time until she does come in. Record that date. After their first heat, most females will be in heat again fairly regularly every six to eight months. Although the entire heat cycle lasts approximately 21 days, the female can only become pregnant when she is ovulating. The problem is that there is no clear-cut rule as to which of the *approximately* (and I emphasize the word approximately!) 21 days she will be ovulating on.

More general rules are applicable to the normal initial signs of a female's impending estrus. In most cases, there is a noticeable swelling of the vulva and an increased sensitivity to just about every situation she encounters, regardless of how calm she's been in the past.

This stage is usually followed in a few days by a dark, bloody vaginal discharge. After you see any signs at all, your female should be watched very carefully and kept away from all males to avoid any accidental matings. She should also be confined to an area of the house where the discharge, which she is unable to control, will not soil carpeting or furniture.

I can't caution you enough to be extremely watchful while your female is in heat. You cannot imagine how many unwanted litters have been born in spite of the fact that the female was "only with a male too young (or too old) to breed" or "in the yard by herself just a few minutes."

Fences give bitch owners an extremely false sense of security. You would be amazed at how innovative the ready female and the always-ready male can be when the time is right! Males and their intendeds look at something like fences as minor and momentary inconveniences to be traveled over, under, or if necessary *through* in order to accomplish their mission. You don't think dogs can breed through a fence? Ha!

It is commonly accepted that females of almost all breeds are not ready to accept the male until *about* the tenth day of their heat cycle. Do not, however, allow that information to lull you into believing that your bitch *can't* be bred before or after that time. Although *planned* matings are seldom accomplished prior to the tenth day of the heat cycle, it seems *unplanned* matings are productive at almost any time the female is in heat and often before and after you believe her to be out of heat.

Psychological factors

Yes, the lady-in-waiting's emotional state has to be considered in this ritual as well. As strange as it may sound, lack of canine socialization and travel trauma can have significant effect upon her psyche and readiness to accept a male. These stressors can even affect conception.

If your female has been the treasured and pampered love of your life and has not been in the company of other dogs often, she may consider herself above a love tryst with, heaven forbid — *a dog!* Some bitches of this mind-set will resort to no less than murderous intent in order to repel the advances of her amorous intended.

To a bitch who has never traveled or never traveled in a shipping crate, shipping can be very traumatic as well. It would be hard to believe that a breeding quality female would never have traveled to a dog show, but in the event her travel history has been minimal, prior crate training is a must.

The bottom line to all this is that you want your valuable female to arrive at the home of her husband-to-be as all that she can be — both physically and psychologically. A calm and healthy female has a far better chance of producing calm and healthy puppies than one who is bred in a high state of anxiety and in run-down condition.

Timing

The traditional method to predict ovulation is observing a reduction of blood flow, diminishing color of the flow, and a softening of the vulva. Bitches then begin to develop a greater interest in the attention of any male present. When the base of the female's tail is scratched, she will arch her tail and raise her rump.

A veterinarian can be extremely helpful in advising the right days on which to breed your female. The advice of a vet is especially useful if you plan to ship your bitch to the stud dog. Your vet has a somewhat more scientific and accurate method of determining ovulation and the best days to breed — the days when your bitch is most apt to conceive.

Three hormones — estrogen, luteinizing hormone (LH), and progesterone — govern the estrus cycle. Shifts in the levels of these hormones control the time of ovulation and the resulting fertile period. Vaginal smears and a blood test known as the ovulation timing test are relatively accurate in determining just when the female's ovulation has or will begin and the right time to have her bred.

Even when ovulation has occurred, hours or even a couple of days may have to pass before the eggs are receptive to sperm. Because of the gradual ovulation, even after the first successful mating has been completed, repeating the breeding again once or twice is wise, skipping a day between each breeding.

Even though your female has been successfully mated to the dog of your choice, do not assume that she cannot be impregnated by another dog. She must be closely watched until she has completely ended her heat cycle.

Bitches can produce litters that have two or more entirely different sires — some of the puppies by the sire of your choice, and others by the dog of *her* choice! Should this unfortunate situation occur, it does not mean that your female is "tainted" for life. The female's eggs and the male's sperm only live for a maximum number of days, so there is no possibility of their having any effect on future breedings. However, in the case of multiple sires, modern DNA testing may be required to determine the parentage of every puppy.

Some experienced breeders, and very often experienced stud dogs themselves, have an uncanny knack of being able to determine the correct day on which a female should be bred. One stud dog in particular who I owned had a near 100-percent success rate when he was allowed to pick the days on which a bitch should be bred.

It was not unusual for bitches to arrive for my stud dog with exacting instructions as to what day (even what *time* of day!) they should be bred. My dog would almost always comply (albeit at times reluctantly) with the dictates of the bitch owner and we would have both successes and failures. However, when he was allowed to choose the day, we seldom experienced a miss.

Tying Up Loose Ends

Customarily, the bitch travels to the home of the male. Totally aside from custom, a stud owner is not about to allow his prize stud to risk life and limb by trying to invade the domain of the female. After a male realizes that the female arriving on his turf is up for a love affair, his libido overcomes any protective inclinations he might have and he becomes Welcome Wagon and Good Will Ambassador all rolled up into one.

Although Old Nell who had her puppies under the shed may have gotten it on with Speck the hound dog completely unassisted, hits and misses in their case were of little or no consequence. Breeding purebred dogs is another story. There's too much thought, planning, time, and money involved in a breeding to leave its accomplishment to luck.

Young males may need assistance until they know the what's and how's of getting the job done. Nor should the owner of a valuable stud dog risk the visiting miss attacking his dog. Close supervision of the two in a confined area is prudent, prevents accidents and injuries, and keeps disappointments to a minimum.

Controlling the Bitch

Females in season seldom attack males during the breeding sequence, but many stud owners like to have complete control of the bitch just to be on the safe side and to avoid accidents. Maiden bitches are sometime startled by the proceedings and may snap at the male or try to escape. If he's not quick enough to anticipate her objections, permanent injury could result. The following can help:

- **Muzzles and collars:** Leather muzzles can be purchased from a pet shop. A discarded nylon stocking can be an improvised muzzle. Nylons are strong and will not cut or irritate the female's muzzle. Snugly wrap the center section of the stocking twice around the female's muzzle. Not so tight that it is uncomfortable, but firm enough so that she cannot use her jaws to bite. Tie the two ends under the jaw and draw them back behind the ears and tie them there. In addition, a collar can keep the bitch from making sudden movements during first penetration by the male and while they are tied.

- **Assistance:** Having two people assist at a mating — one person to hold onto and steady the bitch, the other to assist the male when and if he needs help or guidance. I prefer that the owner of the bitch not be one of those assisting, as the owner's presence seems to unnerve rather than calm the bitch.

✔ **Tables and enclosures:** Toy breeds are usually mated on a table or elevated platform for easy control and to help things along when necessary. Larger dogs should be contained in an exercise pen or small room. Wild romps are fine for the preliminaries, but when you get down to business, escape or even sudden departures are the last thing you will want to have occur.

Tying the Knot

Before they're introduced to each other, the male and female should be allowed to exercise separately in order to take care of bodily functions. After this is completed the two can be introduced in a quiet area away from other dogs and humans, other than those humans involved in the breeding itself. Both animals should be on leash to prevent a sudden amorous rush from the male. An inexperienced bitch could panic and attack the male or try to escape.

Normally, the bitch who is ready to breed will entice the male by backing up to him, flagging her tail, and tilting her rear up toward his inquiring nose. The person managing the female can facilitate this by placing one hand under the female's abdomen with the fingers pointed rearward so that the rear end of the bitch can be waved back and forth in front of the male, enticing him on. In the case of bitches of the larger breeds, tilting the vulva up and outward and rocking the female's rear quarter will be equally effective.

A helping hand

An experienced male will very quickly mount the female and begin thrusting to make entry. Many young and inexperienced males hit everywhere around, but not *on* target. The youngster can become so excited he will spend himself before he even comes near making entry.

It's helpful in situations like this to guide the thrusting male's penis into the vulva. If the bitch is experienced and willing, she may well stand patiently, allowing the person handling the male to give him all the attention and direction needed. However, in the case of the inexperienced or unwilling bitch, both attendants may need to give their full attention to keeping the bitch in position and guiding the male.

Although making decisions on this basis is not always possible, I have always hoped that the young stud dog in training will be given a seasoned bitch for his first breeding. Conversely, having a thoroughly experienced male service the novice female usually makes the whole operation progress far more smoothly than having two greenhorns.

Using the hands-on approach to entice and assist the young male in his early breedings is extremely important for a number of reasons. Making the owner's help a normal part of the breeding will prevent the stud from developing an "I'd rather do it myself" attitude that some males develop. They refuse to let anyone touch the bitch or themselves during the mating.

Believe me when I say that there are just as many females who will not allow a male to mount and breed them as there are females who are anxious and willing to be bred. Some bitches become violent in their refusal and others simply will not stand.

If your stud dog has not learned that assistance is a part of breeding, you could end up with just as many aborted attempts as you have successes. And it never fails that the mating you've always wanted to make is the most difficult to get accomplished. In the beginning, *insist* that your stud dog allow you to be involved — doing so will save you agonizing hours and disappointments later on!

The money shot

When the male is fully aroused, his penis becomes engorged as he attempts to fully penetrate the vagina. This is followed by a swelling of the bulbous glandis that is located at the base of the penis. The swelling, coupled with contraction of the sphincter muscles of the bitch's vulva, locks or *ties* the dogs into position while sperm pumps into the bitch. This is what is referred to as an *inside tie.*

When the tie is complete and secure, the pair normally relax. The male's two front legs can be lifted to one side of the female and they will be tied end to end for the remainder of the breeding.

The male's sperm is ejaculated in three stages. The first sperm is released before full erection and is usually clear and has little or no active content. The second and most important release occurs just after thrusting. This ejaculate has the highest active sperm content. The third stage of an ejaculation takes place while the pair is tied. The content is clear, with some active sperm present.

It is important that the pair be supervised while tied, or at least kept in a very small enclosure. You don't want the female to decide that she has had all the fun she wants for a day and is ready to leave for home. Ties can last anywhere from 5 minutes to over an hour. Although firm ties of over 10 to 15 minutes usually inspire the greatest deal of satisfaction for stud and bitch owners, neither a long tie nor an inside tie are absolutely necessary for conception.

Post coital care for the male

After the male has done the deed, make sure to do the following:

- ✔ Check to make sure the male has fully retracted the penis into the sheath.
- ✔ Wipe the penis and sheath with an antibacterial solution as a precautionary measure.
- ✔ Allow the male to walk around, drink water, and relieve himself if he wants to.
- ✔ Provide a quiet area for him to rest up from his ordeal.

Post coital care for the female

Take care of the female by doing the following:

- ✔ As soon as the female is released from the tie, elevate her hindquarters for at least 5 minutes. Do this to keep what has been deposited safely stored in her vault.
- ✔ After you've elevated her hindquarters, give her a 5- to 10-minute supervised, on-leash walk.
- ✔ Do not allow her to urinate, if at all possible.
- ✔ Keep her crated in a calm, quiet area away from other dogs for several hours.
- ✔ If she is to be shipped back home, wait at least 24 hours after the last breeding.

When the Party's Over: Making Arrangements for the Litter

After the breeding has been completed, the stud dog owner should record the dates and times of all breedings and the length of ties. This information should be provided to the breeder of record.

The breeder of a litter or an individual dog is defined by the AKC as: "The owner (or, if the dam was leased, the lessee) of the dog *when the dam was bred.*"

The first thing the owner of the female will want to know immediately is whether or not she was bred and if there was a successful tie. After those questions are answered, the breeder will want to know how many puppies the litter will produce and what sexes the puppies will be.

TECHNICAL STUFF

The makeup of the litter

The number of puppies in a litter is the domain of the female. Were it up to the male, your litter could easily produce somewhere between 200 million and 2 billion puppies, because that's how many active sperm a healthy, fertile male can produce in a milliliter of ejaculate. But it's the number of the female's eggs (ova) that the little fellows impregnate that tell the tale and regulate the number of puppies your female will have.

Sex of puppies, on the other hand, like all mammals, is determined by the sire of the litter. If the decision were up to the dam of the litter, all her puppies would be female because of her chromosomes for sex. (I know, I know — I promised no more genetics, but this is easy and it's important.)

The female's chromosomes for sex are expressed as XX. All females are XX, and one of those Xs is all a female can contribute in sexual reproduction. The male's chromosomes for sex are expressed as XY. All males are XY, and in reproducing he can contribute an X chromosome or a Y chromosome. If the male's X-bearing sperm reaches the ovum first, then a female (XX) results. But if a Y-bearing sperm gets there first, a male (XY) results.

If at First You Don't Succeed . . .

So, little Fluff arrived at your boy's doorstep with all the credentials and test results. She was bred, had a long tie, went home, got pregnant, and had a healthy litter of puppies.

Isn't dog breeding easy? Sure. *In your dreams!*

I haven't talked much about all those things that can go wrong. What if you can't even get that visiting fraulein *bred?* What then? Give up?

Although at times "forgeddaboudit" seems to be the most prudent option, take heart. There are other ways to get the job done: the various forms of artificial insemination, also known as *AI.*

Perhaps the stud can't get the job done. He might be too young and inexperienced, and hard as it may be to believe, he could be a shy guy without the aggressiveness to put his lady callers in their place. Then too, young dogs often become so excited at being given an opportunity for some action that they have used up their resources prematurely.

And it's not always just his fault either. Maybe the female is the problem child. I've known of a few females who cooperated with all the steps leading up to being bred, but when it came time for the actual deed, they positively and adamantly refused to comply! No coaxing or cajoling altered the situation, nor did physical exams reveal any reason for their determination not to be bred.

Back to the well

In days gone by, after a male had gone on to greener pastures his contributions as a sire were forever lost to a breed. Not so, today. Stored frozen semen allows us to return to the well, so to speak, and avail ourselves of the producing ability of dogs who have left us but who had the capability of making great contributions to breed progress.

In Chapter 12, I relate tales of how profoundly some stud dogs contributed to their breeds. I also give examples of how those great contributions were lavishly squandered in succeeding generations through haphazard and ill-advised breedings.

In these cases, the positive contributions of the great sires were eventually so diluted that, irrespective of the number of times the sires appeared in pedigrees, their value was totally lost. The breeds then foundered in mediocrity for generations. What a boon to those breeds it would have been if breeders could have returned to the source that had initially made such a great contribution.

The complexities and continually soaring costs of shipping bitches by air has made that option less and less viable over the past decade. Frequent delays, weather embargoes, and cancellations of flights, to say nothing of bomb threats and terrorism, make the airways a less-than-desirable way of delivering a valued brood bitch to the stud of choice. AI brings the stud dog from the opposite coast or across the ocean to the bitch owner's doorstep.

Regardless of the reason, AI is here to help and here to stay. There are a whole lot of options and approaches that rely upon the full cooperation of the owners of the sire and the dam, the agencies licensed to collect and store semen, and a vet who has been successfully trained in the field. Various methods can be used to collect and prepare semen for transfer to the bitch. Some of these methods prolong the semen's life a few hours, others indefinitely.

Methods of collection

Depending upon the circumstances, the owner of a bitch can choose to use fresh, fresh chilled, or frozen semen. After the type of semen is determined, the method, vaginal or surgical, of implanting the semen into the female's genital tract must be decided.

Fresh semen

Short of a natural breeding, using fresh semen is the next best option. Any reason, from lack of interest on the part of the male to vaginal strictures on the part of the female, may require the transfer of fresh semen to the bitch who is ready to be bred. The transfer of semen is accomplished most easily by a veterinarian, with both dogs present. Some breeds, such as Chow Chows, French Bulldogs, and Bulldogs, rely on the AI process so heavily that stud owners have become fully adept at the process themselves.

In this process, the male is stimulated by the scent of the female in estrus or with an artificial estral scent. When fully engorged, he is massaged by hand until ejaculation into a container or artificial vagina is accomplished.

If both the male and female are present, the ejaculate is withdrawn from the container with a sterile syringe and injected directly into a flexible sterile tube that has previously been inserted into the bitches' vaginal canal. The contents of the syringe are slowly and completely injected into the tube. After the semen is fully injected, a syringe of air is injected into the tube to help drive the sperm deeper into the vagina.

The appropriate steps to be taken for care of the male and female following a breeding of this type are exactly the same as if the animals had been bred naturally.

Fresh chilled semen

When semen is prepared for storage, only the portion collected during the second stage of the male's ejaculation, with the highest active sperm is preserved. The portion preserved is diluted with extenders and the temperature reduced to 40 degrees Fahrenheit.

Six days seems to be the maximum length of time that fresh chilled semen stays viable. Maximum fertility is limited to the first 48 hours. Sperm cells that have been chilled at 40 degrees are viable for 24 to 72 hours in the uterus. This narrow window of viability means that timing is of the essence in respect to ovulation and insemination.

Frozen semen

Properly collected semen that has been treated with appropriate extenders can be stored indefinitely. The reverse of cooling and freezing is carried out to prepare frozen semen for artificial insemination. More and more owners are collecting semen from their important stud dogs and having it frozen and stored to be used at a later date or by breeders from other countries. Stud dog owners will provide on request information regarding the availability of frozen semen.

Methods of insemination

Rapid advances are being made in improving the success rate of AI breedings. In addition to the insemination process where the semen is transferred directly with both animals on site, surgical insemination receives high praise and has an equally high rate of success.

- ✔ **Surgical insemination:** Semen is injected into the exposed uterus through a needle. Experienced proponents of the methods say it has a success rate closely matching that of natural matings. Surgical implantation also provides an opportunity to see if there are uterine obstructions or infections that might be causing poor conception rates.

- ✔ **Laparoscopic insemination:** A small telescope is injected into the bitch's abdomen. The telescope locates and identifies the uterus for semen injection. This new technique is rapidly gaining popularity, in that it is a less invasive and potentially faster than surgical insemination.

When the Cupboard Is Bare: Failing to Conceive

There's probably nothing more disappointing than having a bitch fail to conceive. The hopeful breeder spends countless hours doing research and studying pedigrees. Eventually, the right stud dog is found and the bitch is shipped off (at no little expense, mind you!). The owner of the stud dog reports all signals go, and then in a few days advises the owner of the bitch that the mating went perfectly.

The carrier of all the prospective breeder's hopes and dreams returns with a starry look in her eyes. Then, both bitch and owner sit back and wait, and wait, and wait. And then, *nothing* — no puppies. What a let down!

Misses do take place, and there's nothing to be alarmed about if a miss happens, especially if it is the first time for either the male or female to be bred. However, in some cases and in spite of proper timing, willing participants, and repeat breedings — still no puppies arrive. The bitch simply, or perhaps not so simply, does not conceive.

I say *not so simply* because there are a host of reasons why she may not become pregnant. The problem can be physical or emotional, due to external or internal forces. Some reasons are very common and easily correctable; others are not. You can go on guessing and repeating fruitless breedings from now till doomsday, or you can do the sensible thing and consult your veterinarian.

Not all vets are experts in female fertility, but most are better equipped than a layman to know where to start looking for what the problem might be. Your own vet might even recommend seeing someone who is an expert in the field of fertility. But before that, he will probably ask you some questions, so you might as well start making notes ahead of time. The more information you can give your vet, the more likely it is that he is going to be able to help you solve your problem.

Input on your part might save your veterinarian's research staff a great deal of time and costly research.

Contraceptives

One of the first questions you might ask yourself, or whoever it was who showed your dog, is whether or not your bitch has been given contraceptives to keep her from coming into season. These products regularly appear on the market, indicating they will not interfere with normal heat cycles or conception after you stop administering them.

I find it interesting, however, that almost invariably after a few years on the market the products are withdrawn, never to be heard from again. However, we do hear of a whole host of bitches who experience nothing but problems in resuming regular seasons and in becoming pregnant after having used these products. Unless you don't plan on breeding your bitch, I would think long and hard before resorting to any product that keeps her from having regular, normal seasons.

Nutrition and environment

Obese or malnourished bitches and those confined to cramped living quarters without the benefit of regular exercise are poor risks when it comes to breeding. Such conditions are not normal for dogs, and it is asking a good deal of bitches to have normal seasons and conception rates when they are not afforded the opportunity to be physically fit.

Structural defects or general infections

Has your bitch ever been in an accident or been injured while working in the field or doing rescue work? Structural damage can realign reproductive organs in such a way that she becomes unable to breed or conceive. Sometimes, these injuries can cause the vulva do become lacerated, probed, or irritated. This can result in infections of the cervix and the uterus, causing temporary or permanent sterility.

Immunization cocktails

A great deal of controversy surrounds the number and frequency of vaccinations given dogs from puppyhood on to protect them from contagious diseases. Many long-time breeders are fully convinced that combination vaccines and annual boosters can have direct and negative effects on the fertility level of breeding stock. Many university and teaching schools are now doing *titres* (taking blood samples to determine the level of resistance to a disease still remaining in the bloodstream) to preempt unnecessary vaccinations. It is highly recommended that owners of all dogs discuss this issue with their veterinarians and give full consideration to what the vets recommend.

Chemical exposure

The fertility rate of dogs can be seriously compromised when they are exposed to farming and manufacturing chemicals over a long period of time. Even regular digging in a garden plot that is heavily infused with chemicals can have adverse and long-range consequences.

Part V

Prenatal Care, Whelping, and Raising Puppies

The 5th Wave   By Rich Tennant

©RICHTENNANT

"She's a model dog, alright. When she's not on a catwalk, she demands a lot of attention, requires constant grooming, and is a picky eater."

In this part . . .

When Mama dog decides "it's time," life changes. Pundits call it "the miracle of birth"; I call it the *trauma* of birth" (my trauma, not hers!). And even if the birthing goes textbook smoothly, (which they usually do) you can pace the floor and wring your hands in support.

While the pups are those little nursing angels all lined up at Mama's Milk Bar, there's not a whole lot the brood requires. But one day, Mama looks up at you with those big soulful eyes that say, "You wanted puppies? Here, take care of them. I'm outta here!"

Just about the time you've become accustomed to the fact that you're now running a maternity ward, the little sleeping angels suddenly sprout legs and start practicing to become tiny tornadoes of terror, or, at the very least, team members of the Minnesota Wrecking Crew. Each pup needs special care and special treatment, and when you're not doing that, you'll be extricating them from the roof and out from three levels under the house foundation. Little inter-litter gang fights. Special meals. Oh, what fun. Don't worry too much, though. This part shows you how to get ready for all that (and more!) and how to handle those squirming bundles of joy.

Chapter 14

The Wonders of Pregnancy

She's bred, she's home, and she's pregnant — at least you *think* she's pregnant. There are surefire ways of finding that out, and your vet can help. You won't notice major changes at first, but as the weeks tick by, she'll change, and her needs will change as well.

What changes take place immediately after conception? Not many, at least not that you can see. Most breeders are sure there are changes: "I can tell, she's acting just, I don't know . . . *different*." Sure. Ask what that "different" is and you probably won't get much of an answer.

What You Can't See

Providing the timing was right, so that the male-of-your-choice's sperm reached your golden girl's ova, fertilization occurred. Conception took place in her fallopian tubes — the channels that pass down from the ovaries to the womb. During the few days following fertilization, eggs pass to the uterus and implant on the wall of the womb.

While this is going on, that single cell that was formed when the sperm joined the ovum has begun to divide and become a little ball of individual cells, each of the cells forming a specific part of the individual puppy's body (as I explain in depth in Chapter 9).

Registering AI litters with the AKC

The American Kennel Club will register a litter that is produced through artificial insemination, provided that the following conditions are met.

For fresh semen:

The sire and dam of the breeding must both be present during the extraction of semen and the insemination of the bitch.

The breeder completes and submits a Litter Registration Application and an Artificial Insemination Using Fresh Semen certification form, with the proper fee.

For fresh extended semen:

The semen must be extracted and extended by a licensed veterinarian.

The insemination of the bitch must be performed by a licensed veterinarian.

The breeder completes and submits a Litter Registration Application and an Artificial

Insemination Using Fresh Extended Semen certification form, with the proper fee.

The breeder submits a DNA certification for dam and sire.

For frozen semen:

The collection of semen for the artificial breeding must be reported to the AKC with DNA certification.

The collector/storer must be on record with the AKC as familiar with and complying with the AKC regulations for record keeping and identification of dogs.

The Frozen Semen Application must be submitted, containing the certifications completed by the owner of the semen, the owner of the dam, and the veterinarian who performed the artificial breeding, with the proper fee.

The spinal cord and the brain form first. Next, and in rapid succession, come the organs, the limbs, the skin, and finally the hair. Canine pregnancy lasts approximately 59 to 63 days, but the fetus itself is completely formed in just over the first three weeks of the pregnancy! What happens from that point on is simply growth and development.

The growing fetus is surrounded by a system of membranes called the placenta. The placenta nourishes the fetus and grows along with it. The fluid-filled placental sacs cushion and protect the fetus from shock and damage.

The placenta is associated with the wall of the womb in such a way that it is supplied with blood vessels from the fetus. These blood vessels form the umbilical cord. The blood that circulates in the placenta is therefore the puppy's own blood and it is being circulated by the fetus's own heart. When the puppy's blood passes through the area attached to the womb, the blood vessels pass close to the mother's blood vessels that are in the womb.

JUST FOR FUN

More old wives' tales

I would give my eyeteeth to have known some of those old wives everyone always talks about. They really must have been characters, because some of the tales they told were so totally off the wall that we still repeat a lot of them for the entertainment value.

Now when I say old, I'm talking *old!* For centuries, our folklore has included myths and legends, many of which trace as far back as ancient Rome and Greece. The Greeks and Romans were actually pretty good dog breeders, but it's hard to understand how they did what they did. They reported crossing dogs with all kinds of other animals, including lions, foxes, and tigers!

One interesting story tells us that crossing an African Hunting Dog with a hyena produced one heck of a hunter. But you had to be very careful in doing so, because the results of the cross were capable of changing their sex each year. The year that your hunter was a female, you could barely get out of the back door for all the footloose local hyena boys she attracted to her doorstep. Seems the boys were especially attracted to those gals of mixed background!

In China way back when, someone saw to it that a wolf got it on with a bear and *voilà* — out came the first Chow Chow! You don't believe it? Well, tell me why Chow Chows and bears are the only two animals that have black tongues?

Did you know that you could influence the color of your litter by parading your female back and forth in front of a horse of the desired color just after she was bred? Or if you wanted to avoid having too many female pups, you could wait until a moonless night to breed her? Guess that's so the fertility gods couldn't see you were trying to pull a fast one on them.

Even my childhood author-hero Albert Payson Terhune passed along stories that I'm sure were inspired by the old wives' stories he knew. At least one of his all-but-perfect, Best in Show Collies was the result of a purebred Collie who had mated with a Bull Terrier! (It appears the cross just made him faster, tougher, and stronger than other Collies. Didn't affect his looks any.)

That's no big deal, though. I can't tell you the number of stories I read where our young hero Jack Patriot's old nag of a plow horse got mated to Man O' War or some other famous Thoroughbred stallion (through the fence, I guess!), and gol' dang it if good old Jack's colt didn't grow up to win the Kentucky Derby *and* the Belmont Stakes!

However, despite Jack's success story, if your female dog was defiled even once by a male of another breed or, God forbid, by a mongrel(!), you may as well get rid of her. Her subsequent offspring were forever cursed and tainted and would never be or look purebred again, no matter who you bred her to. Go figure that one out. Guess it all goes back to that universal truth that what people don't know, they make up.

A unique exchange takes place at this point. Oxygen and nutrients pass from the mother's blood to the blood of the fetus. Waste products and carbon dioxide pass in the opposite direction.

The fetus is completely reliant on its mother for survival. Any disruption of the placenta can lead to death of the puppy.

This amazing series of events takes place without conscious effort or concern on the part of the mother. Even the breeder, who would be more than happy to take a hand in the proceedings, is completely out of the picture. Nature is taking a course which, to be completely honest, never ceases to boggle this nonscientist's mind, even after all these years.

What You Can See (And Do)

Continue providing the mom-to-be with regular meals and ordinary exercise. Nothing need change in the way you care for your pregnant female. You won't be able to detect anything until around the 22nd to the 29th day of pregnancy. At that time, the fetuses can be felt by *gently* palpating the abdomen. The size of the breed determines what you might expect to feel at this stage. A fetus of a medium to medium-large breed will be the size of something between a walnut and golf ball.

Ultrasound can be used to check for fetal shapes and their heartbeats. Ultrasound scanning allows the viewer to observe the little fetuses moving. The breeder can only hope that one of those little moving shapes is destined to become that superstar whose production all the planning and hoping has been directed at.

Although rarely resorted to now because of their potential danger to the fetuses and the availability of ultrasound, x-rays can be taken after the 43rd day of pregnancy. At this stage of development, fetuses can be seen as faint skeletons.

Is She Or Isn't She?

I can't tell a thing about a bitch I've bred until several weeks after the breeding. Even though I've been through it all countless times before, I still invariably lapse into what I call my staring mode. While caught up in this phase, I get nothing else done because I'm too busy gazing intently at the mother-to-be, scrutinizing every little movement (each has a meaning all its own, you know!) and noting every little grunt, groan, and yawn that I will optimistically translate into confirmation of her pregnancy.

I change my mind daily, sometimes hourly, but in the end, just like everyone else, I have to wait about five weeks before I can tell anything at all (unless, of course, I've resorted to what my vet might tell me). At about five weeks a swelling of the female's teats will indicate that the breeding *may have* taken.

May have? Yes, may have. There is such a thing as a false pregnancy. Some bitches are so fully convinced that they are pregnant that they would have had me completely fooled if I weren't in the practice of staying in close touch with my vet.

False Pregnancy

Any bitch who hasn't been spayed can experience a false pregnancy, even bitches who haven't been bred. My experience is that when this condition occurs once, you can almost bet that it will happen again — possibly a number of times in the bitch's lifetime. Many long-time breeders have been known to blame the condition on an overwhelming drive for motherhood.

The solution for those ascribing to this theory — go ahead and breed her, because she's going to go through the whole process anyway, except that she won't have any puppies for all her efforts. The only fly in this ointment is that many of the bitches who have false pregnancies without ever having been bred also have nonproductive or false pregnancies when they are bred.

A bitch experiencing a false pregnancy shows all the signs that a pregnant bitch would — appetite increase, weight gain, nesting, morning sickness, swelling of the teats, milk flow — the whole bit.

A bitch experiencing a false pregnancy can exhibit some very odd behaviors. An Irish Setter I owned would resort to adoption when she was experiencing a false pregnancy. Once it was a teddy bear, another time one of my socks. Other bitches I've known made tennis balls or pot holders the object of their maternal instincts, giving them the utmost care and attention.

It is not at all unusual for these adoptive mothers to kidnap puppies from kennel mates. The plus side of this situation is that the whelping bitch may not be able to nurse all her puppies. A bitch in false pregnancy is fully capable, usually *anxious,* to take on the maternal chores and will nurse the puppies on through to weaning time.

One such devoted adoptive mother in Australia got worldwide coverage. A Golden Retriever female in false pregnancy somehow came upon an abandoned newborn fawn and successfully nursed the orphan until it grew beyond the Retriever's ability to serve as a milk bar. The two remained devoted companions long afterwards. The owner of the Retriever said, "Stormy, our Golden, is quite fond of her adopted child, even though she thinks most of the time he hasn't a brain in his head!"

Although overwhelming desire to be a mother may well be the cause of false pregnancies, science also offers an explanation. The condition is the result of hormonal imbalance. A bitch experiencing the condition, particularly one who is repeatedly in the state, needs special care. Hormone injections and oral medications can alleviate the condition — sometimes permanently. However, in some cases not even extensive hormonal therapy creates a change. In these cases, spaying the bitch is the only real cure.

Prenatal Care

If your bitch is not in top physical form, she should not be bred in the first place. Obesity, depravation, worms, and any other condition indicating lack of care are all matters that have to be taken care of well ahead of the time a bitch is bred. Attempting to cure health problems after the bitch is bred will only complicate an already bad situation. The loss of the pregnancy, and even the dam, is possible.

If you've attended to your responsibilities and you had your bitch in optimum shape before breeding, you need to do very little for the first several weeks of her pregnancy. Food intake should remain basically the same — perhaps a trace more, in total, and you may want to divide the daily rations up into several small meals rather than just one large one.

Exercise

Do not, and I repeat *do not,* think that a pregnant bitch has to wait out her nine weeks lounging on a chaise lounge. This is the worst possible thing that could happen to her! A whelping bitch needs good muscle for the contractions that assist easy delivery. For the first three to four weeks after she's been bred, the mother-to-be can continue doing whatever it was she was doing before she was bred.

Mom Nature is back in action, and has means to protect the bitch and the puppies. If the bitch has been engaged in activities like hunting, tracking, and swimming, no reason whatsoever exists that she can't continue to do these things during the initial weeks of pregnancy.

Although a bitch can continue with her normal physical routine, don't choose the first few weeks of a pregnancy to have her learn how to jump off the tops of buildings or enter the Dogathon event at the Canine Olympics. She probably wouldn't choose to do those things herself at this time, so don't you go pushing her into situations that test her limits when she's been bred.

After the fourth week you can start regulating — not discontinuing! — her exercise. Something a bit more placid is okay. An invigorating walk around the block at a normal pace two or three times a day will do wonders for her — and get you in shape for all those demanding little strangers who are due to come for a visit.

Diet

Puppies in the womb are entirely dependent on their mother for their nutritional needs. This dependency continues after birth and up until the time the puppies are weaned. You need to start bringing the mom to an optimum level of health so that she can fulfill this need long before breeding time.

The drain of providing her pups nutrition takes its toll on dams who are in the best of health. It should not be difficult to understand that the bitch who is not in optimum health before her pregnancy is going to be reduced to a dangerously low level of well-being as the fetuses develop within her.

A dam in poor health transfers poor health on to her puppies, who are born in a weakened condition, often suffering from fading puppy syndrome, a condition that can lead to poor development, compromised growth rate, and often death.

Every breeder you talk to has a different take on their dogs' diets at any time, and especially so when it comes to feeding a bitch during pregnancy. There is one point that you are apt to find almost universal agreement on, however, and that concerns the use of vitamins and minerals during pregnancy. Overdoses of these additives are now known contributors to congenital abnormalities. As a result, some breeders are adamantly opposed to supplements of any kind when well-balanced and nutritious food is being fed to pregnant bitches.

A wide variety of quality commercially manufactured dog food is available for practically every phase of a dog's life. Foods are carefully produced to supply all the nutritional needs that a dog has at any stage of life, from puppyhood on through to old age. Do not upset the correct balance of these foods by adding anything to them unless you fully understand the consequences.

Discuss dietary supplements with your vet. Clipping the ingredients label off the bag that your kibble comes in and taking it along with you when you visit your vet is a good idea. Ingredient information is required by law to appear on all commercially sold dog food, whether dry or canned.

At about the fifth week of pregnancy, you will likely notice a sharp increase in appetite. By the time D-Day arrives, a bitch will normally have increased her food intake somewhere in the area of 15 percent to 25 percent. Some of the larger Sporting breeds who appear famished around the clock on a normal basis are capable of consuming huge quantities of food during pregnancy. Be extremely careful in these cases. Unreasonable weight gain can occur and can lead to a whole myriad of problems, extreme diarrhea not the least of them.

Environment

Through the years, congenital disorders have been considered the result of heredity. Science and research now reveal that a good many of these disorders can be attributed to exposure to pesticides and herbicides. Although no dog owner would intentionally expose his dog to the chemicals present in pesticides, many of these agents can be absorbed through dogs' feet or if they're present in the plants and grass a dog's toys or bones lie in. Intake of antibiotics and other medications should also be monitored very closely by your vet during pregnancy.

Vet visits

Emergency situations during whelping are the exception rather than the rule, but when they do occur, the last thing you want to waste time on is trying to locate a veterinarian who can handle the situation. As large and fully staffed as many modern animal hospitals are today, they do not handle emergency situations that take place after hours.

Knowing who to call and where to go in the event of complications your bitch might experience during whelping is extremely important. Having this information at hand could save your entire litter, and your bitch's life as well.

Most vets are capable of performing caesarean sections (surgical removal of puppies) if needed. However, not all vets are experienced at dealing with your breed of dog under these circumstances. Different breeds do not react to surgery, pre-anesthetic agents, or anesthetics in the same way. What works for some breeds may be fatal in other breeds.

If your vet is not fully experienced in dealing with the peculiarities of performing caesarean sections for your breed, it is imperative that you provide this information for him or locate a vet who has had the experience. The breeder from whom you purchased your bitch or long-time breeders of your breed who reside in the same area as you do will be able to provide you with the information that you need.

Chapter 15

Whelping the Litter

. . . .

In This Chapter

▶ Setting up your maternity ward

▶ Whelping — "Go boil some water!"

▶ Dealing with whelping problems

▶ Feeding pups yourself

. . . .

As highly civilized and evolved as you think your mother-to-be is, when it comes time to heed nature's call and unload that burden she's been carrying around, her lupine ancestry kicks back in. An underground cave, a hole dug under the foundation of the house, or even the back corner of the guest room closet are the places that Trixie is most likely to select for the blessed event.

For her, it's all about secrecy and privacy. Convenience and accessibility are the last things on her mind. If none of the options I just mentioned seem viable, you are going to have to make preparations that are a compromise between what you want and what the anticipating mother can live with. This chapter helps you put together a maternity ward that's fit to house your eagerly awaited royal rascals.

The Maternity Ward

The gestation period of pups is normally 59 to 63 days, so you have more than enough time to be well prepared for the birth of the coming litter. One of the first orders of business is deciding which room in the house is going to serve as your delivery room. You can change locations after the pups are born and as they grow, but initially you probably won't have a whole lot of choices. The room has be one that affords the nursing mom some privacy and quiet, away from the mainstream of household traffic.

The room must be one that enables you to provide a constant temperature for the newborn pups. With few exceptions, a chilled pup is a dead pup! This applies to pups of any breed and size, but it's particularly true for the tiny and more constitutionally fragile breeds. The ideal temperature for newborn and nursing puppies is somewhere between 80 and 85 degrees Fahrenheit at all times.

Hanging an infrared heat lamp above the whelping box is an ideal way to make sure newborn pups are kept at the proper temperature.

Do not clip a heating lamp to the side of the whelping box. It can easily be dislodged and start a fire. A heating pad in the whelping box is not much safer because most mothers are constantly scratching and digging in their whelping box and, if you aren't there, electric shock could occur or the pad could bury the puppies.

The whelping box

The whelping box is sort of the canine baby crib — a quintuplet-type baby crib, that is. This is where the pups will be born and where the mother and her brood will spend the first several weeks of the pups' lives together.

You can purchase a whelping box ready-made from pet emporiums or build one at home. The boxes can be made out of just about anything, from a cardboard box or wooden shipping crate to a kiddies' plastic wading pool. It all depends on the size and chewing proclivities of your breed of dog.

If you are going to have more than one litter in your lifetime as a breeder, I would suggest that you buy or build a box constructed of well-sanded wood, because the puppies will continue to use it as their bed even after they have been weaned. As the puppies grow, you will find them leaving the whelping box to relieve themselves, thus assisting you in the first stages of their housebreaking. When the pups move on to adult quarters, you can scour and sanitize the box and have it ready for the next litter.

The box should be large enough to allow your bitch to lie down on her side and fully stretch out. The box does not have to be covered, but if it is, the top should be high enough to allow the mother to stand completely upright, and at least one side should be low enough to allow her easy access. You don't want to make it necessary for her to leap over the side and into the box, as she may land right on top of one of her pups.

The best whelping boxes have one side that is either hinged or slatted. The slats can be removed or the sections let down as necessary, leaving easy access for mom but making it hard for the newborn pups to tumble out.

When the pups start toddling around, all the slats can be removed and they can enter and exit at will. You'll be amazed at how quickly the little guys learn that outside the box is the place to relieve themselves!

In some breeds, the moms are slightly less than bright about infant care. They are known to roll over onto their pups and fall asleep before they realize that the comfy cushions they are lying on are their own pups! Bulldogs and Bull Terriers are prize winners in this respect. I guess it's because they have such a high tolerance for discomfort they don't realize that little lump they're lying on is alive. Not good for the fragile babies! For this reason, many of the professionally constructed boxes have what is referred to as a *pig rail* around the interior. This is a shelf along the inside wall that gives the pups a bit of a crawl space to protect themselves from clumsy mothers.

The important thing is that your female should be able to hop in and out of the whelping box easily without injuring her puppies. Once in, she should be able to stretch out fully on her side so that all her teats will be available for the puppies to nurse on.

Keep the bottom of the whelping box lined with several layers of newspaper or unprinted newspaper stock, which can be obtained at most printing shops and will keep mother and puppies much cleaner looking. A blanket can be placed on top of the papers prior to the delivery of the pups, but when the female goes into labor, you should remove the blanket as it will only be in the way when the bitch scratches and digs her nest. Also, pups could get tangled up and lost or smothered in a blanket very easily during whelping.

Your own ER

As the time draws near for the actual whelping, it helps tremendously to gather all the equipment and aids you'll need and have them sterilized and in working order. After you put a piece of equipment in your whelping room, leave it there! And make sure you promise the firing squad to anyone who takes anything out of the room. After whelping starts, you'll not be pleased to find that sister Susie has taken away the exact item you need and has stashed it in her doll hospital. A well-equipped and organized whelping room will assist you in insuring that the delivery goes smoothly. Here's a list of necessary standby whelping equipment:

- ✔ Patience. For some reason, the birth process never takes place when you think it should.
- ✔ Whelping box.
- ✔ Unprinted newspaper stock. Newsprint makes for soiled pups and the ink isn't good for the pups.

- ✔ Toweling. Use it to dry off and stimulate pups that are slow to start breathing.

- ✔ Gauze pads.

- ✔ Small box with adjustable heating pad. This is a good place to put the newborn pups when the mother is working on the next delivery.

- ✔ Emergency supplemental feeder.

- ✔ Patience.

- ✔ Mother's-milk replacement.

- ✔ Glucose. A drink of warm milk and glucose is a great energy restorer that can be offered to a bitch having a difficult time or who is whelping a large litter.

- ✔ Rectal thermometer.

- ✔ Disposable latex gloves.

- ✔ Blunt sterilized scissors. Use them for cutting the umbilical cords.

- ✔ Cotton thread. Use it if you need to tie off the umbilical cord.

- ✔ Lubricant.

- ✔ Scale.

- ✔ Spiral notebook and pen.

- ✔ Infrared lamp.

- ✔ The telephone number of your vet or 24-hour emergency clinic.

- ✔ Patience.

- ✔ *More patience!*

The Miracle of Birth

Some breeders believe that nature provides a bitch with all the instinctual birthing knowledge necessary and that the owner should interfere as little as possible — that is, of course, other than stepping in when complications arise. Those who subscribe to this approach believe interference robs dogs of their natural abilities and perpetuates lines incapable of caring for themselves.

Other breeders leave nothing to chance and perform a good many of the steps (removing birth sacs, cutting cords, and so on). Their approach rises from the belief that any puppy lost could have been the best puppy in the litter — the very reason for making the breeding in the first place.

Personally speaking, I feel that if a breed is basically healthy, with none of the abnormal breed points that make whelping difficult, the female herself will take care of everything. My role is always that of a careful observer, and I always have all necessary equipment on hand to forestall complications that would endanger the life of a healthy puppy.

A good part of the equipment I've so obsessively assembled goes all but untouched. But it's there when and if I need it. But on the other hand, I have never owned or assisted at the birth of puppies of a breed in which dams are physically unable to perform the necessary functions themselves. The bull breeds (Boston Terriers, Bulldogs, French Bulldogs) have difficulty delivering their puppies naturally because the heads of the puppies are usually too large to pass through the birth canal. These breeds are normally delivered by caesarean section. In the case of breeds of this kind, I feel it is the breeder's responsibility to supervise and assist in each and every detail until veterinary help is obtained.

Inexperienced breeders who specialize in the more exotic breeds need to keep in close and constant touch with their veterinarian. Many of these breeds require caesarean sections. Timing is critical in these cases.

Whelping a litter for the first time usually proves to be more traumatic for the owner than for the dog. Mom Nature has provided your female with a whole set of instincts that rise to the surface when the proper time comes. On the very rare occasions when a female does not respond properly, or if you suspect something is wrong, call your veterinarian at once. A veterinarian is trained to know what to do and when to do it. There is no reason for you to try to guess your way along when years of study and experience are as accessible as your nearest telephone.

Getting ready ahead of time

Be completely prepared for the whelping at least a week before your female is actually due. (Be prepared for it to happen in the middle of the night, as well. That seems to be the preferred time for puppies to arrive!) Some females are a few days early, others a few days late. When one of my females was running late, especially if it was her first litter, I usually took her to our vet just to make sure that there were no complications.

As the time approaches for your female to give birth, don't allow her to be outside unattended. You can't imagine how inventive some mothers-to-be can become in finding a little den under the house or some other inaccessible place to whelp. Keep her in or near her whelping box as much as possible.

Signs that she's ready

The female's temperature will usually drop from a normal 101.5 degrees Fahrenheit (38.6 Celsius) to 99 degrees Fahrenheit (37.2 Celsius) within 48 hours of the time she begins whelping. General restlessness, shivering, and panting often accompany this temperature change.

There will often be a clear mucous discharge from the vulva that acts as a lubricant during the whelping process. The female will begin scratching in her whelping box, preparing a nest in which to deposit her puppies. Some females will vomit during this stage.

These signs can continue for up to 24 hours before contractions actually begin. Although the female is obviously experiencing discomfort, there is no need to get overly concerned unless she appears to be in pain.

Delivery begins

Uterine contractions increase in frequency and intensity and the vulva and vagina slowly begin to dilate. Often, the laboring mother will swing around to investigate her rear end and then lie down, stretching her rear legs to press against the sides of the whelping box or squat and strain as if she is trying to relieve her bowels. She may howl or whimper during these contractions.

If contractions continue and no puppies arrive within the next two hours, seek the advice of your veterinarian. In some cases, a puppy is too large to be passed naturally and a caesarean section may be needed.

The puppies arrive

The first puppy is usually preceded by a water bag that breaks and serves as a warning that a puppy is about to be whelped. After a few minutes and more contractions, the first puppy will work its way along the birth canal and begin to emerge from the vulva, usually head first, as shown in Figure 15-1. After the head has emerged, the female may rest a moment or two before expelling the rest of the whelp. It will be contained in a membrane sac sometimes connected by the umbilical cord to the placenta.

The puppy must be removed from the sac either by the mother or by you. Normally, the mother immediately gets to work and does all that is necessary, breaking open the sac, biting through the umbilical cord, and licking the puppy until the pup starts breathing and gives a loud cry.

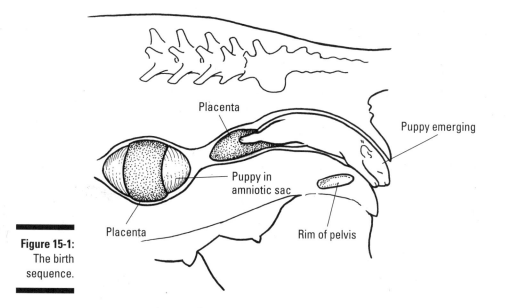

Placenta

Puppy emerging

Puppy in
amniotic sac

Placenta

Rim of pelvis

Figure 15-1:
The birth
sequence.

On rare occasions, a female whelping her first litter may seem to be totally surprised by the arrival of her first puppy and, lacking the maternal instinct, will only look at it in complete amazement. It is then time for you to act. If the puppy remains in the sac, it will drown and die.

If you need to intervene, break open the membrane at the puppy's head and grasp the umbilical cord about two inches from the abdomen, draining the fluid in the cord toward the puppy. Immediately sever the cord at this point with the sterilized scissors. Rub the puppy vigorously with rough toweling to stimulate circulation.

It is wise to make sure that the puppy's nose and throat are clear of mucus at this time. Support the puppy in the palm of one hand with the head toward your fingers. Cover and hold the puppy securely with your other hand. Raise your arms above your head and swing the puppy downward in an arc. The centrifugal force will expel any fluids remaining in the nasal or throat passages.

Newborn puppies are far less fragile than most people imagine, so do not be afraid to be vigorous in stimulating the newborn whelp. Use a drop of disinfectant to sterilize the cut end of the umbilical cord that is still attached to the puppy.

Breech births

Normally puppies are born head first, but *breech births,* in which the puppy is born hind legs first, are not entirely uncommon. You don't really need to worry about this if your breed is a normally constructed one without structural exaggerations that in themselves lead to difficult whelping. Breech births in large-headed breeds like Bulldogs, Boston Terriers, and so on can be difficult because the head of the puppy may not be easily passed. Drowned puppies can result.

You can gently assist a breech birth if your help seems necessary. Help may be required if the breech occurs further along in the whelping process, when the female may be tired and her contractions not as strong. In this case, slip on the latex glove and firmly grasp as much of the puppy as has emerged.

As the contractions occur, simultaneously ease the puppy out. It is important to have a firm grasp on as much of the puppy's body as possible when you do this. Do not pull sharply, as you risk injuring the mother. Should you be unable to dislodge the puppy in this manner after ten to fifteen minutes, consult your veterinarian.

Some puppies are slow to start breathing. If the mother does not see to this immediately, rub the puppy vigorously and follow the procedure I just described to remove any fluid from the lungs. After you are sure that the pup is breathing regularly, you may return him to his mother.

If the placenta has not been expelled along with the puppy, the female will normally expel it shortly after the puppy is born. There is one placenta for every puppy born, and they must each be accounted for. The mother instinctively wants to eat the placentas. Allow her to have one, because the placenta contains useful nutrients. However, allowing her to eat them all can lead to severe diarrhea. I suggest quickly removing the rest of the placentas as they are passed. Wrap them in newspaper and place them in the trash.

Barring unforeseen circumstances, the puppies will usually follow each other in irregular succession. Litters vary in number from breed to breed, but again, nature has never fully understood the meaning of the word *average* and can be very arbitrary in deciding such things as numbers.

There is no need to be concerned if the female takes time out to rest between births. But if she continues to strain and no puppies are passed, consult your veterinarian.

After Whelping

After a puppy has been dried and is breathing properly, weigh him and record the time he arrived along with the color or distinguishing marks he may have. You'll need this information to be able to track weight gains and losses.

WARNING!

Caesarean delivery

In some situations, surgical intervention is required to deliver a litter. Pelvic malformations, poor muscle tone, and hormonal imbalance on the part of the bitch or overly large and abnormal presentation of puppies can impede or totally block normal birth. Caesarean delivery is required in these cases.

In a good many cases, your vet will be aware of the impending need well ahead of actual delivery time and surgery can be planned for. This is not always the case, however. Be certain you know what number to call at your regular veterinary hospital in case of an emergency. If your vet does not provide emergency service, you should be familiar with the location of a clinic that does and you should have that telephone number available.

Plan on being present during the surgery. While the veterinarian in charge of the surgery is concentrating on delivering the puppies, the assistant may be absorbed with caring for their mother. You can give the puppies the attention they need as they are delivered. Anesthetic delivered to the mother makes puppies groggy, and even the healthy ones are too sleepy and depressed to put much effort into breathing. Making sure they do breathe will be your important job.

Because of the anesthesia involved and the lack of the natural birth process, you may need to make some extra efforts to get the pups to bond with their mom. But after the light dawns, both mother and puppies normally progress as if nothing unusual has happened.

Then allow the puppy to nurse on the mother until contractions begin again. You'll be amazed at the vigor of most newborn pups and how quickly they find their mother's milk bar! Sometimes you'll have a puppy who needs to be guided to her mother's teat or given assistance to nurse. More often than not, it is a case of insuring that the larger, stronger puppies do not push their smaller littermates out of the way and keep them from getting their fair share of milk.

When the mother's birth contractions resume, remove the previously born puppies and place them in a small box right next to the whelping box so that the female can see that her puppies are safe as she prepares to give birth to the next one. On the bottom of the small box, place a heating pad or not-too-hot water bottle covered in towels. Doing so keeps the puppies warm while they are away from the mother. It is critical that newborn and nursing puppies not become chilled! Their temperature-regulating systems are not fully functional at this stage.

Throughout the whelping process, keep water available for the female and also a bowl of broth or milk at room temperature. After whelping has been completed and you have cleaned up the whelping box, offer the nursing mother light food, such as chicken and rice or even scrambled eggs.

Veterinary checkup

It is wise to have this checkup performed within 24 hours of whelping to avoid any complications and to make sure that the mother has not retained any puppies. The veterinarian will also inspect the puppies at this time to make sure that there are no abnormalities.

Retaining a placenta can cause serious infection in the mother. If you suspect one has been retained, mention this to your veterinarian when you take the mother and puppies in for their first checkup. Your vet can administer an injection that will insure the bitch expels any undesirable afterbirth.

Dewclaw removal

The first checkup is the time when the puppies' dewclaws should be removed, if removal is customary and recommended for your breed. Removal of dewclaws is standard procedure for most breeds. But some breed standards require dewclaws if a dog is to be shown. The dewclaws of Great Pyrenees, Briards, and the rare Norwegian Lundehund and Beauceron must not be removed.

Tail docking

If it is customary for your breed to have its tail docked, the first checkup is the time that most veterinarians like to do the dock. There are exceptions, however, and in some cases, like if the breed is very small or the puppies are born prematurely, a vet may want to wait a few days for tail docking.

Not all veterinarians are familiar with correct tail docking for all the breeds that require the procedure. Nothing destroys a dog's balance more than having a tail that is too short or too long. Be sure that your veterinarian has had experience in this respect. If not, it is imperative that you have an experienced breeder supervise the procedure or find a vet who knows the appropriate place to dock the tail for your breed.

Many breed standards prohibit any docking, and if the tail has been dealt with in this manner, the dog is barred from the show ring. It is important that you know what is required for your breed in this respect.

Many breeders dock tails themselves. A popular method is *rubber-band* docking. A rubber band is tightened around the appropriate place on the tail The banded tails shrivel and fall off within three to five days. Those breeders who use this method feel it is cleaner and causes less discomfort to the puppy than using a knife or shears.

Rubber-band docking is not a method for the novice to attempt without instruction from an experienced breeder. However, observing a breeder band the tails on a litter or two should prepare the new breeder to do so as well.

Peace and quiet

Other than the important first trip to the veterinarian, the mother and puppies should be given as much peace and quiet as possible. Undoubtedly, everyone in the household, if not the entire neighborhood, will want to see the puppies. Remember that the mother wants and deserves privacy. Many diseases can be carried from one household to another on clothing and shoes. Young puppies are extremely vulnerable at their early age. It is best not to let anyone outside of the immediate household touch the youngsters.

Some breeds are highly protective of their offspring, and strangers coming and going can be upsetting. An otherwise calm and friendly family member is quite capable of greeting people she does not know well with a threatening growl.

What the new mother needs is privacy. Giving it to her permits her to settle in with the important duties of motherhood. Warmth and sustenance are primarily what young puppies require. A constant flow of strangers upsets the mother and disturbs the puppies.

Water and food

Make sure that the mother has plenty to drink at all times. She must not become dehydrated. The female's appetite will begin to increase significantly a day or two after whelping and she should be fed several times a day. Give her as much as she wants to eat. Her regular nourishing meals should be resumed and supplemented with meaty soups and thick broths. Many breeders switch to puppy chow in place of the regular adult kibble because there are more nutrients in these specially prepared formulas.

Post-whelping complications

Occasionally, post-whelping complications do arise. Being aware of the symptoms is important, as your vigilance can prevent serious complications. Potential complications include the following:

- **Mastitis:** An inflammation of the mammary glands usually associated with bacterial infections, the infection is introduced into the bloodstream through a skin lesion or through the teat canal. An excess of milk in the female can also cause the breasts to become hard and painful. This is common when nursing females have only one or two puppies and too much milk, as some nipples rarely get used. Examine breasts regularly and massage them gently if milk is building up. If your female seems to be in pain or if one or more glands seem excessively red or hot to the touch, call your veterinarian at once.

- **Eclampsia:** This is a much more serious condition but far less common than mastitis. It is caused by a shortage of calcium in the bloodstream. It may occur just before or any time after whelping, but usually at about three to four weeks after the puppies are born. Symptoms are the mother's extreme restlessness, often accompanied by shivering and vomiting. Her legs or entire body can go stiff, and convulsions may occur. Veterinary treatment must be sought at once. Massive injections of calcium are usually administered, and recovery is normally rapid, but the mother should not be returned to her litter as she will undoubtedly relapse.

- **Metritis:** Metritis is an inflammation of the uterus, and is usually the result of contamination entering the uterus during whelping, or from a retained placenta, or sometimes as a result of bacterial contamination during mating. Fever, abdominal pain, discharge from the vulva, and straining may be seen. Veterinary care is essential to treat this condition.

- **Pyometra:** Pyometra is not directly related to the birth process but occurs between heat periods. Bacteria in the resting uterus multiply and the resulting infection fills the uterus with pus. The bitch often exhibits depression and a fever, and there may be a bloody or foul-smelling discharge from the vulva. In some cases, there may be no discharge, but the uterus may be swollen and the abdomen tender. Advanced cases are very serious and may be life threatening. Only a veterinarian can treat this condition, and surgery that ends in having the female spayed may be necessary.

Hand Rearing

Sometimes a puppy or an entire litter will have to be given supplemental feedings or be completely hand raised. This may be necessary for a number of reasons. At times, individual puppies in the litter are too weak to obtain the necessary amount of milk to maintain optimum growth, or the mother may not be able to nurse any of her puppies because of complications of one sort or another.

Providing warmth and feedings every two hours is critical if you're hand raising a puppy.

Keep mother's-milk replacement and all the necessary feeding apparatus on hand prior to whelping day, just in case you must give assistance. Veterinarians are probably the best source of these items, and you can get necessary instructions in how to hand feed should you have to do so.

Follow all instructions from your veterinarian, as well as the instructions on the feeding product's container. A puppy's digestive system is very delicate and can easily be upset, causing diarrhea, dehydration, and even death.

Many different methods used by breeders and recommended by veterinarians can be used for supplemental feeding. Discuss this issue with your veterinarian, who can not only provide you with any equipment you may need, but also can give you instructions on how to properly proceed with hand rearing or supplementing for one puppy or an entire litter.

Bottle feeding

For newborn puppies of medium to large breeds, a human baby bottle with a baby-sized nipple will do very well for hand feeding. The puppies will learn to use these nipples quite easily. Puppies who nurse naturally on their mother suck far more than just the nipple itself into their mouths; therefore, they have little or no trouble using the baby bottle.

Place the puppy on a rough bath towel on your lap. This surface allows the puppy to dig in with her hindquarters and gain traction, enabling her to knead with her front legs while she is nursing. I find that this method most closely approximates natural nursing and has been the most successful, causing the fewest problems in the long run.

The puppy may not accept the nipple at first. You may have to gently open her mouth. Make sure the puppy's tongue is at the bottom of the mouth, so that she can suck properly. Inserting the nipple into the puppy's mouth will be easier if the nipple is squeezed flat.

If the puppy doesn't start sucking immediately, squeeze a few drops of milk into her mouth. Usually, a taste of what is to come will inspire most puppies to start chowing down in earnest. Still, there is the reluctant pup who is bound and determined that Mom is the only way to go, and you will have to be a bit more persistent and patient. Be sure to keep the bottle tilted at an angle so that the nipple is continually filled with milk, as you do not want the puppy to suck in air.

Newborn puppies need small quantities of food often. Healthy puppies' appetites will increase in small increments every day or so. They will usually pull back and turn their heads when satisfied. As long as their abdomens seem firm and filled, but not bloated, they are doing just fine. If a puppy seems gaunt and isn't gaining weight, consult your veterinarian.

Syringe feeding

Many breeders use the syringe method of hand feeding newborn puppies because it is so easy to control the rate of formula flow, even for those middle-of-the-night feedings when you may not be fully awake. Use an insulin syringe with the needle discarded.

Place the puppy on a bath towel and gently open the puppy's mouth with one hand, using the thumb and index finger. Place a drop at a time on the center and back of the puppy's tongue. When the puppy begins to swallow, add another drop or two. Most puppies will take to the procedure very quickly and begin to swallow with little difficulty. You can then very slowly increase the flow.

Tube feeding

Tube feeding is a great timesaving method that is especially useful when a good number of puppies must be fed. A tube is inserted into the puppy's stomach through the mouth and formula is inserted into the tube with a syringe.

This is not a technique for anyone to attempt without instruction. Your veterinarian can teach you how to feed this way and will be able to supply all the equipment you will need to do so properly.

Tube feeding insures you that each puppy receives the proper amount of formula and is especially helpful for the puppy who is a reluctant nurser. But do not attempt to tube feed until you are confident you can do it correctly!

Cleanup time

If you are completely taking over for the puppies' mother, you will have to perform the functions the mother normally assumes. Clean the puppy's mouth of any milk that has accumulated there with a piece of cotton slightly dampened with warm water. Using another swab, gently rub around the area from which the puppy urinates to stimulate it to pass water. This also must be done under the abdomen and around the anal region, encouraging the puppy to empty her bowels.

When this has been accomplished, rub these same areas with a very small amount of Vaseline to avoid chafing and irritation. This procedure must be repeated every time the puppies are fed from a bottle.

Obviously, this procedure is going to take a significant amount of time. Hand rearing puppies is no mean feat, especially during the first two weeks when the newborn whelps must be fed every two hours. After the second week, feeding times may be spaced to two-and-a-half to three hours apart. By the end of the third week, you can begin introducing the orphans to solid food.

Puppies who have been nursing on their mother's milk will have derived a degree of natural immunity from her that will last several weeks. After that, they need individual immunization. Puppies who have been completely hand raised will not have this immunity, and must be protected from coming in contact with any of the airborne contagious diseases. These diseases can be transmitted through contact with infected dogs or by coming in contact with the clothing worn by people who have been around infected dogs.

Chapter 16

Growth and Development of Puppies

There they are, that box full of wiggling little lumps, none of whom would be there if it weren't for you. And they all depend solely on you for — *everything!* Unlike a human child, a puppy never reaches that stage where you wash your hands, say you've done all you can and then pack them off to seek their fortune while you cool your heels down in Fort Lauderdale or Acapulco.

Nope, you supervise a pup's well-being from birth to weaning, through the growth period, and, in fact, for the rest of the dog's life — or at least its life with you. Your responsibility is to see that each pup you breed becomes "all that he or she can be." And if the pups don't live up to that potential, you get all the blame! Remember, you're the breeder. People judge you on the dogs you send out into the world.

That plump and content pup in the box in front of you will spend its entire life in the company of humans. Regardless of where one of your puppies shares its time with humans — show ring, field, police beat, or as a rescue dog — it will be done in the company of mankind.

Because it's by your design that the puppy made its way into this world in the first place, it becomes your responsibility to do everything in your power to provide the groundwork that will enable the youngster to one day achieve its full potential. When you do so, you will be know that you've done everything possible to make sure the dog you've bred earns the respect of everyone it encounters.

By this point in your career as a dog breeder, you should be well aware of what it takes for a dog of your breed to be considered an ideal representative. Whatever those elements are, they are the ones you must concentrate on developing as your puppies take their first wobbly steps out of the whelping box and catch their first glimpse of the world in which they'll spend the rest of their lives. This chapter helps you take an inventory of all those things that make your breed, your litter, — and each puppy in that litter — unique. You'll also find out what you can do to help the dogs you breed achieve that distinction.

Charting the Course from Day One

When your puppies first arrive, you can't worry about whether or not that little snoozing wonder in the box is going to be a Best in Show winner or Field Trial star. Right now your concerns are about making sure that everything required for getting from day one to day two is in place.

What the puppies need

During the first 24 hours of life, what the puppy consumes from its mother's breast is called *colostrum*, and this nourishment is what provides the puppy with passive immunity. Although a puppy absorbs a certain degree of immunity while still in the womb, the pup acquires almost 90 percent of its immunity from the colostrum. Orphaned puppies or puppies born to dams who are unable to nurse them, have a far greater chance at survival if colostrum is collected from the mother and given to the puppies.

Warmth, quiet, and the mother's milk supply are what bring the puppy to its next important stage of life. The eyes open, and the youngster gets up on its feet to investigate the world around it, Experiments with food other than mother's milk take place and socialization begins.

What you need to be doing

Recording your puppies' weight gains daily from birth and daily for the next two weeks is very important. Puppies have tremendous growth potential and should gain weight daily from the day of birth on. The weight gain is not as rapid during the following two weeks and, therefore, weighing can take place every three to four days. Then weigh every two weeks up to eight weeks and once a month thereafter.

Sometime between seven to ten days a puppy's birth weight should double. By six weeks it should increase by at least six times its birth weight. Recording all birth weights, daily gains, and weights at specific points of development assist a breeder in making educated guesses, if not fairly accurate predictions, of mature size in some breeds. The breeder can choose these points of development, but in order to be of any value in making comparisons, each litter should be weighed at exactly the same intervals.

Even if weights taken at these intervals do not predict mature size in your breed, they do provide information that allows a breeder to compare the progress of the current litter with that of the parents or of other litters. Accurate weight records also allow the breeder to compare progress rates and differences that might exist between linebred and outcrossed breedings. See Chapter 8 for more information on linebreeding and outcrossed breeding.

Birth weight and gain is information that can and should be an addendum to an individual dog's Type Tracking Chart (see Chapter 7). Growth and maturation rates are an important part of a dog's and a breeding program's records.

What to expect as your pups mature

Some lines mature very early. They're ready to hit the show ring as puppies and often "peak" at well under a year. By peaking, I mean the individual dog comes into full bloom and is at the height of his conformation and character while still in puppyhood.

This early maturation point is by far the norm rather than the exception in some breeds — American Cocker Spaniels, to name just one. The point of concern here, however, is how long the early bloomer is able to hold its quality when the peak of development comes at such an early stage.

On the other hand, the Bichons Frise, a breed not a whole lot smaller than an American Cocker, is much slower to mature. Males are seldom really mature enough to cut much of a swath in the win department until they are near to two years old. This slow rate of maturity does lend itself to a longer period in which the breed remains in competition form. Generally speaking, this point holds true for the breeds in general: The slower the rate of maturity, the longer a dog maintains its peak form.

Careful record keeping becomes more useful as the years pass and the number of breedings increase. This information lets a breeder know if his show prospect is maturing at a satisfactory rate or not. Is the fact that the dog lacks size at five to six months significant? Will size come in a short, rapid spurt or over a long period of time? This information is particularly important in measurable breeds — that is breeds that are disqualified from the show ring if they don't achieve or if they surpass certain height or weight limits required by their breed standards.

Birth weight bingo

It is interesting to note how little difference there is in actual birth weights from one breed to the next in respect to what weight at full maturity will be. The average Chihuahua's birth weight is approximately three to five ounces while the Great Dane's is normally four to five times that. But stop to consider the weight of the two breeds at maturity. The well-bred Chihuahua matures at a maximum of 6 pounds and the Great Dane tops the scales well past 100 pounds. Note that the rapid growth experienced by the Great Dane on its relatively short journey to maturity takes a heavy toll on the breed's physiology and longevity. A Chihuahua might live well into its teens, but six to seven years is considered the average life expectancy of the Great Dane.

Food, Glorious Food

At about 10 or 12 days old, most puppies' eyes will have begun to open. Weaning hand-fed puppies can begin at this time, but if the litter has been nursing on their mother, then some animal behaviorists suggest that weaning not begin until the puppies are 28 days old. The reason is that puppies are extremely sensitive to abrupt changes of any kind between the ages of 21 to 28 days. Weaning can be extremely stressful to puppies before this age, so it is best to avoid doing so unless it's absolutely necessary.

At about this time a number of things also begin to occur simultaneously. Mom's milk supply begins to diminish, the pup's first teeth begin to appear, and the pups develop an interest in solid food.

Weaning the pups from mom

When the pups are ready for some solid food, you can introduce the litter to puppy food specifically designed for the weaning period. The easiest way to assist the transition of puppies from entire dependency upon their mother to a self-sufficient state is to allow the transition to happen gradually.

Consider the following transition tips:

- The tiniest sliver of raw lean ground beef on the end of your finger usually delights a pup and introduces it to the fact that all good things do not necessarily have to come from mom. A very small amount of the beef can be added to a puppy gruel to tempt the litter into eating on its own.

- There are now good quality "puppy chows" available that can be soaked and made into an easily digestible mixture from the first day of weaning.

You can use cow's milk, goat's milk, or any one of a number of commercial brands prepared especially for dogs.

Mother should have some outdoor time while you are feeding her brood or she'll eat what you've put down and then regurgitate the food for the puppies. In the wild, Mama Wolf would come back from the hunt and regurgitate half-digested food in front of her brood to get them interested in a food source other than what she provided. This instinct has been handed down through the ages to canine mothers who take up the practice as their offspring come toward the end of their nursing phase and are ready to eat on their own.

Most humans find the dam's regurgitating her food for her puppies a disturbing and offensive habit, but it is not harmful to the puppies in any way unless the mother has passed back large lumps of meat or other solid food. To avoid this, it is best to keep the mother away from her puppies for at least an hour after she has eaten.

After weaning has begun, start cutting back on the time the mother is with her puppies to the point where she is allowed to be in with them only to relieve her of an accumulated milk supply. Doing so hastens the reduction of milk flow and gives the puppies greater incentive to eat the food you give them.

Feeding puppy food

By two months of age pups should be fed puppy food. The pups are in an important phase of life growth! Skeletal development is at its peak for the first six months of life. Nutritional deficiencies and/or imbalances during this period are far more devastating than at any other time and result in long physical damage as well.

During this phase puppies develop a functioning immune system, dramatically add bone and muscle mass, and learn all about their new environment; all the while developing proper socialization behaviors. This period is the most critical time to ensure proper nutrition.

Keep these guidelines in mind:

- Feed a high-quality diet that meets the specific nutritional needs of your breed.

- Purchase a food specially designed for this growth period, and be certain that the manufacturer has conducted feeding trials.

- Keep your puppies on this diet until they are at least 12 to 18 months of age, again depending on the nutritional needs of the breed. Most large breeds don't mature until at least 18 months of age and so benefit from a longer period on these fortified rations.

Adult food considerations

The amount and kind of food fed to the adult dog depends entirely upon the breed and how the individual dog spends its day. "Speck" the working Australian Cattle Dog is going to require far more food per day for his size than his pal Polo the Great Dane, who though much larger, lives in a Downtown Manhattan apartment and gets his exercise by walking a sedate mile or so a day around Central Park.

Pups should be fed four times a day for the first two weeks after they are no longer nursing. The first meal should be given early in the morning and about every four to five hours thereafter. At least three of these meals should be semisolid food. The other one or two meals can consist of milk with perhaps a small amount of baby cereal or puppy kibble added.

When the puppies are completely weaned, they should also learn to eat from separate dishes. One or two bullies in the litter are likely to stand in the middle of a communal food pan and intimidate the less bold littermates. Separate dishes allow you to see how much each puppy is eating; you can feed the slow eater alone if necessary.

After at least two full weeks of four meals a day, you can cut down to three meals (morning, noon, and night). At five tosix months old, you can substitute dog cookies or hard biscuits for the midday meal. Maintain that routine until they convert to adult food.

Puppy Behavioral Development

Following the work of canine behaviorists John Paul Scott and John Fuller, character development in puppies is now generally divided into five fairly distinct stages. In truth, it's the behaviorists who pay the most attention to these stages because dogs do what they do when they're ready to do it and not before. Therefore, as in most things with nature, the stages are not a cut-and-dried affair. A puppy doesn't wake up on the morning of its 14th week of existence and take on a brand new set of behaviors appropriate to its new stage of adolescence.

Behavior development is gradual and you'll see a great deal of sliding back and forth. Don't be surprised when young Rover acts like a sane and sensible adult one day and a goofy puppy the next. That said, you can look at the following as transitions each of the pups in your litter will experience at some point or another:

✔ **Neonatal** (birth to 2 weeks): During this time puppies do little more than eat and sleep.

✔ **Transitional** (2 to 3 weeks): As the senses begin to develop puppies begin to become increasingly aware of their environment.

✔ **Socialization** (3 to 13 weeks): Along with this growing sense of environment, the littermates develop an awareness of each other and begin to interact.

✔ **Adolescence** (13 weeks to 6 months +/–): The length of this stage varies considerably from breed to breed and with the individual dog.

✔ **Adulthood:** Sexual maturity is probably the most defining characteristic of this stage, although the behavior of many males indicates a great reluctance to let go of the previous stage for a considerable length of time

Breed character

Most people who are raising a young dog for the first time will wonder just *when* the dog will arrive at the point where it will start acting like what would seem appropriate for the breed. Rest assured what's meant to be there *is* there and if the dog is properly dealt with, breed character will eventually surface right along with full physical maturity and all the things that attracted you to the breed in the first place.

What is also a fact, however, is that breed character is not something that a dog is taught. You can try to teach your Greyhound to behave like a Newfoundland until you're worn to the bone, and you just might possibly get him to feign mild interest in someone cast adrift in the briny deep or to ignore sister Suzie's pet bunny. Don't turn your back, however — not even for a minute — or good old Streak will turn his own back on the drowning man so fast it'll make your head spin and he'll be off in full pursuit of said bunny with malice and forethought.

Now, Greyhounds have many sterling qualities but don't expect them or any breed for that matter to be what they're not. Greyhounds are not water dogs nor are they rescue dogs or inclined to be best buddies with the local rodent population. Thousands of generations of selective breeding made them what they are and no one is going to change that overnight or over a lifetime.

The same principles apply to breed character and sound temperament. It's in the genes or it's not. Plain and simple. It is futile to expect the dogs you breed to be reliable in the capacity for which the breed was created if they don't come from stock that was bred to that purpose.

On the other hand, you can't expect a dog, even the one that has inherited all the right stuff, to excel in those respects if what he has isn't developed.

Inherited natures and abilities normally prevail to some extent, but not always in the manner that we would find appropriate unless properly channeled.

We admire and respect the naturally protective nature of our guard dog breeds but on the other hand we don't want our homes to be protected from everyone we know! "Rajah" has to understand that there are rules to be followed and you are in charge of making those rules.

The easiest way to get Rajah to understand concepts like that is by understanding Rajah. All breeds have highly developed instinctive natures, but how they conduct themselves within the framework of those natures is remarkably individualistic.

Understanding Rajah's individual personality is the key to bringing out his best, whether it's the best scenting ability, protective nature, herding acumen, or deportment in the show ring.

This tenet applies to any dog of any breed you might be involved with.

The "characters" in your litter

As the puppies from your litter emerge from the whelping box and explore the world around them so do their individual personalities emerge and assert themselves. These personalities and the degree to which they are expressed can run the entire spectrum of types. The average litter most often includes the following types.

Leader of the pack

You'll always have one pup in the litter that has declared itself the leader of the pack. You won't miss this one. Pack leaders are first at everything. (Even if they don't get there first they'll bully their way through to the top spot.) The Leader invariably winds up with the best toy and is first in line to be picked up when the service is available.

Some behaviorists believe that the leader types also have the fastest heartbeats of any of the puppies in a litter — up to 25 percent faster in many cases. Naturally you aren't expected to follow the little extrovert around with stethoscope in hand, but in handling the puppies in the litter you may well detect the difference in heartbeats.

Leader-type puppies may throw themselves headlong into doing what's being taught (ring procedure, hunting technique, and so on), but there's just as much chance that the pup can put that determination into defiance. Leader-type dogs need leader-type owners!

Finding amusement in the leader-type pup's aggressive behavior — growling, mouthing, puppy biting, and generally indicating what a little toughie it is — has a very serious down side. This behavior may be cute in puppyhood but encouraging that behavior enforces the tendencies and changing the dog's mind in adulthood can be impossible.

Although the dominant, leader-type dog can be great at what it does, you can't allow the dog to make choices on its own. This point is particularly true of large breeds of dogs. The combination of size and aggressiveness can be lethal, and the unaware or negligent owner will undoubtedly have to pay the consequences at some point.

The adventurer

The adventure lover in the litter puts up with the leader type and stands its own ground if it has to. This pup, however, would rather quietly investigate what is going on in its world.

The adventurer is better in the "wanting to please you" department than the litter's pack leader but that doesn't mean the pup is a total pushover either. This pup could be inclined to be a bit independent simply because it does like to investigate. The adventurer is usually inclined to be somewhat gregarious and capable of sharing its affection with all members of the family and is the kind of dog that would do just as well on the road with a handler as it would traveling to shows with its owner.

You might think of this pup as a sleeper in that it may not stand out from its littermates — neither terribly aggressive nor shy. But in the right hands this pup could be one of those wonderful dogs that is a joy to own and show and could be one that presents relatively few problem behaviors. Do note, however, that I did say *"could be,"* not *"always!"*

The passive pup

Don't confuse the passive type of puppy with one that is downright shy. The passive pup is apt to allow its littermates take what they want and will avoid serious tussles at all costs. While the passive pup doesn't run and cower, it would probably be more than happy to walk the proverbial mile to avoid a confrontation. This fellow (or lass, as the case may be) is usually best at home. Strange situations like air travel, crowded and noisy buildings — the usual things of the average dog shows — may not be passive pup's cup of tea. This type of pup does best with a steady, supportive owner who offers lots of attention and patience.

The passive dog needs lots of reassurance, and though I've had a few of this kind who completed their championships because of their excellent conformation, I was never quite sure how the circumstances of the day would affect them.

In the right hands, the more passive pup can be a whiz at learning because its goal in life is usually to please. Compliance won't be a problem as much as being careful you aren't too aggressive or heavy handed in your training techniques.

The shy one

The shy one, too, is a problem child but one who comes at the opposite end of the spectrum from its pack leader littermate. This puppy seems to react in fear to almost everything, including littermates who play too rough, loud noises, strange people. People who do not know what the situation really is are apt to assume the puppy has been abused when that is not the case at all.

Shy puppies can be born to a litter in which all the other puppies have absolutely delightful temperaments. Shy pups show their temperament right from the time their eyes first open and when they begin to walk around the whelping box. Their treatment and experiences are no different than those of the other puppies. Try as you might, you many never really be able to conquer the puppy's unfounded fears.

You may be able to find a kind and sympathetic owner for this kind of pup. A mature person with no children who understands temperament difficulties and is still happy to provide a home for the pup is most suitable. Even when this is the case, the puppy should always be placed with a proviso that in the event any problem arises that the new owner is not able to cope with, the puppy will be returned to you.

I have seen situations in which shy puppies grew to adulthood as quiet, devoted pets of elderly or at least mature couples. While the stability of the pups improved somewhat, new situations, strange people, or sudden loud noises were a problem throughout the dog's entire life.

Should you find the right home for a puppy of this kind, make sure that the new owners are very clear on what shyness is all about and what kind of behavior they can expect from the puppy all through its life. Homes with children are not an ideal situation for the shy dog. Children can be extremely persistent in what they want, and shy dogs can become not only fearful, but fear biters.

The suspicious one

I would be very concerned about any young puppy that was properly social-ized like its littermates and was still suspicious of strangers or openly aggres-sive toward littermates or especially people. Character of this kind is totally uncharacteristic of young puppies and could lead to dangerous behavior. Even puppies of the guard dog breeds should love the world. The protective nature of even the guard dog breed does not begin manifesting itself until adolescence. Before that time, the pup should be willing to meet all strangers and never show evidence of hostile behavior.

You should never have any thought of breeding the extremely shy, suspicious, or hostile puppy. If a dog of any breed can't be trusted around humans, euthanasia is the only real recourse. A dog of this nature is mentally deficient to be a companion to humans and could cause serious injury if not under guard every moment of its life. This treatment may sound harsh, but, again, there is no purpose for any dog unable to coexist with humans.

Should any breeding you make produce a very shy or hostile puppy, I would take great pains to follow the producing histories of littermates. Bad temperament is something that must be purged from your line at all cost.

Ideal Beginnings for Your Puppies

The ideal environment in which to raise top quality dogs is — emphatically — in a house full of kids who are brought up well! This may not always be possible for all breeds, but the socialization they get in this way is irreplaceable. Whether the litter is Great Danes or Pomeranians, there is no better place for them to spend time (especially their first weeks and months on earth) than in close and constant proximity with humans and especially humans of the youthful kind.

Bringing on the kids (and other folks too)

Puppies and children have a natural affinity for each other and those children who are well trained in puppy care and sufficiently supervised have no equal in the socialization department. Children seem able to teach puppies things like eating from their own dish and behaving for cleanup with relative ease. They have a knack of breaking up puppy squabbles and it seems to take children minutes to leash train a puppy while the same pup will balk and refuse when an adult tries the same thing.

Secluded, sheltered puppies who never see a stranger until they are ready to go off to their new homes are a poor risk in the temperament department. Their ability to take strangers and strange situations in stride lacks cultivation. With reasonable care, after the puppies have had their first inoculations, they should be given the benefit of as many strange sights, sounds, and people as is possible.

Playing dress-up

Friends of mine who raise Rottweilers have a young next-door neighbor who comes to call with a whole wardrobe of doll clothes to dress their puppies in. The puppies get rides in a doll carriage and sit around a tea table fully dressed as if it was the thing every self-respecting Rottie would do. The pups adore all the attention and go to their new homes thinking that children are the greatest playmates in the world.

Getting the puppies out of the house

Savvy breeders make it a point to introduce their puppies to strange environments. For example, if the gang has been raised in the kitchen, a trip outdoors, weather permitting, is arranged. One puppy at a time gets special attention in the family room.

Puppies destined for the show ring should go everywhere with you: the post office, along busy streets, to the shopping mall — wherever. Be prepared to create a stir wherever you go. The public loves puppies of any kind and while they might not want to approach a mature dog, most people are quite taken with the baby puppy and will undoubtedly want to pet your youngster. There is nothing in the world better for the puppy!

It's up to you to make sure the puppy is safe at all times. Don't allow overly rambunctious children or strange dogs to come rushing up to the puppy. Pick the pup up before something like that occurs.

Should your puppy back off from a stranger give the person one of the little snacks and have that person offer it to your puppy. Be sure, of course, that the person holds the puppy correctly so that the puppy doesn't become frightened and struggle to get away. *Insist* your puppy be amenable to the attention of any strangers you approve of, regardless of sex, age, or race. It is not up to your puppy to decide who it will or will not tolerate. You are in charge. You must call the shots.

Dealing with temperamental breeds

Some breeds had a long-standing reputation for difficult temperaments until dedicated enthusiasts admitted to the problem and took the situation in hand. Chow Chow fanciers as a whole owe a great debt of gratitude to long-time breeders such as Dr. Samuel Draper of Lion tamer Chow Chows, Joel Marston of Starcrest, and Bob and Love Banghart of Rebelrun fame. These dedicated breeders have relentlessly preached good temperament and the socialization principle to people in their breed through the years. It shows in their dogs and in the effect their efforts have had on today's Chows.

The Chow Chow by its very nature is somewhat wary of strangers. Some attribute its hand-shyness to poor eyesight. Whatever the reason, if the Chow Chow youngster is not socialized early and well, the inherent wariness can turn into problems. The socialization campaign undertaken by responsible breeders has turned around the reputation of the Chow Chow to where one seldom hears so much as a minor incident due to poor temperament.

Temperament test techniques

Several techniques can reveal a great deal about an individual puppy. Cradling a puppy in your arms and holding it on its back can tell you how willing the youngster is to comply with what you want it to do. Checking ears and feet can bring a number of different reactions. Some pups will comply easily; others will offer mild resistance. The puppy to avoid is one who becomes terrified at something strange occurring or the one who snaps at being intruded upon. No puppy should be anything less than happy and friendly and reasonably able to cope with your little experiments.

Behaviorists can give tests that are more formal and which reveal significant detail in regard to puppies' potential temperament as adults. These tests begin as early as three weeks of age and continue on up to three months.

Good temperament in the kennel?

Socialization with people and exposure to strange situations are important to a puppy's development, but that doesn't mean good temperaments can't be produced in a kennel environment. It just takes diligence and some extra thought. A perfect example of this approach is Rick Tomita and Bill Scolnik's Jacquet Boxer kennels. There, an intelligently planned number of litters are whelped each year. The kennel owners emphasize the parents' temperament, and this characteristic is obvious in the many winners emerging from that bloodline each year.

When the Jacquet puppies make their eventual move from the house to the kennel environment, they are placed in the most strategic of locations. Every person who enters the kennel, employee or stranger, must pass directly by the area where the puppies are kept.

Who could possibly resist stopping to play with a pen full of loving Boxer puppies? As a result, that all-important support and development of the inherited temperament continues. This early and continuous socialization is critical for all dogs, particularly those destined for a show career.

The Vin-Melca approach

Pat Craige Trotter, of Vin-Melca Norwegian Elkhound fame, had a unique way of ensuring that her "high hope" puppies got the socialization they deserved. Often she would have two puppies she especially liked and found too close in quality to make an early decision on which to keep. Because she was a full-time school-teacher while she was campaigning her dogs, these promising puppies were at risk of not getting all the socialization she felt they needed.

On occasion she would place both puppies with a family interested in owning a quality Elkhound. She was particularly partial to families with young children. The agreement was that Pat would return at a given time to reevaluate the puppies and select the one she wanted to keep. The other pup remained with the family. This practice produced beautifully socialized puppies and provided the family with a quality Elkhound it may not otherwise have been able to afford or have access to.

Evidently, the Vin-Melca program worked. No matter what kind of criticism the detractors of her dogs might have come up with through the years, no one could ever say the Vin-Melca Elkhounds were anything less than consummate show dogs with reliable temperaments. Her unprecedented record over the years of ten Hound Group First wins at the famed Westminster Kennel Club held at Madison Square Garden was earned with dogs whose steadiness and willingness to cooperate were legendary.

Evaluating Puppies

A good friend and one of Mexico's most notable judges, the late Robin Hernandez, once made an interesting observation regarding the changes that have occurred in the dog game over these last several decades. "When dogs moved out of the large kennels and into our homes as members of the family, our attitude toward them changed," he said.

"They became 'little people,'" he went on. Unfortunately this was accompanied by a disintegration of our ability to view the dogs objectively — as breeding stock. It isn't too easy to objectively critique a dearly beloved member of one's household.

Allowing sentiment to interfere with your ability to evaluate a dog you've bred or want to breed to is one of the most debilitating blows you can strike against your breeding program. Love dear sweet "Trixie" or "Rover" and let them live on with you for the rest of their lives, but dear memories and the fact that they may be "last of the line" have no bearing on their quality as individuals.

You may want to keep an entire house or kennel full of dog show "rejects" or dogs who carry a long, sad history. That is certainly your prerogative, but you must also consider that with each dog you keep that you don't need, there is one less that you *can* keep that will make a contribution to your breeding program.

When evaluation begins

Some breeders say they select their puppies at birth. Possibly so, and if this is the case, I give these people all the credit in the world. How one keeps track of good, better, and best from a litter of all black Cocker Spaniels, white Bichons or red Irish Setters has always proven a bit of a challenge for me. I am not saying this "at birth" selection process cannot be done, only that it is a unique gift, indeed. Author (and my childhood idol) Albert Payson Terhune claimed he made his selections at birth regularly, and who am I to doubt the word of that venerable icon? I, on the other hand, would be hard-pressed at times to determine so much as the *breed* of some newborn litters because of their at-birth similarity. I leave this method of selection to others.

I used to get quite a chuckle when young breeders would call to report they had a litter, often their first, sired by my Bichon Frise, Champion Chaminade Mr. Beau Monde. Mr. Beau Monde, whelped in 1969, was a very prepotent stud and eventually became the top-producing sire in the breed, a distinction that he holds to this day.

Obviously a litter by him created high hopes for the owners of the bitches bred to him. In their enthusiasm, neophyte breeders would make some astounding claims: "Three could well be Group winners, and there's one that I'm willing to bet will be our first Best in Show dog!" When I'd ask how old the pups were, they would respond, "Oh, they're already eight weeks old now!"

I've never been sure I had a Group or Best in Show winner until the dog had won a Group or Best in Show. I have had some dogs I felt *should have* and never did. Others have surprised me completely with just how much they did win. Know ahead of time? One can always hope, but *know?* I think not! That is up to the whims of nature and the very subjective opinion of the judge.

I like to evaluate my puppies over a long period of time, tracking and eliminating as I go. In a good many breeds, eight weeks is that "magic" age in which, for some inexplicable reason, the pups are almost a miniaturized version of what they will be as adults. This "magic" age varies from breed to breed but most breeders seem to agree it is at about eight weeks that it takes place.

The charting system

Using a charting system (see Chapter 7) to track the development of puppies from a litter takes time and some careful attention to detail, but the payoff is far greater than what you might imagine.

After a generation or two, used in tandem with pedigrees, the charts begin to reveal answers to problems that some breeders never seem able to solve. Complete and accurate charts reveal developmental stages and patterns that can be compared to future litters and individuals. The charts can eventually provide a very accurate picture of what a specific sire or dam is dominant and weak in passing along to their get. Kept over an extended period, the charts can paint a very clear picture of how one's line nicks with other lines, pointing up consistent faults and virtues along with gains and losses made each time an outcross breeding is made.

Beginning the system at the time the litter is first graded is important. Puppies seem to stay in that "miniature adult" stage of eight weeks or so only briefly. Shortly after this, many breeds begin to go through all kinds of peculiar stages. Few puppies "enlarge" in proportion. Some breeds get very gangly and long legged, others appear cloddy and long bodied.

The notes made at eight weeks include both faults and virtues. Simply record at this point. Don't be too hasty with an otherwise good puppy with an obvious flaw. Being patient is especially important until you have been charting enough over several generations to know which shortcomings are temporary and which will not go away or may even get worse.

Here, the question to ask is the same as one would ask of any dog of any age, in the ring or out — "*How much good* is there in this individual?" If the answer is anything less than, "Quite a lot!" there is little point in running the puppy on.

The second evaluation should be made one month later. Even in that short time, it will be obvious that some problems may well have already changed: bites can change, a pup can come up on leg, ear carriage can change, and the runt of the litter can suddenly catch up or even surpass its littermates in that brief period.

Be aware that some faults are highly unlikely to change, which is why taking notes is important. You want to be able to observe the *direction* a pup is taking. Is the low-on-leg pup getting more so, or is it improving? What has the bite done? The point here is to see if the problem is correcting itself or if it is growing worse.

Those whose breeding programs are the result of consistent, closely monitored line breeding will find that charting enables them to predict what given combinations will produce with a reasonable amount of certainty. The system will also reveal where their lines are dominant and where they are weak.

All these elements are factors in helping determine the direction a promising puppy might take or where a disappointing puppy might improve over the course of time.

Part VI
Business or Pleasure?

The 5th Wave   By Rich Tennant

"Watch—I can make him ring that bell just by drooling a little bit."

In this part . . .

One of these days, I'm going to get organized! Sound familiar? If you don't make it happen with your dog breeding program, you'll probably find that the program won't last half as long as you'd like it to. The mantra in the real-estate business is "Location, location, *location.*" In dog breeding, the key is organization, organization, *and more organization.* Budgeting, tax records, registration records, planning litters, charting what you want and what you get — the details are endless. You'll be in a great mess unless you keep accurate records of what's going on. This part helps you organize yourself so that you can conduct your breeding operation, small or large, in a manner in keeping with the top quality stock you've set as your goal.

Chapter 17

No Bizness Like Dog Bizness

Dog breeders want every pup they breed to be the ultimate: a conformation champion, a star in the obedience ring, a Master Hunter, or whatever it is that all the blood, sweat, and tears have been dedicated to creating. Controlling all the variables so they add up to a winner isn't easy, though. Even the best breeders acknowledge that they narrowly miss the mark far more often than they ever actually score a bull's-eye. You need to deal responsibly with all those near misses — but perfectly lovable dogs — who need to have a suitable owner and the right environment in which to live out their lives.

Even if you were to become some miracle breeder who gets exactly what you want in every single litter you breed, there is a limit to just how many of those "perfect" dogs you'll be able to house sensibly. So you need to find homes for these dogs, as well. You'll spend just as much time in locating the right homes for all the dogs destined for family life as you will in dealing with the ones destined for breeding. Save time and effort by knowing just what kind of person you want to own one of your dogs.

Matchmaker, Matchmaker

You know the personality of each pup in your litter better than anyone does. Without thinking much about it, you've given the reticent one a little more encouragement and put the bully in its place every time it was necessary.

Just like the differences that exist within the litter, so will there be differences in those who come to take one of your little darlings home to a new life in their household. It's now your job to match the right dog with the right owner. Above all, you have to make sure that the prospective household is the right one for the breed you have. The biggest supercharged male in your Great Dane litter just might not be the perfect choice for an under 5 foot, 88-year-old retired schoolteacher, nor would a very timid, 3-pound Chihuahua seem to be the right dog for a household commandeered by a quartet of teenaged linebackers.

At the same time, there is a perfect household for the Chihuahua, or you may have just the answer for the football team. It's those matches made in heaven that make all the screening seem worth the effort.

Remember the third degree the breeder you bought your first dog from put you through? Remember what a pain in the neck all those questions appeared to be then? By this time I'm sure you have a much clearer understanding of why you were so intensely grilled. Who in their right mind wouldn't scrutinize someone who was about to go off with what easily represents a good part of their life's work?

After investing as much time, effort, dedication and, yes, *money* as you have in bringing that little pup that's going out the door to its full potential, you want to know that it is leaving your premises for a home that will love and care for it as well as you have.

Anyone interested in obtaining a dog from you has to understand and appreciate the amount of time and work you've invested in your breeding program, and they must also be made aware that your relationship with them does not cease when they walk out the door. What you expect of the prospective owner and what they can rely upon you for should really be stated in writing. In that way, your mutual responsibilities are clearly understood.

Determining whether the potential buyer is someone suitable to become an owner of one of your dogs should begin with the same "Personal Suitability Test" you were screened with when you were starting off. Chapter 3 of this book lists those requirements and you should have answers to all the questions included before you even begin discussing the sale of one of your puppies or adult dogs.

Don't take the screening questions lightly. You've done everything possible to produce top-grade dogs and establish yourself in the dog game as a dedicated professional. The last thing you want to have happen is for your stock or stock your dogs have produced to wind up in some pet shop window or in some commercial dog breeding farm. The best way to avoid this happening is through a *sales contract.*

The Sales Contract: The Ties That Bind!

You, as the breeder, should supply a written agreement that lists everything that you are responsible for in connection with the sale of the dog described. The contract should also list all the things the buyer is responsible for before the sale is actually final. The contract should be dated and signed by both the seller and the buyer. Sales contracts vary, but all assurances and anything that is an exception to the outright and final sale should be itemized.

Some of these conditions might be as follows:

- ✔ Sale is contingent upon dog passing a veterinarian's examination within 24 to 48 hours after it leaves the seller's premises. You should provide a clear statement of your refund policy in the event the examination proves dissatisfactory.

- ✔ Any conditions prevailing regarding seller's requirement for neutering of dog sold.

- ✔ Indication that a "limited registration" accompanies dog (that is, the dog is ineligible to have offspring registered by the respective kennel club).

- ✔ Arrangements that must be followed in the event the buyer is unable to keep the dog regardless of length of time that elapses after sale.

- ✔ Conditions that exist should dog develop genetic bone or eye diseases at maturity.

The contents of sales contracts vary considerably from one buyer to the next and develop in relation to the breed and experiences of the breeder. However, insist that the buyer read the contract carefully to make sure he or she fully understands what is included and what both the buyer and seller are responsible for. The following is an excellent example of what a good sales contract can and should contain. It protects both the buyer and seller.

Of course, you may want to consult an attorney to help you come up with a contract that meets the requirements of the laws of your particular location. The following contract should be considered as an example.

Purchase Agreement/Health Guarantee

DATE_____

This agreement is made between XXXXXXXXX and the BUYER:

NAME_____ PHONE_____

ADDRESS_____

CITY_____ STATE_____ ZIP'_____

for the purchase of the following (enter breed here):

REGISTERED NAME_____

REGISTRATION/LITTER #_____

COLOR_____ SEX____ DATE OF BIRTH_____

SIRE_____ REG#_____

DAM_____ REG#_____

The above said (enter breed here) is sold as a PET_____ SHOW PROSPECT_____ for the total price of $_____. A deposit of $_____($100 minimum) is hereby made and the cash balance is due to Seller before this dog is placed in the Buyer's possession. Registration papers will also be held until balance is paid in full. The Buyer understands that once a deposit is made, it is a commitment to buy said dog and is therefore NON-REFUNDABLE. Buyer will forfeit deposit and said dog may then be re-sold if not paid in full by specified date being _____.

IT IS HEREBY AGREED BY BOTH PARTIES THAT THE FOLLOWING CONDITIONS WILL BE MET AND THAT NO OTHER WARRANTIES OR CONDITIONS ARE EXPRESSED OR IMPLIED.

If this dog has been classified as a PET by Seller, it does not qualify as a Show Prospect/Show Quality dog at this time of sale. This dog is being sold with FULL_____ LIMITED_____ registration.

(Limited registration means that offspring of this dog CANNOT be registered. A SHOW PROSPECT is a dog that goes beyond the definition of a Pet/Companion dog. This dog is not guaranteed to become a Champion of Record, but with the proper care and training on the part of the Buyer and/or Handler, this dog should be a reasonable contender and do well in the show ring.)

Seller guarantees this is a purebred (enter breed here), offspring of the previously mentioned Sire and Dam.

BUYER certifies that he/she is not acting as an agent for another individual in the purchase of this dog, and will not sell this dog to any mass-producing kennel (puppy mill) or business.

The purchaser promises to keep the dog in a proper manner. It shall not be kept permanently in a kennel. If problems arise concerning keeping or training, or if the dog becomes seriously ill, the BUYER agrees to consult the Breeder. If it should prove necessary for the dog to change hands, the Breeder has prior purchase rights for a period limited to two weeks. Selling to a third party is permissible only after prior consultation with the Breeder, whereby the main consideration is the assurance that the dog is passed to responsible owners. This puppy has been bred by us and has been carefully and painstakingly reared. The parent animals were mated with the aim of breeding good and healthy puppies. Seller guarantees this dog to be free of communicable diseases as appears to the eye at the time of sale.

At the expense of the BUYER, this dog should be examined by a licensed veterinarian within 48 hours of possession to validate Health Guarantee. (If purchased on a Saturday, this requirement is extended through the following Monday.) Should this dog be found in ill health, the cause of which is clearly attributable to the Breeder, this dog may, upon written diagnosis from a veterinarian, be returned to Seller for refund of purchase price or for another dog of equal value, the choice to be determined by Seller.

No other warranties are expressed or implied unless explained by Seller below:

In the case of puppy being sold as a pet, the new owner will provide proof of spay/neuter by the age of eight months. Where then Seller will turn over full registration/limited registration to the new owner.

_____

_____

Buyer releases Seller, XXXXXXXXXXXXXX and their estate from any and all liabilities, and/or damages by fault of this dog after the time of sale. These damages include, but are not limited to, destruction of property and/or physical damage to any person or group of people.

This contract is made out in duplicate; the Seller and the Buyer each to receive one copy.

Signed

Buyer_____ DATE_____

Signed

Seller _____ DATE___

Packing the "Bon Voyage" Bag

Before the new owner arrives to take little Trixie off to her new home, a smart idea is to have her travel bag ready and waiting. This preparedness isn't a sign that you're anxious to get her out the door, but rather that you want to make the transition as easy for her as you possibly can.

Little things mean a lot!

A bone, a toy, a baby blanket — any of those things that the pup has been used to and carries the scent of your home will help the little one through the trauma of entering a strange, new world. A good practice is to have a number of toys in the puppy pen while the pups are growing up, so that each pup can take along one of the playthings — particularly his or her favorite — on departure day.

In addition to familiar toys, the bon voyage bag can include

- ✔ **A good supply of the puppy treats that the pup is used to.**
- ✔ **A few days' supply of the diet the puppies have been eating.** No sense in adding an upset tummy to all the other new and different things the pup will have to adjust to.
- ✔ **A little note describing the idiosyncrasies of the individual pup.** Such a note is always a good idea, especially if the pup has shown some marked aptitude or aversions while growing up with you.

Big things mean a lot too, like getting paid for the puppy you are selling! You must make an iron-clad rule: No puppy will leave your premises unless it is paid for in full or you have an agreement *in writing*, signed and dated by both parties, that states ownership and transfer of registration is contingent upon payment in full.

If the buyer has the dog in his or her possession and you have no signed agreement stating otherwise, you are required by the AKC to supply the registration documents.

Treat this sale like any sales transaction you might encounter:

- ✔ Make sure checks clear.
- ✔ Supply receipts.
- ✔ Make sure your contract spells out *every* detail of the transaction other than a direct, fully paid sale.

Important papers

In addition to the all-important sales contract, some other documents should definitely be a part of what the new owner takes along. These documents are ones that you must have completed and are as up-to-date as possible.

Health record

Most breeders have begun the necessary inoculation series for their puppies by the time they are seven to eight weeks of age. These inoculations protect the puppies against hepatitis, leptospirosis, distemper, and canine parvovirus. These are all deadly communicable diseases. A rabies inoculation is also necessary, but in most cases, it is not administered until a puppy is four to six months of age or older. Local ordinances may have a bearing on the age, and the rabies shot may be necessary before that time, particularly if it is necessary to ship the puppy to its new home. Check with your veterinarian, who will know what situations exist that are peculiar to your area or to the destination the puppy is headed for.

At any rate, a puppy should never leave your home before these initial inoculations have been at least started. The prescribed series of inoculations your vet has been following should be recorded in the puppy's health record so that a subsequent veterinarian can follow the series accordingly: the dates the shots were administered and the type and make of serum used are very important.

The health record should also indicate what kind of veterinary treatment the puppy has been given since birth. This health record will include records of exams, along with dates and type of medication used for each worming.

Pedigree

You, as breeder and/or seller of every AKC-registered dog, should supply the buyer with a copy of the pedigree. This document can be a typed or written three-generation pedigree that you have prepared yourself. You can also include a note stating that an official pedigree can be obtained directly from the AKC should the buyer wish to do so. (The UKC automatically supplies an official pedigree as part of its registration process.)

Registration Certificate

The Registration Certificate is the puppy's "birth certificate." As with the official pedigree, the registration certificate is issued by a country's governing kennel club.

Diet sheet

You should provide a diet sheet that indicates the number of times a day the puppy has been fed and the kind of vitamin supplementation or additions to the food it has been receiving. Let the buyer know that the prescribed procedure will reduce the chance of upset stomach and loose stools.

Usually, a breeder's diet sheet projects the increases and changes in food that will be necessary as your puppy grows from week to week. If the sheet does not include this information, ask the breeder for suggestions regarding increases and the eventual changeover to adult food.

Some breeders add vitamin supplements to their dogs' and puppies' diets as a matter of course. Other breeders are adamantly opposed to supplements when well-balanced and nutritious food is given. Be sure to clearly indicate what procedure you have been following and what your thoughts are on this issue so that the buyer can act accordingly and be able to discuss the issue with his or her veterinarian.

Gauging the Sales Climate and Avoiding Fads

If your breed has the misfortune of becoming "fad of the month," you'll probably be besieged with telephone calls from people wanting puppies. Friends of mine who breed and show Chihuahuas told me their phones all but rang off the hook when the Taco Bell Chihuahua became the rage of television commercials. And every call that came in wanted a Chihuahua "just like the one on TV!"

As captivating as the dog in the Taco Bell commercials was, "she" (playing the part of a "he") was an extremely poor example of a purebred Chihuahua. (On the scale of 1 to 10, that dog is probably a low 3!) The dog is the last thing in the world any reputable breeder would want out there as an example of what they breed. So to find one "just like the one on TV," the buyer would have to look to someone who didn't care about breeding quality dogs.

All that aside, trust me when I say a good percentage of the puppies purchased during these fad periods do not "stick." That is, after the novelty wears off, the buyers are looking for a way out of having acted on a whim. If you, as seller, have a binding enough contract the dog will wind up back on your doorstep. If not, you'll probably find the dog at the local animal shelter.

Movies such as *101 Dalmatians* and any film with a Golden Retriever in it create a whole new rush on the sales market. The problem is that the puppies don't arrive with a Screen Actors' Guild card and haven't a clue to all those wonder-dog feats their movie counterparts are capable of.

People who buy these "pop culture" dogs haven't a clue when it comes to training, and before long, the thrill of owning one of these wonder dogs who hasn't yet been taught to do anything wonderful wears off and said wonder dog gets its walking papers. If you're lucky, you'll get the dog back and you can only hope and pray it does come back somewhere near to the mental and physical condition it left in. If not, it will be up to you to put Humpty Dumpty's pieces back together again.

So in reality, those popularity surges are both the best of times (in respect to demand) and the worst of times (as to the kind of buyer they inspire). You'll spend far more time rejecting unsuitable owners than you ever will in selling your dogs to folks who can provide the right homes for dogs you've bred. It can be twice as hard to recondition and rehome those dogs that "didn't work out" than it is to deal with any "problem child" you might have had at home.

Planned Parenthood

Something worth considering when breeding dogs is that a summer litter is infinitely much easier to care for than one born and growing up during seasons when the weather is inclement. Fencing off a good-sized area outdoors is easier than having to find equal space inside the home. Growing puppies need space to exercise and stretch those rapidly growing muscles. The freedom to put those little "wrecking crews" safely outdoors during the summer months can be a godsend, and the puppies seem to love it, as well.

Plan carefully. Your female will not whelp until approximately two months after she is bred. The puppies will spend the first three or four weeks after they are born in their whelping box; it is during the weeks and months following that you will welcome good weather.

Consider the other side of the popularity coin, as well. There are many wonderful breeds that the public knows little about or that don't have pop appeal until you get to experience them on a one-to-one basis. Some of these breeds are magnificent animals and do make wonderful family companions. Others are of a more specialized nature, so it takes a very distinct kind of owner to really appreciate them and provide the kinds of homes they need.

Common sense should tell you that if your dogs are a low-in-demand breed that manages to produce enough puppies in a single litter to populate your entire county, then four or five litters a year is not be the most prudent choice you might make.

Although "marketing principles" might sound as though you're trying to peddle sugar-cured hams, you're better off when you consider the laws of supply and demand than by being forced to build a fence around five city blocks to contain all the dogs you're looking to find proper homes for!

Chapter 18

Getting Down to Brass Tax

. . . .

In This Chapter

▶ Knowing when a hobby becomes a business

▶ Keeping records for Uncle Sam

▶ Looking at legitimate deductions

. . . .

Serious dog breeding is neither something that can be accomplished on a shoestring nor is it a pursuit for the disorganized. If you are like most other good breeders I know, keeping expenses down to a minimum is high on the priority list. A sensible attitude regarding expenditures and income *(income?!)* enables the dedicated breeder to carry on a breeding program through the years without being forced to sell the children off into indentured servitude or having the whole family carted off to Debtor's Prison.

Knowing what you're spending, what you're spending it on, and good record keeping in general, are as much a part of being a good breeder as is carefully selecting breeding stock. And when money exchanges hands, the Internal Revenue Service pricks up its ears. There may come a day when "the man" decides he wants to take a look at where those checks you've deposited into your account came from. He'll also be interested in knowing why you haven't — if you haven't — declared that money as income. In other words you'll have to be clear in advance whether or not your breeding operation is a hobby or a business.

This chapter deals with all the very boring but very important business of keeping good financial records.

You and the IRS

Even if you don't consider your dog-breeding program a business as such, it still must be conducted in a businesslike manner. You already know there are important records to maintain and *selling the dogs you do not keep represents income.* Never mind that you probably spend ten dollars for every one that might have come in. Those expenses mean nothing to the Internal Revenue Service if you don't have itemized records and receipts to prove it!

Telling the IRS that just getting the puppy *ready* for sale had cost you ten times the amount you received for selling that puppy is not about to cut it with these folks. They want to know the how and why for every dollar that comes in, and if you don't expect to pay tax on that dollar, they'll want to see the specific receipts for all your expenditures related to what you call your hobby/business.

Income tax and hobby businesses involve a whole raft of complex rules, regulations, and interpretations that are best left to professionals who are knowledgeable and experienced in these areas. Even the most knowledgeable dog breeder in town is not going to provide you with the information you need if he or she is not right on top of the constantly changing federal and state tax regulations. In addition, the brilliant tax person who has no knowledge of the intricacies of dog breeding and dog showing in not going to be anywhere near as valuable to you as the individual who has a clear picture of both tax laws and what your hobby and/or business really involves.

The normal course of dog breeding involves such myriad expenditures and transactions that a person on the outside looking in would never in a million years even think to ask you about. These expenses could all be very valuable and legitimate tax deductions.

Tax Tips from a Pro

To give you some sense of the complexities of the rules that govern small- or hobby-business income, I went to Kathy Gilliam of Woodland, Washington, who is both an active breeder of top quality German Shorthaired Pointers and a highly respected enrolled agent licensed to practice before the Internal Revenue Service both in audit and collections.

An *enrolled agent* is the only professional licensed by the U.S. Treasury Department that is permitted to practice in all 50 states. Gilliam has been the owner of American Bookkeeping for over three decades and has attended the National Tax Practice Institute at Stanford University. Gilliam's clients include leading dog breeders, handlers, judges, and vendors. Her combined tax and dog breeding experience has allowed her to successfully represent these clients in all tax matters and particularly when they have been audited by the IRS.

Those who are not involved in the business may see the dog world strictly as a hobby and do not realize the true extent of this business of dogs. Gilliam's knowledge of both sides of this important issue enables her to explain its complexities in intelligent and easily understandable detail. Following is an overview of what she feels every dog breeder should be familiar with.

The profit dilemma

When is dog breeding a hobby and when is it a business? You can approach this question in two ways:

- ✔ From a tax standpoint, all income is taxable *up to the extent of expenses* for a hobby business.
- ✔ A business in the eyes of the Internal Revenue Service must be profit-motivated — that is, it must show a profit two out of five years.

The ethical breeder's goal is aimed at breeding *quality* rather than *quantity*. As breeders, your goals are to produce dogs that conform to a standard of excellence (mentally and physically sound and healthy). The question a breeder must ask is, "Would I be willing to alter my breeding program to breed for quantity in order to produce a profit?" Most hobby kennel breeding businesses do not show a profit two out of five years as required by the Internal Revenue Service.

One important consideration would be to capitalize the expense of your breeding stock and the expense involved in acquiring the titles for your breed that would prove their superiority.

Examples of such titles are:

- ✔ Confirmation title: AKC, Canadian, Mexican, and International
- ✔ Performance titles: Hunting, Coursing, Tracking, or Field

Health clearances required for your breed that would enable your dogs to achieve these titles could be capitalized as well. When these animals are then ready to breed, you have an asset that can be depreciated against the income of resulting puppy sales.

Weigh the issues involved here very carefully. You will find very few highly respected breeders who want to — or, for that matter, are capable of — stepping up their breeding programs in order to qualify as a profit-making enterprise. This is not to say that it is absolutely impossible to operate on a profit-making basis. (Anything is possible!) Should this be the case, record keeping *is the key*. (For a list of bottom-line necessities, see the "Legitimate (profit-motivated) breeder business expenses" section that comes later in this chapter.

A diary of your business activities and a carefully constructed business plan are extremely important in proving your intention to make a profit. Write up a business plan and discuss it with professionals in the dog world — for example, long-time breeders in your breed and professional handlers. Keep a log of the experienced professionals you have discussed your business plan with. Tax professionals who are well versed in the dog world should also be consulted in this respect. Record and date their input as well.

A matter of record

You can claim legitimate deductions in many ways, and accurate records prove you are eligible to do so. The following are important parts of smart record keeping:

- Keep a calendar or day planner showing where you have been and how many days and why you were gone. Include your destination (kennel club name, name of the city), *per diem* rate, meal receipts, tips, rental car expenses (gas and insurance), motel expenses, cabs or other public transportation, dry cleaning, and any other expenses incurred from the time you leave home until the time you return.

- Keep copies of any contract you may have with a professional handler you might employ to show your dogs. Contracts should list *everything* that is expected of you financially. Keep copies of all checks issued for expenses or a receipt for cash expenses.

- On your telephone bills, highlight the long-distance calls related to your business.

- Keep postage receipts and receipts for all office supplies and equipment purchases.

- Maintain a log for time on the computer for both business and personal usage.

- Keep a mileage log, noting mileage at beginning and end of the year.

- File receipts for *any* expenses that you feel were incurred in the line of business.

- Don't forget clothing: Business suits, ties, shirts, dresses, and so on, are not a deduction. Gowns and tuxedos by IRS definition are not deductions. However, rain gear, safety gear (by IRS definition), and sun gear are deductible (as long as you have receipts).

- Remember that an item such as sunscreen is a deductible safety precaution.

✔ Consider the In-home Office expense. Is the space used exclusively for your business? You can take the home-office deduction if you use the office space only for work and you have nowhere else to do administrative or management tasks. (The important rule to remember here is for an In-home Office expense on a tax return, a profit must show on a Schedule C.)

✔ Make sure you send a Form 1099 to anyone that you paid over $600 for services or over $1 in the case of an attorney.

✔ Be careful how you classify contract services versus actual employees. *This is a big audit item, and both federal and state auditors scrutinize this issue very closely.* If the state auditors catch you with errors here, then they will notify the IRS or vice versa!

Legitimate (profit-motivated) breeder business expenses

The following are normally incurred expenses a dog breeder would encounter through the year. It is extremely important that receipts be kept in all cases.

✔ Advertising or photographs and photography services

✔ Vehicle or truck expenses

✔ Vehicle expenses for a smaller vehicle for running to vet, airport, feed store, and so on

✔ Insurance

✔ Interest

✔ Mortgage interest

✔ Legal fees

✔ Professional fees

✔ Office expenses

✔ Equipment rent

✔ Supplies

✔ Taxes

✔ Licenses

✔ Meals (number of people times the number of days times the federal *per diem* rate)

✔ Utilities such as electricity, water, garbage, snow plowing, and so on

- ✔ Cell phone, including cost of unit and service. Personal and business use must be noted.
- ✔ Airlines
- ✔ Dog shipping
- ✔ Dog show entries
- ✔ Parking
- ✔ Catalogs
- ✔ Dry cleaning on the road
- ✔ Long-distance telephone
- ✔ Vet
- ✔ Show expenses
- ✔ Dues and subscriptions
- ✔ Feed
- ✔ Laundry for dogs
- ✔ Motels
- ✔ Pest control
- ✔ Employees
- ✔ Contract services
- ✔ Travel expenses
- ✔ Real estate taxes
- ✔ Security system
- ✔ Repairs and maintenance to both property and vehicles involved in breeding operation

Questions for an inquiring mind

As you consider the tax aspect of your business, keep the following list of questions in mind. You should also discuss these questions fully with your professional tax consultant. The clearer you are in regard to each question on this list, the better prepared your tax consultant will be able to assist you.

- ✔ Do I fully understand that *all* income (legal or otherwise) is taxable?
- ✔ Am I paying more than my share?
- ✔ Am I taking all the deductions allowed?

✔ Does my tax consultant have the necessary dog world experience?

✔ How many dog world professionals (kennel owners, handlers, judges) does my tax consultant work with?

✔ Is my tax professional legitimate or will his/her amateur status wave a red flag?

✔ Will he or she be there to defend an audit?

✔ Am I confident I am paying the correct amount of tax?

✔ Am I getting the record-keeping guidance I need?

Living through an audit

"Be prepared!" That's the Boy Scout motto, and it should be yours as well — particularly in the event of a tax audit. If you are fully prepared and have the right kind of representation, everything will go without a problem. Just to make sure you are in step with the Boy Scouts, here are some important tips about audits:

✔ If you receive the IRS Audit Notice, your first call is to your tax professional. Obtain his or her signature on a Power of Attorney for your protection.

✔ You may be given the choice of a meeting place ranging from the IRS office to your own office. *Move all records to your tax professional's office.* Always make the examination at somewhere other than *your* place of business. You may feel more comfortable at your own place of business or residence, but you also provide opportunity for an information fishing expedition that you don't need.

✔ The audit percentages are down for the self-employed and up for hobby businesses. The important question that comes up here is how the real world views dog shows.

✔ Be fully armed with the documentation listed in the section "Legitimate (profit-motivated) breeder business expenses" in this chapter. Most important of all, make sure that your representative fully understands your occupation.

✔ Don't volunteer extra information. Provide answers and documentation only for the questions the auditor asks. Talking about other areas of your business may prompt the auditor to probe into new territory that was previously unquestioned.

✔ Wrap up the audit as quickly as possible and get on with your life. Don't let your representative drag the audit on. Doing so increases fees, but more important, the longer the auditor has, the more time he or she has to ask questions.

Chapter 19

Conducting Transactions

· ·

In This Chapter

▶ Providing a quiet showroom

▶ Putting your kennel on "inspection"

▶ Understanding the importance of written contracts

· ·

"**I**f you build it, they will come," or so film and television have repeatedly told us over the past decade. Quite frankly, I do believe this to be true. I have traveled the world of dogs for almost half a century, and I've discovered that top quality dogs can be bred anywhere by anyone — even those in the world's remotest corners.

I've known individuals with even the most humble incomes who have produced stock that has the world's wealthiest exhibitors standing in line for an opportunity to own one of their dogs. Although finances for their breeding programs had to be strictly maintained, their money was invested wisely in nothing but superior stock, and no breeding was ever made without serious thought and high expectations.

These efforts and accomplishments seldom go unnoticed. I have always been amazed how the dog game's "information pipeline" extends itself to wherever good dogs are being bred. Somehow, some way, the cream rises to the surface. For example, I've seen dogs of a bloodline developed by a Corgi breeder of strictly limited means in a remote little town in New Zealand gain worldwide interest and respect. The reason for this was that the breeder's extremely high standards produced animals of exceptional quality, and only the finest were sent off to other breeders around the world. News, both good and bad, travels very fast in this world of dogs.

I remember traveling to the Philippine Islands many years ago to judge an all-breed show and being surprised and delighted to find some of the finest Miniature Pinschers I had ever judged in my entry. They were bred there in the Philippines by a woman who very carefully imported foundation stock. With endless hours of study, research, and comparison, she eventually established a MinPin line capable of standing alongside the best bred anywhere else in the dog world.

All this is to say that with the necessary study, dedication, and a little help from Mom Nature, you may have developed such a highly regarded reputation that enthusiastic beginners may now be calling you to provide their start. It is in you they are placing their confidence in hopes that your expert guidance will send them off in the right direction with quality foundation stock.

If you already enjoy such high regard, then allow me to congratulate you! It takes a reputation for honesty and quality to bring people to your door. But, at the same time, I would like to offer you a very important bit of advice: No matter how successful you are, no matter how many top awards you win in your field, never lose touch with the person who you were at the beginning of all this — when you were an earnest, knowledge-hungry novice. Don't ever forget how important the right start was in getting you where you are today.

If you keep that picture of yourself in mind and do your best to give every novice who comes to you as much as you possibly can, you will have repaid, in part, the debt you owe to those who set you off on the right path. And at the same time, you will be making yet another giant contribution to your breed by assisting someone to carry on the torch of quality.

A Suitable "Showroom"

Having a quiet space to talk with clients is very important. Set aside an area somewhere in your home or kennel in which you can sit down with a prospective buyer and calmly discuss your transaction. Regardless of whether the puppy you are selling is going into the buyer's home to be a member of the family or to someone who has as many aspirations as a breeder as you had in the beginning, there should be some place away from the barking and interruptions. This is the place where you and your buyer can get a sense of each other and fully understand what is required of from each of you.

The tour

Any sensible buyer will, of course, have requested a "kennel tour." Even if yours is not that large an operation, prospective buyers will expect at the very least a meeting with the sire and dam of the puppy or dog they might be buying. Arrange to have that take place at a specific time, never at an unannounced whim. The buyer may also request to see the entire litter from which their puppy will be selected. Whatever the arrangement is, get that done first and then move on to where you can sit down and talk.

The room

If space allows, a special office-type room is ideal for this meeting. If this is the room where puppies that aren't housebroken will be viewed, make sure the floor is of a surface that can be cleaned up quickly and easily. You don't want to have to call in a carpet cleaning team to rescue your oriental rugs in the midst of what you want to get accomplished. This is another point in favor of having just one pup at a time in the "meet the folks" room. If one pup in the litter has to take care of its elimination duties, every single one of them will have to.

You don't have to fly in an architect from some high-powered firm that just made the cover of "Architectural Digest" to design your space. Buyers are not coming to see what kind of interior decorator you are. Just have the room comfortable and *interesting*.

The room can be set up attractively with pictures of your winning dogs, scrapbooks of their accomplishments, pedigree books, and books you recommend on the breed you are involved with.

The talk

Give the buyer an opportunity to become more acquainted with your line, your goals, and what you might be expecting from them if the transaction includes more than a simple sale. This is a good time and place to impress the fact that the welfare of each and every dog you breed is very important to you and that you expect anyone who gets a dog from you to care for it in that same way.

Kids and puppies

If children are a part of the family that is purchasing a dog from you, this is the perfect time and place to demonstrate exactly how they should pick up, hold, or carry a puppy. Children do not come equipped with this knowledge and, in fact, most parents don't either.

Puppies — and even adults of the small, fragile breeds — can be permanently injured or killed by dropping them; and puppies of breeds too large or too heavy for a child to hold securely are just as prone to injury. Demonstrating all this is far more effective than expecting new owners to follow some illustrations in a book.

A new or first-time owner needs to know lots of new information, so be prepared to explain pedigrees, diet and feeding schedules, and health and inoculation records. I highly recommend that you put down all this information in writing. Emphasizing the importance of what is included in your paperwork can only serve to ensure the well being of the dog he or she is buying from you.

The thing you shouldn't do is confuse the issue by having the pup's sire and dam and umpteen littermates flying around the room creating general havoc! There is no way you or your buyer will be able to concentrate on the important discussion at hand.

Some breeders like to treat this meeting like a social event and offer the buyer not only tea and crumpets but also a personal life and family history. I don't think this is entirely necessary and probably not what the buyer is looking for in the first place. However, if adopting the buyer and his or her entire family is a part of what you want to offer, then go ahead. Just let the prospective buyer know that your meeting may last a bit longer than what they might have expected, and if you are planning a gourmet meal as part of the meeting, advise them not to stop off at the local hamburger palace on the way.

The Inspector Cometh

Legally speaking, only government officials with proper documentation and the organization with which you choose to register your dogs are entitled to enter and inspect your kennel. I would be highly suspect, however, of any kennel that would not allow me to at least view their breeding stock and where it was housed. Nor would I be particularly enthused about buying stock from a kennel where I could not come in direct physical contact with adult dogs and, particularly, the parents of the dog I was contemplating buying.

When you do take someone through your kennel, point out the special qualities in conformation or temperament that distinguish the individual dogs. You might also explain how the dogs they see are related to their prospective purchase and what similarities the buyer might expect in the way of such things as adult size or temperament.

A buyer who plans to plans to become a breeder could be well served by having the conformation qualities of individual dogs pointed out to them. Those of us who have been involved in dog breeding for a long time are apt to assume a great deal on the part of the beginner. Giving someone information they might already have is far better than missing an opportunity to provide them with something they may not know.

Meet mom and dad

Experienced breeders are aware that females are very often bred to males other than those they own or keep and that just as often, these breedings are to dogs that live far away from where the breeder resides. In situations like this, it isn't possible for a buyer to meet the sire of the dog they intend to purchase.

On a rare occasion, the dam of the litter is not available for one reason or another. She may be away being shown, or sometimes a breeder leases or sells a female to someone and part of the agreement includes a puppy coming back to the breeder. This could be the puppy that is offered for sale.

Other than exceptions of this nature, there should be no reason for a buyer not to have direct contact with the sire and/or dam of the dog they are considering. If the temperament of a dog or bitch cannot be trusted on its own premises and with the owner present, then *that dog should not have been bred from!*

I think most buyers would understand exceptional situations when they exist and are fully explained. I do think, however, that the buyer is entitled to names and addresses of where the respective parents of their dog are located. Even when situations of these kinds exist, I still feel the buyers should have the opportunity to come in contact with other adults in your breeding program. This information gives them some sense of size and temperament and the general "look" you are attempting to produce.

A prospective buyer might get the idea that he or she is free to drop in and take a quickie tour of your kennel any time the buyer gets the notion. Make it clear in your earliest conversations with the buyer that all this takes place *by appointment only!*

Don't be a stop on the tour

Another point you should be emphatic about is that your kennel should not be one stop on a "tour of kennels." Let interested parties know you would prefer they not visit your kennel within 48 hours of having visited someone else's kennel. Explain there is no way of your knowing what diseases may be present elsewhere and that you do not want to run the risk of exposing your dogs and, particularly, your puppies, to problems that might possibly exist elsewhere.

If a prospective buyer were not able to abide by these conditions, I would be very reluctant to allow that person to have a puppy or dog I had bred. Disease control is an important part of dog ownership whether you own just one dog or a kennel full; and someone that treats this practice lightly should not be given the opportunity to own or breed dogs of your bloodline.

Verbal and Written Contracts

The late film mogul Samuel Goldwyn, known as a "master of the malaprop," is quoted as once having said, "Verbal contracts aren't worth the paper they're written on." As ludicrous as it may sound, there's an element of truth to what the oft-quoted Mr. G. had to say. Relying upon the "he said, she said" of a verbal contract is courting disaster that is most often resolved to the dissatisfaction of all concerned in a court of law.

Unless you are totally comfortable that your association with the dog you are selling and the person buying it is over when they walk out the door, *write everything down!* Every contingency agreed upon by both buyer and seller must be put in writing and signed by both parties. (See the sample contract in Chapter 17.) Experience has taught me that all too often, in their enthusiasm to get what they want, buyers will agree to almost anything. This scenario is particularly true if their agreement is with something that doesn't come due until some vague date in the future.

If you want to participate in a scene worthy of an Oscar, Emmy, and Golden Globe nomination all rolled into one, rely upon a buyer to "just remember" that it was *your* choice of puppies from their female's first litter that is due you. In verbally agreed upon situations like this, I find that selective memory quickly falls into place. Inevitably, the puppy you select is just the one that everyone in the household has decided life will cease without. Be prepared for husbands guarding the compound, shotgun in hand, children lying across the threshold sobbing hysterically, and mother Rottweiler posted in front of the whelping box baring her teeth and ready for action.

Signed contracts for everything due you and what you owe the buyer are an absolute *must*. There are no exceptions to this rule. You may not think this is necessary with your best friend Sue, whom you've known since kindergarten. But if you want to risk a friendship of this magnitude on something that could have been avoided with a mutually signed piece of paper, go ahead and trust the good will of Sue. You may find yourself "good will hunting" if you'll excuse the pun!

This is the part of dog breeding that *is* business — *strictly business*. Maintaining hard and fast allegiance to this principle will save you a lot of legal grief and just might avoid the loss of a key element in your breeding program.

Part VII
The Part of Tens

The 5th Wave   By Rich Tennant

He's a mix.

In this part . . .

You should read and reread every single pearl of wisdom contained in this book until you have fully and completely committed each one to memory. Yeah, right — as if you had the time. Don't despair. If you're long on interest but short on the time it might take to go pearl diving, this part will help. In this part, you'll find lists of the stuff that is bottom-line important to your success as a breeder.

Chapter 20

Ten Characteristics of a Good Breeder

So you own more than one gorgeous purebred and are thinking, "I just love owning dogs, and wouldn't it be great to become a breeder!" Before you go further, find out if you have the right stuff for what you think might be an interesting pursuit. Carefully determining if dog breeding is for you is important because dog owning is one thing, breeding is another.

The following list of considerations can help you decide:

You have no doubts whatsoever that dog breeding is a hobby you want to pursue.

Dog breeding is not a project like photography or painting that you can shelve when you're bored and then pull down and restart as the mood hits you. As soon as you take on the responsibility of the lives you've collected, that responsibility is noncancellable. That responsibility remains yours until and unless you find a dependable party who is willing to assume what is really your obligation.

Dog breeding is entirely your idea, and you will be completely responsible for the care of all dogs included in the project.

If success in this project depends upon anyone other than yourself, you must be positive that they are ready, willing (make that *absolutely willing!*) and able to assume all the drudgery involved. No "maybe's," or "if I have to's" suffice here!

Your lifestyle allows plenty of time for care, training, and exercise of the breed you've chosen.

Everything that has to be done with the dogs in your breeding program has to be done whether you are ready or not. Even multiday business trips or frequent getaways to the Bahamas don't alter the fact that those little (or big) canines are waiting to be taken care of.

Everyone you live with agrees entirely with your pursuing a dog breeding project.

Being involved with dog breeding isn't a "some of the people some of the time" kind of situation. The hobby/business is full of little nuisance factors that don't even faze people who love and want dogs around. For people who aren't dog lovers, however, it's a different story. You and your dogs can become a thorn in their sides very quickly. Neither you nor the dogs are going to be entirely happy living with someone who is just waiting for the next (ahem) bone of contention.

The environment in which you live is completely suitable for the kind of dog you've chosen to breed.

Great Danes in a studio apartment or huge, coated Standard Poodles in the Costa Rican rain forest are arrangements that don't have much of a chance of working. Think long and hard about where and how you live and what kind of dog will do best in that living arrangement.

You are physically capable of handling a fully grown dog of your chosen breed.

Would I advise an elderly, arthritic retiree to take on a kennel full of Rottweilers? Hardly. No sooner than I would send a 3-pound Chihuahua into a home full of kindergartners who have yet be introduced to the word "discipline." Know what you can handle and what the breed that interests you is capable of handling.

Your character and personality are compatible with that of the breed you've chosen.

Don't expect Bufford the Bulldog to go along to Hawaii to accompany you on the Iron Man marathon. He just isn't cut out for that kind of life. And as much as you might admire some of the Herding breeds, joining you as a fellow couch potato is simply not going to happen. I assure you that in the case of the latter, one or both of you will have a nervous breakdown long before that scenario becomes reality. Some breeds require long, hard exercise, and some don't. Know the needs of the breed that piques your interest and "know thyself."

You are financially able to incur the cost of food, upkeep, and sometimes extremely expensive veterinary bills.

When you start deducting even the basic expenses from any anticipated profits in keeping dogs, you'll quickly see that a breeding program that pays its way is more dream than reality. In addition, consider all those medical emergencies that seem to happen just when you don't need them to. Expensive? Very!

Seeking advice (and following it!) comes easily to you.

Successful breeders are who they are because they (a) have experienced all the pitfalls and have learned what works and what doesn't, and/or (b) they've had the good fortune of having a mentor who helped them avoid their mistakes.

If your way is the only way, then be prepared for a long, rocky road as you seek success.

You're satisfied only with the very best.

A good breeder realizes that in dealing with nature, perfection remains ever elusive. But that never deters the successful from constantly trying to achieve it.

Chapter 21

Ten Tips to Help You Breed Better Dogs

*T*his chapter shows you the most essential guidelines to breeding quality dogs. Taking shortcuts or being frugal can prove disastrous to your dog-breeding efforts. Take the following tips to heart to save yourself a fortune in time and money on your road to success.

Make sure you've chosen a breed you really like.

You will do best with the breed with which you have great rapport and whose character is something you can relate to. Naturally, the breed's "look" should have great appeal, but never make your decision on that basis alone. Make sure that you and the breed you select have something to offer each other.

Study long and hard before you even think about investing in foundation stock.

Attend dog shows, visit kennels, see as many good representatives of the breed as you possibly can. Purchase the best books available on the breed, and ask veterans in the breed to recommend articles and magazines you should add to your collection. If possible, attend the National Specialty shows that are held for your breed.

Find the best breed mentor you can locate.

Breed mentors — there is absolutely no one who can be of greater assistance to your education than someone who has spent many years in your breed and who has bred dogs of outstanding quality. Longevity in a breed helps an individual see the overall picture and see through trends that are apt to cause a breed to drift from its intended origin and purpose.

Clearly understand the elements that constitute breed type in your breed.

Breed type is made up of more than any one characteristic, and it is up to the young breeder to clearly understand what these characteristics are. Without clarity in this respect, it is impossible to appreciate the important dogs in a breed when they come along.

Find out which lines have historically produced the best dogs.

Almost any decent line or pedigree can produce an occasional "flyer" — a dog that has a celebrated show career. That's the fun part, but what's of consequence to a breeder is not a collection of ribbons but the strength of the pedigree behind the winner. Make sure the dogs you use in your breeding program are the result of generations of carefully considered breeding.

Buy the best foundation bitch you can possibly afford.

No single thing that you do as a beginning breeder will have a more profound effect upon your success than purchasing the proper foundation bitch. You'll take many steps along the path to success, but none is more significant than this critical first step.

Buy the best foundation bitch you can possibly afford.

Am I repeating myself? Yes, intentionally so! This emphasis is to encourage you to pay more attention to this step than any other you'll ever make as a breeder. The key to success is here, so use it!

If possible, concentrate the bloodlines of the breed's top producing bitch lines in your pedigrees.

Some breeds have the good fortune of having more than one very good producing bitch line. Smart breeders attempt to combine the best of these lines in their pedigrees. Smart line-breeding and outcrossing can get you there, and you'll reap the rewards if you do it well. (For more information about outcrossing, see Chapter 8.)

Make no breeding other than to the right male.

No excuses here! Breeding to a dog because he's handy or somehow related or less expensive than the dog that should be used will prove to be the most costly mistake you'll make as a breeder. Avoid the temptation to succumb to convenience or cost. Better no breeding than the wrong one. Those mistakes live on in your pedigrees forever.

Breed to the best available sons of your breed's best bitches.

Experience in my own breeds and studies of pedigrees in other breeds clearly indicate that a good percentage of males that produce real quality are the sons of those bitches figuring prominently in quality female lines. I would gamble on breeding to an unproven male only if I had the assurance that he was a son of a top-producing female or the result of a pedigree that concentrated on the breed's top-producing females.

Chapter 22

Ten Signs You're a Responsible Breeder

*A*nyone can put two dogs together in the backroom, see to it that they are mated, and then, after 63 days of standby, watch puppies being born. The resulting puppies can later be sold to anyone who can plunk down the selling price. None of that action takes any great talent, and it certainly doesn't make the person a dog breeder. A dog breeder is someone who views what they're doing as an art and a responsibility — someone who doesn't make a breeding unless he or she feels fairly certain that the offspring resulting from a breeding will be even better than the parents that produced them.

A responsible breeder has many admirable characteristics — here are just ten of them:

You use sales contracts.

Without exception, a responsible breeder clearly defines the rights and expectations of both buyer and seller. Both parties discuss these rights and obligations and agree upon them in writing.

You ensure buyer suitability.

A responsible breeder does not permit any dog to go to a home or environment that has not proven to be entirely suitable for the breed of the dog.

You stay involved.

Responsible breeders are members of their breed's national club and participate in activities that support the origin and purpose of the breed such as Conformation shows, Field Trials, Obedience Trials, and Agility and Herding competitions.

You keep abreast of medical advances.

Following recommendations for testing and keeping a watchful eye on research developments aid the responsible breeder in the ongoing quest to eliminate medical problems.

You spay and neuter all pet stock.

A concerned breeder does not release any companion stock, whether puppy or adult, to a new home before it is sexually altered. Only those individuals specifically designated as show or breeding stock are released sexually complete.

You arrange for permanent identification.

A responsible breeder does not release any puppy or adult dog until it has been permanently identified or until specific arrangements have been made to do so. Identification can be accomplished by tattooing or by having a microchip implanted.

You make socialization for the dog a top priority.

The responsible breeder takes all the necessary steps to make sure every dog he or she raises is given all the socialization advantages appropriate for the dog's age and breed.

You maintain proper housing and exercise.

Housing appropriate for breed, age, and location are provided at all times. Surveillance and upkeep of the facilities are maintained without fail. All breeds need to be given the space to exercise regularly and to the degree that will maintain their health and well-being.

You guarantee the health of all stock sold.

The health of any dog sold is confirmed in writing and verified by the breeder's veterinarian, along with certification that all appropriate inoculations have been administered. When genetic problems exist in a breed, a responsible breeder addresses them in the sales contract and outlines the buyer's recourse should they arise.

You assume a lifetime responsibility for your dogs.

The responsible breeder makes a lifetime commitment to every dog he or she sells. That commitment is expressed in writing, stating that the seller must be given the opportunity to take back any dog sold if the buyer is unable to keep it.

Appendix A

Resources

● ●

*T*his appendix lists a variety of media that you can explore as you develop your dog-breeding pursuits. You'll find plenty of resources from books and magazines, videos, Web sites, and trade organizations.

Books

American Kennel Club. *The Complete Dog Book.* Howell Book House, New York.

Burns, Marca and Fraser, Margaret N. *Genetics of the Dog: The Basis of Successful Breeding.* J.B. Lippincott Company, Philadelphia.

Craig, Patricia. *Born to Win.* Doral Publishing, Sun City, Arizona.

De Prisco, Andrew and James B. Johnson. *Choosing a Dog For Life.* T.F.H. Publications, Inc., Neptune City, New Jersey.

Fiennes, Richard and Alice. *The Natural History of Dogs.* The Natural History Press, Garden City, New York.

Fiorone, Fiorenzo. *The Encyclopedia of Dogs.* Thomas Y. Crowell Company, New York.

Gilbert, Edward M., Jr. and Thelma Brown. *K-9 Structure & Terminology.* Howell Book House, New York.

Hancock, Colonel David, *The Heritage of the Dog.* Nimrod Press Limited, Alton, Hants, England.

Hastings, Pat and Erin Ann Rouse. *Tricks of the Trade.* Dogfolk Enterprises, Aloha, Oregon.

Lane, Dick, BSc, FRAgS, FRCVS and Neil Ewart. *A-Z of Dog Diseases & Health Problems.* Howell Book House, New York.

Mery, Fernand. *The Life, History and Magic of the Dog.* Grosset & Dunlap, New York.

Monks of New Skete. *How to be Your Dog's Best Friend.* 1991, Little, Brown & Company, Ltd., Toronto.

Paramoure, Anne Fitzgerald. *Breeding and Genetics of the Dog.* Denlinger's Middleburg, Virginia.

Serpell, James. *The Domestic Dog.* Cambridge University Press, England.

Smythe, R. H. *The Breeding and Rearing of Dogs.* Arco Publishing Company, Inc., New York.

Spira, Harold R., D.V.M. *Canine Terminolog.* Harper & Row, Publishers, Sydney, Australia.

Willis, Malcolm B., BSc, Ph.D. *Practical Genetics for Dog Breeders.* Howell Book House, New York.

Magazines

AKC Gazette
260 Madison Avenue
New York, NY 10016
Tel: 800-533-7323

Journal of Veterinary Medical Education
Dr. Richard B. Talbot, Editor
VA-MD College of Veterinary Medicine
Virginia Polytechnic Institute and State University
Blacksburg, VA 24061

Dog World
9 Tufton Street
Ashford, Kent TN23 6LW
England
Tel: 44-123-362-1877

Dogs In Canada
Canadian Kennel Club
89 Skyway Avenue #200
Etobicoke, Ontario
Canada M9W 6R4
Tel: 416-674-3672

Dogs in Review
P.O. Box 30430
Santa Barbara, CA 93130
Tel: 805-692-2045

Videos

AKC and the Sport of Dogs, American Kennel Club

Breed Standard Videos, American Kennel Club

Canine Legislation: Taking Command, American Kennel Club

Dog Steps, Rachel Page Elliot, American Kennel Club

Puppy Puzzle, Pat Hastings, Dogfolk Enterprises

Right Dog for You, American Kennel Club

Web Sites

American Kennel Club
www.akc.org

American Rare Breed Association
www.arba.org

American Veterinary Medical Association
www.avma.org

Australian National Kennel Council
www.ankc.aust.com/

Canadian Kennel Club
www.ckc.ca/info

The Kennel Club (England)
www.the-kennel-club.org.uk

United Kennel Club
www.ukcdogs.com

National Registry Sources

American Kennel Club
5580 Centerview Drive
Raleigh, NC 27606-9767
Tel: 919-233-9767

American Rare Breed Association
9921 Frank Tippett Road
Cheltenham, MD 20623
Tel: 301-868-5718

Australian National Kennel Council
PO Box 285
Red Hill South
Victoria 3937
Australia
Tel: 011-61-2-9-834-4040

Canadian Kennel Club
89 Skyway Avenue #200
Etobicoke, Ontario
Canada M9W 6R4
Tel: 416-674-3672

The Kennel Club
1 Clarges Street
London W1J8AB
England
Tel: 011-44-870-606-6750

States Kennel Club
1007 W. Pine Street
Hattiesburg, MS 39402
Tel: 601-583-8345

United Kennel Club
100 E. Kilgore Road
Kalamazoo, MI 49001-5598
Tel: 616-343-9020

International Organizations

Federation Cynologique Internationale
13 Place Albert 1er
B6530 Thuin
Belgium

Special AKC Departments

General Customer Service Inquiries
Tel: 919-233-9767
Fax: 919-233-3627
info@akc.org

Artificial Insemination
ai@akc.org

Companion Animal Recovery
Enrollment: 800-252-7894
found@akc.org

Foreign Registrations
foreign@akc.org

Foundation Stock Service (FSS)
fss@akc.org

Performance Events
Tel: 919-816-3907
Coonhound Events: coonhounds@akc.org
Earthdog Events: earthdog@akc.org
Herding Events: herding@akc.org
Hunting Tests: huntingtest@akc.org
Lure Coursing Events: coursing@akc.org
Tracking Events: tracking@akc.org

Appendix B

Glossary Plus

*M*ost ordinary books have what is simply called a Glossary. Dog breeding is not just an ordinary activity, and for sure, this book is not just an ordinary everyday approach to the subject. So the following is what I call "Glossary Plus," which includes scientific definitions (simplified to the best of my ability), commonly used terms, and that extra-special lingo you probably hear only when you're hanging out with doggie friends.

achondroplasia: A form of dwarfism that affects growth in certain breeds of dogs. Usually affected are the leg bones, so that the breed has a normal size head and torso but the legs are severely foreshortened. Examples are the Basset Hound and the Dachshund.

American Kennel Club (AKC): Organization that registers purebred dogs and sanctions dog shows and other competitions.

angulation: The angles formed by the meeting of the dog's bones. Usually in respect to the bones of the forequarters and rear quarters.

balance and proportion: Used to signify a dog is symmetrically and proportionally correct for its breed.

Best in Show (BIS): Designation for best dog at an all-breed show.

Best in Specialty Show (BISS): Designation for best dog at a Rottweiler-only show.

Best of Breed (BOB): Designation for best Rottweiler at an all-breed show.

Best of Winners (BOW): Winners Dog (WD) and Winners Bitch (WB) compete to see which is the better of the two.

Best Opposite Sex (BOS): Once Best of Breed (BOB) is awarded, the best individual of the opposite sex is chosen to receive this award.

bitch: A female dog (even the well-behaved ones!). This term can also be used to describe what some exhibitors do about not having won with their dog.

bitter apple: A liquid used to discourage dogs from licking or chewing on themselves or household objects.

body language: A dog's method of communicating their reactions.

breed character: The sum total of all those mental and physical characteristics that define what a breed should look like and how it should act.

Canine Good Citizen: Basic test of a dog's good manners and stability. Passing the test earns an official CGC designation, which can be added to the successful dog's name on the pedigree.

castration: Surgical removal of the testicles of the male dog. Also known as *neutering.*

CERF: Canine Eye Registration Foundation, which tests and certifies eyes against genetic diseases.

Champion (CH): Winner of 15 American Kennel Club (AKC) championship points under three different judges. Two of the wins must be "majors" (three or more points).

character: The general appearance and/or expression that is considered typical of the breed.

chromosomes: Threadlike structures that consist of deoxyribonucleic acid (DNA) and protein, and which carry the factors for heritable characters, the genes. All living creatures are made up of microscopic cells, each of which has a membrane-bound nucleus containing chromosomes.

coat: In dog parlance, coat includes amount, color, texture, and very often, trim.

colostrum: The milk secreted by the mother immediately after birth and through the next several days.

Companion Dog (CD): Official initial Obedience degree that can be earned by competing in the Obedience Novice class. Comparable to a person's high school diploma.

Companion Dog Excellent (CDX): Next up from the initial Companion Dog Obedience degree. Comparable to a person's college degree.

condition: A dog's overall appearance of health or lack thereof.

conformation: Form and structure of a dog as required by the respective breed standard of perfection.

cryptorchid: Male dog whose testicles are not visible.

dentition: Arrangement of the teeth.

dog: This is a tricky one because it can mean any member of the species *Canis familiaris,* or it can mean only the male of the species. Examples: "All dogs enjoy a romp in park," or "The litter contained three dogs and four bitches." To further complicate matters, dog fanciers are inclined to use the term interchangeably.

dominant gene: A gene that masks the presence or appearance of an unlike gene.

dysplasia: Abnormal skeletal development.

estrus: See *oestrus.*

expression: The resultant facial expression created by the formation of a breed's head characteristics. Examples: the "Oriental" and "far away" expression of the Afghan Hound, the "lordly" expression of the Chow Chow, the "keen" expression of the Wire Fox Terrier, "inquisitive" expression of the Bichon Frise, and the "keen, piercing varminty" expression of the Scottish Terrier.

"eye" for a dog: A natural ability to assess quality in dogs.

FCI (Federacion Cynologique Internationale): Controlling body of pedigreed dogs in most of the European and Latin American countries.

free whelper: A female dog (bitch) who has her puppies naturally. Because of their conformation, the females of some breeds frequently require Caesarean section.

gene: The basic unit of heredity carrying individual characteristics.

genetics: The science and study of heredity.

genotype: The inherited characteristics a living thing is able to pass on to a succeeding generation.

Group First–Fourth: Designation indicates a dog has earned a placement in Variety Group competition at an all-breed show.

head: In a general sense, *head* refers to skull-muzzle configuration. In dogs, there are three basic types but many variations within the three: **1.** *dolichocephalic* (narrow skull and muzzle, usually of great length as in a Collie or Borzoi. **2.** *mesaticephalic* (typified by medium skull and muzzle proportions as one might see in the Springer Spaniel or German Shepherd. **3.** *brachycephalic* (broad skull and short muzzle length, as in a Pekingese or Bulldog.

Herding Trials: Trials designed to test a dog's ability to control livestock.

hip dysplasia (HD): Abnormal development of the hip affecting the dog in varying degrees of intensity.

hybrid: The offspring of parents who have dissimilar genetic make-up.

International Championship (Int.Ch.): An award given only by the FCI.

lure coursing: Working trials for sight hounds.

monorchid: A male dog that has only one apparent testicle.

movement: The action taken by a dog's legs as he goes from one place to another. The respective breed standard dictates correct movement for a breed.

National Research Council (NRC): The company that researches ingredients before they are permitted to be used in dog foods.

neutering: Surgical removal of the testicles of the male dog. Also known as *castration.*

oestrus (estrus): Stage of the reproductive cycle in which the female will stand willing for mating.

OFA (Orthopedic Foundation for Animals): Certifies X-rays of hips and elbows.

phenotype: The physical appearance of a living thing. Genotype as influenced by environment.

recessive gene: A genetic trait that is not expressed unless matched with a matching gene and is completely covered in the presence of a dominant gene.

Schutzhund: German dog sport that tests a dog's excellence in obedience, protection, and tracking.

Sieger: Best male in a German Rottweiler show.

silhouette: An outline portrait in profile of a dog. The proportions called for in a breed standard, or in its origin and purpose, establish the correct silhouette for each breed.

sound: Overall good construction and health of a dog.

spay: Surgically removing the ovaries of the female dog.

specialty show: A show restricted to only one breed of dog.

stacking: The act of posing the dog for examination or for having its picture taken.

stop: The juncture at which there is a step-up from muzzle to skull.

SV (Verein fur deutsche Schaferhunde): Largest and most influential breed organization in the world of which Schutzhund training is an integral part.

therapy dogs: Dogs so trained as to bring comfort and companionship to hospitalized and elderly people.

tracking: Trials that test a dog's ability to track humans or lost articles.

type: The distinguishing characteristics of a breed, as called for in the standard of the respective breed.

undershot: When the front or incisor teeth of the lower jaw extend beyond the front or incisor teeth of the upper jaw.

Utility Dog: Advanced Obedience trial degree comparable to a person's master's degree.

withers: The top of the first dorsal vertebra or highest part of the body just behind the neck. Often referred to as the top of the shoulders.

Index